JAPANESE IMPERIALISM TODAY

Jon Halliday
and Gavan McCormack

JAPANESE IMPERIALISM TODAY

'Co-Prosperity in Greater East Asia'

MR

Monthly Review Press
New York and London

Library of Congress Cataloging in Publication
Data
Halliday, Jon.
Japanese imperialism today.
(Pelican books)
Published as a rough draft in Association for Radical East Asian Studies pamphlet, autumn 1971.
Includes bibliographical references.
1. Japan—Economic conditions—1945—
I. McCormack, Gavan, joint author. II. Title.
HC462.9.H213 330.9'52'04 72-92027
ISBN 0-85345-271-1

First Printing

Monthly Review Press
116 West 14th Street, New York, N.Y. 10011
33/37 Moreland Street, London, E.C. 1

Manufactured in the United States of America

Contents

Tables

Acknowledgements

This study grew out of discussions within the Association for Radical East Asian Studies (AREAS). The present book appeared in a rough draft as an AREAS pamphlet in autumn 1971. We are grateful to many members of the AREAS collective for their contributions and assistance, particularly to Walter Easey. Our thanks also go to Bernard Béraud, David Bergamini, Herb Bix, Alain Bouc, Don Burton, John Clark, Inoue Kiyoshi and Kitamura Hiroshi.

List of Abbreviations

BCAS:	*Bulletin of Concerned Asian Scholars*
FEER:	*Far Eastern Economic Review*
JCA:	*Journal of Contemporary Asia*
JEJ:	*Japan Economic Journal* (English language weekly of the *Nihon Keizai Shimbun*)
JER:	*Japan Economic Review*
JI:	*Japan Interpreter* (formerly *Journal of Social and Political Ideas in Japan*)
JQ:	*Japan Quarterly* (*Asahi* publication)
NLR:	*New Left Review*
PR:	*Peking Review*
PR & WET:	*Pacific Research and World Empire Telegram*
TKP:	*Ta Kung Pao*
WSJ:	*Wall Street Journal*

Bibliographical Note

In addition to the above, a good deal of information on Japan is to be found in the following English-language magazines: *Ampo; Developing Economies; Eastern Horizon; Kyoto University Economic Review; Looking Back; JCP Bulletin; Japan Socialist Review; Oriental Economist; Pacific Imperialism Notebook; Pyongyang Times; Ronin; Sohyo News; Tsushin.*

The three leading Japanese dailies all publish English language daily papers: the *Mainichi* and the *Yomiuri* in the morning, and the *Asahi* in the afternoon. There is also a pro-governmental English-language daily, the *Japan Times*.

Note that in all references to articles from the *Asahi Journal* (*Asahi Janaru*), *Sekai, Chuo Koron, Gendai no Me, Nihon Keizai Shimbun*, etc., the translated title only is given here, the original articles being in Japanese.

Since some of the above sources are not widely known, we include here some addresses to facilitate further research:

Bulletin of Concerned Asian Scholars
604 Mission St, Room 1001, San Francisco, California 94105, U.S.A.

Ampo
P.O. Box 5250, Tokyo International, Japan

Journal of Contemporary Asia
37 Macaulay Court, Macaulay Road, London SW4, U.K.

AREAS Bulletin
6 Endsleigh Street, London WC1, U.K.

Pacific Imperialism Notebook
P.O. Box 26415, San Francisco, California 94126, U.S.A.

Notes

1. An earlier version of Chapter 5 ('The Tokyo–Taipei–Seoul Nexus') appeared in *Journal of Contemporary Asia*, vol. 2, no. 1, spring 1972.

2. Japanese names are given in the Japanese order – i.e. surname first, except where quoting from English language articles in which the usual Japanese order has been reversed.

3. *South-East Asia.* In all Japanese government publications the term covers all non-Communist Asian countries including Afghanistan and Pakistan, eastwards to South Korea and Taiwan.

4. The Japanese yen was up-valued by 16·88 per cent against the U.S.$ in December 1971. All conversions from yen into U.S. dollars, pounds sterling and other currencies are given at the rate operating at the time to which the conversion refers. Up to August 1971 the rate was ¥360 per U.S.$; from August to December 1971 the ¥ floated upwards until the December 1971 revaluation fixed it at ¥308 per U.S.$ (with flexible exchange band of 2·25 per cent); as of early October 1972 it stood at 301 to the U.S.$. It should be noted that the revaluation of the ¥ against the $ makes for great difficulties in establishing international statistical comparisons; overnight, calculations of, say, the Japanese military budget in $ terms may move it from seventh to sixth place in the world league – whereas it did not, at that moment, change in ¥ terms; likewise, Japan's trade with, say, Indonesia, may suddenly jump by $200 mill., whereas it remains the same when measured in ¥.

5. *Nomenclature.* Several problems of nomenclature arose in writing this book. For the sake of convenience, we have referred to the Democratic People's Republic of Korea as 'North Korea', and to the Democratic Republic of Vietnam as 'North Vietnam'.

The southern parts of Korea and Vietnam are referred to, respectively, as 'South Korea' and 'South Vietnam' – usage which is in no way meant to imply recognition of the regimes in Seoul and Saigon. Likewise, where something like the Tokyo–Seoul 'normalization' agreement of 1965, which is conventionally referred to as 'the Japan–R.O.K. Treaty' occurred, we have kept this terminology, again without this implying recognition of the so-called 'Republic of Korea'. China's Taiwan Province is referred to as 'Taiwan', and where existing institutions, such as the 'Japan–Republic of China [R.O.C.] Cooperation Committee', are mentioned we have maintained the conventional name without qualification, and without specifying that 'R.O.C.' refers to Taiwan Province under Kuomintang control.

The names of Japanese companies pose another problem. Recently many of the major Japanese firms have been changing or simplifying their names and adopting English names for international usage: the most important of these are:

Mitsubishi Shoji Kaisha	now Mitsubishi Corporation
Mitsui Bussan	now Mitsui Trading
Marubeni-Iida	now Marubeni Corporation

In many cases Japanese companies have adopted English names which are not literal translations of the Japanese originals. We have tried to be as clear as possible by providing either the company's own English version of its name, where this was available, or by supplying a literal translation of the firm's Japanese name.

6. References to the *Guardian* and *The Times* are to the London daily papers.

Preface

Japan is now the second largest capitalist economy in the world, and the third largest economic power – preceded only by the U.S.A. and the U.S.S.R. Yet the lack of analysis of Japan's current activities is almost universal. To a very large extent, this lack of analysis stems from a simple lack of knowledge.

In this brief book we have tried to achieve a limited aim: to provide the basic economic and political information on Japan's relationship with the South-East Asian area. We have set this in the context of Japan's relationship with the dominant imperialist power, the United States. Where necessary, we have added immediately relevant political and economic considerations – particularly involving Japan's relations with China, the U.S.S.R. and Australia. To have enlarged the study to cover Japan's relations with Europe, Africa and Latin America would have involved a completely different kind of book.

The relationship of Japan to America is crucial throughout the postwar period: it is discussed at several points in the main body of the book, and also, from a theoretical point of view, at the end. But it should be said at once that this is not a primarily theoretical work. We are well aware that serious, extended discussion of Japanese capitalism and Japanese imperialism is almost completely absent from political and theoretical debate in the Western world. But the work of Marx, Lenin and Mao has shown that theoretical constructions can only be based on hard facts. Up to now these simply have not been available to anti-imperialist militants and to scholars and students in the

West. It is remarkable, for example, that the valuable and wide-ranging work on imperialism carried out in recent years by Nicolaus, Sweezy, Magdoff, Mandel, Gunder Frank, Emmanuel and others has almost totally neglected Japan – both in its relationship with the United States and vis-à-vis the less developed areas of South-East Asia. It is also clear from reading the imperialism debates in the West that this neglect is largely due to lack of information.

We have not thought it necessary to justify our use of terms such as 'imperialism'. In the final section we discuss, briefly, the nature of Japan's relationship with the U.S.A. and South-East Asia, and this also involves some observations on the nature of the Japanese state, and the relationship of the economy to politics. We consider these a necessary adjunct to the core of the text. Yet, we would like to stress that we consider that the primary task at the present stage is to provide the data for study and research in an easily accessible and organized form. By indicating fairly fully the sources we have found useful we also hope that the book may be of help to those who wish to research further. Indeed, we consider this book very much as only an immediate transitional step towards a further objective: the full-scale integration of Japan into political theory and action in the West. In this way we in the West hope, by making known the activities of Japanese imperialism now, to assist people everywhere to defeat all imperialisms, Western and Japanese, which are the joint enemies of all the peoples of the world.

March 1972

Postscript. In view of the important changes which have taken place since we completed this book in March 1972, we have added a postscript at the end, resuming major developments in the intervening period.

3 October 1972

Chapter 1

JAPAN AND AMERICA

THE AMERICAN OCCUPATION OF JAPAN AND THE ATTEMPTED INTEGRATION OF JAPAN INTO THE AMERICAN EMPIRE

At the end of the First World War the Far East was convulsed by a series of revolutionary upheavals, following on the victory of the Bolshevik Revolution in Russia. Japan exploded in 1918, Korea and China in 1919. For several months in the years 1921–2 the four major imperialist powers involved in the area, the U.S.A., Japan, Britain and France, met at Washington to try to re-stabilize their positions in the Far East and reorganize their respective holdings in the light of the great changes which had taken place during the war, both in relations between the imperialists, and between the masses in the area and the various imperial powers.

The Washington Conference probably represented the most painstaking and prodigious effort ever made to systematize inter-imperialist relations over a major area of the globe. On the whole, the Western powers were extremely keen to maintain good relations with Japan, and had difficulty reconciling themselves to the final break with Japan which came with the Second World War. America was traumatized by Pearl Harbor. But as the war progressed, the main task became to ensure that the contradictions between the Western imperialists and Japan should be solved in a more effective way than they had been at Washington. Whereas the Washington Conference had opted on the whole for a *division* of interests, the thinking of the American ruling class during the Second World War moved towards *integration* under U.S. hegemony.

Well before the end of the Second World War, the U.S. government set up a task force, largely made up of intellectuals, to study the coming problem of how to absorb Japan into the Western imperialist system. This task force included such figures as Ruth Benedict (author of *The Chrysanthemum and the Sword*) and Talcott Parsons. The core of America's problem was how to demobilize the antagonistic elements within Japanese capitalism without undermining the entire system. Parsons, for example, warned agitatedly about the dangers of a rural-based revolution if the absorption programme were not handled with care.[1]

America's liberal scholars, however, were unable to produce a scientific analysis of Japanese capitalism and imperialism: in particular, they could not specify the respective roles of the military and business leaders in the process which had brought about the war with the U.S.A. In addition, the war with Japan ended much more quickly than envisaged, and the U.S.A. had to install its occupation regime without having worked out a unified political programme for Japan, and without the necessary number of trained personnel. Besides this, of course, there was the fact that General Douglas MacArthur, enjoying the prestige of victory in the Second World War, was able to install himself with virtually dictatorial powers in Tokyo. MacArthur was, on the whole, close to the right wing of the Republican party; many of his close advisers were also extremely conservative, and some were outright cranks. But there were also a number of New Dealers involved in the administration of occupied Japan, both in Tokyo and in the U.S.A., and MacArthur tended not to see eye-to-eye with them.

The American occupation of Japan did not follow a linear pattern: policy changed several times, and during each of these phases there were more or less serious contradictions.

1. Talcott Parsons, 'Population and Social Structure', in Douglas G. Haring, ed., *Japan's Prospect*, Cambridge, Mass., 1946.

With this important proviso, the following points should be stressed: the occupation made a major attempt to draw Japan away from contact with Asia, particularly socialist Asia after 1949, and tie it in to the American-dominated 'Western' world; Japanese currency was not convertible, and the Japanese were not allowed to travel abroad in the early postwar years; during the entire period of the occupation, the U.S.A. provided nearly two thirds of Japan's imports, while taking less than a quarter of Japan's exports – in other words, Japan was transformed into a huge captive market for U.S. exports. At the political level, MacArthur imposed an American-drafted Constitution whose two most important features, as regards future developments, were a clause downgrading the status of the Emperor and locating sovereignty in the Japanese people; and a clause (Article 9) banning the maintenance of land, sea and air forces, as well as all armaments, without qualification. By international agreements, Japan was deprived of all territories it had acquired by force: these included all the areas on the Asian mainland, including Korea; Taiwan and its surrounding islands, which included both the Penghu (Pescadores) and the Tiaoyu Islands; Sakhalin and the Kuriles. Two groups of islands, the Ryukyus and the Bonins (Ogasawara), were taken over as colonies by the U.S.A.

Western imperialist writers have long sustained the myth that the occupation smashed the Japanese *zaibatsu*.[1] This is completely false. The occupation attacked only a handful of businesses, mainly trading companies like Mitsui which had been involved in flagrant slave labour operations, mainly in China and Korea; and a few industries closely tied to the wartime regime, mainly through arms production. Very few businessmen were purged, and even when they were formally disqualified, this was done in such a way as to enable them to

1. Financial-industrial combines. The pre-1945 *zaibatsu* were closely controlled by family holding companies. The postwar *zaibatsu* are superficially more loosely organized around banks. For a full analytic definition, see *Pacific Imperialism Notebook*, vol. 3, no. 1, December 1971–January 1972, pp. 1 ff.

retain power behind the scenes, or to delegate it to reliable deputies. A number of American businesses did, of course, try to use the occupation to weaken their competitors: this group included American textile manufacturers, rayon and ceramics producers, and most big trading companies. A second group, the more powerful, lobbied successfully for tight limitations on the de-cartelization programme (and for its rapid reversal); this group, dominated by General Electric, included Associated Oil, Westinghouse (which had a prewar tie-up with Mitsubishi), Owens Libby (tied up with Sumitomo), American Can (tied up with Mitsui) and Goodrich (tied up with Furukawa).

A second myth which has been widely perpetrated in the West is that only with the outbreak of the Korean War in June 1950 did America decide to reverse its occupation policy and build up Japanese industry. This is false. America had begun to turn and crack down on the Japanese working-class movement as early as May 1946, less than one year after the start of the occupation. By 1948 the U.S.A. was already actively seeking out a way to restart Japanese industry at full pitch, and this process was already under way in 1949, fuelled by Washington's hostility to *both* the Japanese working masses *and* the Chinese Revolution, which were the two determinants in the process. The Korean War was, certainly, important in accelerating the process, and in promoting the militarization of Japanese industry, but it is important to make clear that America's promotion of Japanese capitalism predated June 1950, and was directed against socialism throughout Asia – not only in Korea, but also in China and, above all, in Japan itself.

The Korean War, and its attendant boom, was, of course, extremely profitable to Japanese business, which benefited greatly from the increased American expenditure connected with the war: the war itself thus solidified the position of Japan as America's counter-revolutionary ally in East Asia.

AMERICAN CAPITALISM AND JAPANESE CAPITALISM

American Investment in Japan

The only sizeable hunk of foreign capital in Japan is American. In June 1970 total foreign assets in Japan amounted to ¥2,444,922mill. ($7 billion) of which the American share was believed to be between 60 and 70 per cent (the $7 billion figure represented about 2 per cent of total Japanese corporate assets then – some $350,000mill.).[1] Direct U.S. investment accounted for about one fifth total American assets: $1,491mill. out of the $7,232mill. total as of the end of 1970.[2] American business operations in Japan are largely financed by U.S. banks there (the biggest foreign bank grouping in Japan).

Official Japanese figures showed that U.S.A. firms accounted for 477 (61.5 per cent) of the 776 foreign companies operating in Japan as of 30 June 1970. Of America's top 200 industrials, eighty-three were represented in Japan. Of the top 200 non-American firms, a mere sixteen had a footing in Japan (excluding Japanese firms). In the key sectors, the figures are as follows: of the twenty-three major U.S. electricity firms, twelve are represented in Japan; in the petroleum industry, eleven out of twenty; of the sixteen biggest chemical firms ten are active in Japan; and of the seventeen major manufacturers nine are operating in Japan; six of the seven big U.S. pharmaceuticals manufacturers operate in Japan.

In most sectors of the economy, foreign interests control only around some 5 per cent of the market. However, there are

1. Except where stated, these figures and those immediately below are taken from *FEER* no. 27, 3 July 1971, pp.74–6, 90 and from *FEER* no. 34, 21 August 1971, p. 37. An indication of the difficulty of assessing foreign investment in Japan is that a special EEC Commission on its own members' investment in Japan acknowledged that it was quite unable to come up with an answer on total EEC capital in Japan: the 1969 figure (new EEC investment in Japan in that year alone) was extremely small – a mere $17mill., of which $11mill. was Italian: see *The Times*, 26 October 1970.

2. *Survey of Current Business*, vol. 51, no. 10, October 1971, p. 21.

some important exceptions. Prior to 1964 Tokyo allowed foreign firms to set up 'yen-based' companies.[1] Among those who took advantage of this were IBM, which now has about 70 per cent of Japan's computer market (with the exception of table-top machines), through a wholly-owned subsidiary.[2] Major oil interests, Coca Cola and Pepsi Cola also took advantage of this arrangement. The petroleum industry is particularly important, as foreign capital controls well over half the Japanese market,[3] and non-U.S. foreign capital in the sector is negligible. Foreign control of the rubber manufacturing industry is also high: 20.3 per cent in 1970. Thus, the fact that the major round of capital liberalization, announced on 4 August 1971 by the Japanese government, excluded seven key items (the so-called 'negative list') means rather little. The 'negative list' included oil refining and marketing, as well as computer manufacturing and data processing, but American-owned 'yen-based' companies are not affected by this 'exclusion', and the 4 August measures were, therefore, not expected to hit the big U.S. companies at all.

Other U.S. giants which already have a stake in the

1. To our knowledge, there is no available study of the structure of these 'yen-based' companies. Since there are still strict limits on the repatriation of funds out of Japan, they are not wholly comparable to, say, a U.S.-dominated subsidiary in Western Europe.

2. National Cash Register Co. (Japan) is 70 per cent owned by the U.S.A. parent company.

3. 'After the surrender, Standard Oil affiliates quickly emerged as the largest foreign investors in Japan, with a stranglehold on its oil industry – a timely move since Japan subsequently became the world's largest importer of petroleum.' (John G. Roberts, 'The American Zaibatsu', *FEER*, no. 30, 1971, p. 51). Roberts gives a figure of 58.3 per cent foreign control of the Japanese market in 1970 – this is presumably in refining. The company with the biggest sales of petroleum products in Japan, Nippon Oil Co., is in partnership with the U.S.A. giant, Caltex. The Japanese government White Paper of October 1971 on Resources estimates that American capital controls the supply of 80 per cent of Japanese imports of crude oil (*The Times*, 8 October 1971). Roughly a further 10 per cent is controlled by other foreign capital (*JEJ*, no. 475, 1 February 1972, p. 20).

Japanese economy, like United Fruit, have recently been moving to take over control of the joint ventures they entered into earlier: United Fruit was moving in late 1971 to raise its holding in the Far East Fruit Co. (a joint venture) from 44 per cent to 77.6 per cent.[1]

It should, however, be added that in certain sectors American participation has been declining. This is particularly the case in the important sector of aluminium. All the U.S.–Japanese joint ventures in this sector have shown a deficit: Sky Aluminum Co. (Kaiser Aluminum, Chemical Co., Nippon Steel and Showa Denko), Furukawa Aluminum Co. (Alcoa Co. of U.S.A. and Furukawa Electric Co.), and Mitsubishi Aluminium Co. (Reynolds Metal and Mitsubishi). In the case of the Reynolds–Mitsubishi venture, Reynolds has simply declined to pay up its share for capital increases in the joint project, and its percentage of the holding has fallen steadily from 33.3 per cent at the beginning to 8.7 per cent at the end of 1971.[2]

The major area in which U.S. capital penetration has recently been felt is the motor car industry. The American car industry has been badly hit in the past few years by its complete failure to envisage the overall evolution of motor car production. The traditional American monstrosities are no longer welcome on the roads of any country in the world, for pollution as well as cost and convenience reasons. Even in America itself, medium and small cars have been becoming more and more popular. The big American manufacturers tried to capture this sector when it was already too late. First Volkswagen, and now the Japanese producers, have seized an apparently unassailable portion of the market.

The American response has been two-fold: to try to buy into the Japanese car industry, on the one hand, and to exclude Japanese cars through higher tariffs, etc., on the other.

Two tie-ups are under way: Chrysler with Mitsubishi, and General Motors with Isuzu. The impetus for these has come mainly, but not exclusively, from Detroit. The two largest

1. *JEJ*, no. 463, 9 November 1971, p. 14.
2. Ibid. p. 4.

Japanese companies, Toyota and Nissan, both of which have been swallowing up smaller Japanese firms in recent years, hold more than 70 per cent of the domestic Japanese market and more than 90 per cent of the export market.[1] It is the smaller, rather vulnerable Japanese firms which have gone into mergers with the American giants: together, Isuzu and Mitsubishi held just under 13 per cent of the domestic market in the first half of 1971.

The Japanese government has imposed fairly strict terms on the Americans. Chrysler is to be allowed to buy only 35 per cent control of Mitsubishi Motors – for the sum of $100mill. – buying in gradually over a three-year period. GM already holds 34.2 per cent of Isuzu (a major truck company), and has guaranteed that it will not increase this stake before 1976.

The advantages of Japanese tie-ups to American firms are many: cheaper production costs and higher productivity; the greater attractiveness of Japanese cars in the Third and Second Worlds; in addition, Japanese producers are better geared up to shifting production to yet cheaper labour areas: one calculation recently had it that perhaps 70 per cent of some Japanese cars were manufactured in the Taiwan–South Korea area; Toyo Kogyo opened up a plant in Malaysia in mid-1971 to build its new rotary-engined passenger car. Japan also offers a better springboard for China than does the continental U.S.A.: when the then GM Chairman Roche visited Japan in April 1971 he stated that he was more interested in China as a potential market than he was in Japan which, he opined, had reached near-saturation as far as foreign car sales were concerned. Chrysler's Dodge Colt is already being produced by Mitsubishi in Japan, and an Isuzu–GM car is planned for 1973. It should be added, however, that this movement of capital and production to Japan by U.S. companies is already encountering stiff resistance from the UAW, since it is bound further to cripple the U.S. automobile industry. (The

1. *FEER*, no. 32, 7 August 1971, pp. 66–7; cf. *FEER*, no. 5, 30 January 1971; *Newsweek*, 3 May 1971; and *Time*, 10 May 1971, for surveys of the Japanese car scene.

TABLE ONE The Japanese Automobile Industry: Domestic Market Share

Toyota Motor	29.3	Toyota group (43.9)
Daihatsu Kogyo	6.9	
Hino Motors	1.1	
Suzuki Motors	6.6	
Nissan Motors	23.7	Nissan group (28.1)
Fuji Heavy Industry	4.0	
Nissan Diesel	0.4	
Mitsubishi Motors	9.8	Chrysler tie-up
Isuzu Motor	3.1	GM tie-up
Toyo Kogyo*	7.7	
Honda Motor	6.9	

Source: *JEJ*, no. 459, 12 October 1971, p. 20. The figures show the domestic market share in percentages for the period January–June 1971.

*Toyo Kogyo started negotiations with Ford in 1969 for a tie-up (Toyo Kogyo have developed a revolutionary rotary engine). After three years of fluctuating information, the negotiations were reported to have broken down definitely early in March 1972 over the issue of Ford's participation in the management of Toyo (*The Times*, 10 March 1972).

contradictions of U.S. capitalism which it is bound to aggravate are discussed more fully below.)

America's big advantage over its competitors came through the occupation, when numerous contacts were made and some Americans learnt Japanese. The overwhelming presence of American machinery, from fighter aircraft to office equipment, played a major part in steamrollering Japanese industry into cooperation with American capital. This association has been particularly noticeable in the military–industrial area and in the field of technical tie-ups.

U.S.–Japanese ties in the Military–Industrial Sector

The extent of U.S.–Japanese links in this sector has been admirably detailed by Herbert Bix in an excellent study.[1]

1. Herbert P. Bix, 'The Security Treaty System and the Japanese Military–Industrial Complex', *BCAS*, vol. 2, no. 2, January 1970.

TABLE TWO U.S.–Japanese Military Aircraft Manufacturing Tie-ups

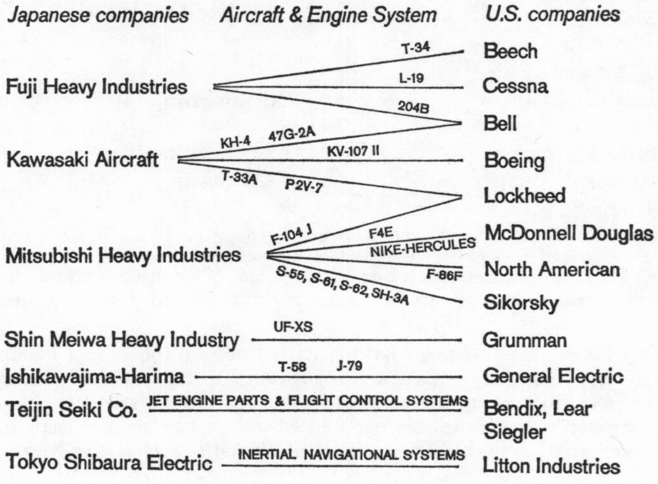
Japanese companies
Aircraft & Engine System
U.S. companies
Fuji Heavy Industries
Kawasaki Aircraft
Mitsubishi Heavy Industries
Shin Meiwa Heavy Industry
Ishikawajima-Harima
Teijin Seiki Co.
Tokyo Shibaura Electric
T-34
L-19
204B
KH-4
47G-2A
KV-107 II
T-33A
P2V-7
F-104 J
F4E
NIKE-HERCULES
F-86F
S-55, S-61, S-62, SH-3A
UF-XS
T-58
J-79
JET ENGINE PARTS & FLIGHT CONTROL SYSTEMS
INERTIAL NAVIGATIONAL SYSTEMS
Beech
Cessna
Bell
Boeing
Lockheed
McDonnell Douglas
North American
Sikorsky
Grumman
General Electric
Bendix, Lear Siegler
Litton Industries

Table 2 sets out U.S. planes, helicopters and engines manufactured in Japan from 1954 to 1966.[1] The two most important tie-ups since then have been the agreement between Hughes Aircraft and Kawasaki Heavy Industries and Nippon Electric to develop an 'early warning defence aircraft',[2] and an agreement between General Electric (U.S.A.) and Hitachi over jet engines.[3] There have also been a number of important agreements recently in the field of rocketry.[4] The crucially important question of precisely how many and what elements of military

1. ibid., p. 39, adapted from G. R. Hall and R. E. Johnson, *Transfers of U.S. Aerospace Technology to Japan*, Rand Corporation, 1968, p. 13.

2. *The Times*, 15 July 1970. Rolls Royce, through its Anglo-French subsidiary, Turbomeca, was involved in manufacturing the engines for the new Japanese supersonic fighter aircraft, the XT2 (*The Times*, 23 March 1971).

3. *JEJ*, no. 459, 12 October 1971, p. 4.

4. See particularly *JEJ*, no. 478, 22 February 1972, p. 12.

hardware Japan would purchase direct from the U.S.A. or manufacture itself, was too obscure at the time of writing to allow for any definite statement.

It is hardly necessary to stress the fact that Japan's role as a huge American base and repair facility in both the Korean and

TABLE THREE U.S. Defence Expenditure in Japan and Vietnam 1964–9[1] (in $mill.)

Year	Japan	Vietnam
1964	321	64
1965	346	188
1966	484	408
1967	538	564
1968	581	558
1969	320	303

1. *Survey of Current Business*, vol. 49, no. 12, December 1969. Of course, this refers only to a limited sector of real expenditure: in effect, it excludes the actual *cost* of the war in Vietnam.

MITI* figures for U.S.A. special procurements are as follows:
1965: $320mill.
1966: $470mill.
1967: $510mill.
1968: $590mill.
1969: $640mill.

*MITI: Ministry of International Trade and Industry (henceforth: MITI).

Source: Hayashi Naomichi, 'The Economic Basis for the Revival of Japanese Militarism', *Gendai to Shiso* 1, October 1970, p. 245.

Vietnamese wars has produced myriad occasions of technological collaboration. The extent of the American military–technological presence can be shown graphically by the figures for U.S. defence expenditure: right through the years of massive expansion of the Vietnam War American military expenditure in Japan was higher than it was in Vietnam, with the single exception of the year 1967.

The total boost to the Japanese economy from the Vietnam war was made up of this, plus the figures in Table 3, plus the enormous purchasing power in South-East Asia directly attributable to the war. Some Japanese sources have calculated the total 'benefit' to Japanese business at around $2 billion p.a. at the height of the war (direct 'benefits'). In addition, concentration by U.S. manufacturers on war production may have enabled some Japanese exporters to make inroads into the U.S. market.

Added to this one must consider: (a) the virtually complete destruction of Japan's arms industry by 1945, and (b) the fact that it grew up again in close liaison with the American military–industrial complex, and with negligible contact with other capitalist weapons industries.

In examining the American–Japanese relationship in this area, one should also bear in mind the fact that Japan has recently been working hard to develop a series of special weapons for use in South-East Asian terrain: a new-style ('72') tank capable of underwater use that will be appropriate to the paddy-fields of South-East Asia (of which a prototype has already been produced by Mitsubishi),[1] special small flying boats, hovercraft-type vessels for swamps and jungles, and, in particular, a new infantry rifle designed for smaller men than the cumbersome American rifles – and, of course, more efficient than the defective American issue. With at least a dozen client armies composed of soldiers about one foot smaller than the average American, it is more than possible that Japan will develop as the arms plant specifically for these forces . . .

Japan's subordination in the important field of technical tie-ups, patents and licences has been extreme. Over the two decades 1950–70 Japan paid out over ten times what it took in on technology royalties: ¥929.4 billion (c. $3,175) to ¥86 billion (c. $279.2mill.) in receipts.[2] Japan is closing the gap

1. *Asahi Journal*, 4 June 1971.

2. Japanese Government White Paper on Technology Imports, 1972, as cited in *JEJ*, vol. 10, no. 477, 15 February 1972, p. 10. All information below from same. Cf. *JEJ*, vol. 10, no. 478, 22 February 1972, p. 20 for a chart of the composition of Japan's technology imports. The *JEJ* regularly carries a complete listing of all business tie-

only very slowly: in fiscal 1970, the last year for which full details are available, Japan paid out ¥155.9 billion ($506.1mill.) for imported technologies (17.7 per cent over the 1969 total); its technology exports came to ¥21.2 billion ($69mill.) – a rise of 27.7 per cent over 1969. 1970 was the first year when the ratio of exports to imports rose above 13 per cent. In that year Japan took in about $\frac{1}{37}$ the U.S.A. figure, one quarter France's receipts, and about half the sum West Germany received. A very large proportion of Japan's out-payments must go to the U.S.A.: for example, nearly 70 per cent of the 2,563 technical agreements signed with foreign interests between 1949 and 1963 were with U.S. companies. In the words of the *Far Eastern Economic Review*, 'reciprocity in this field is minimal'.[1] And, although the sums involved may not seem very large, every visible dollar in a licence (or a loan) may signal much more below the surface.

In order to be able to give some idea of the importance of the U.S.–Japan relationship, several other factors must be noted. First, the sizeable role of U.S. banks in Japan – again, with virtually no reciprocity, as Japanese banks play a negligible role in the U.S. economy.[2] These U.S. banks

---

ups (investment, licensing, etc.) carried out by Japanese interests. To give an idea of the speed with which things are changing, it should be added that Japan's 1970 earnings were double the 1968 figure of $34mill.

1. *FEER*, no. 5, 1971. *The Times* of 11 September 1968 carries a useful survey of U.K.–Japanese licensing agreements.

2. Towards the end of 1971 there were seventy-four foreign banks in Japan – more than double the 1968 figure of thirty-four. The total deposits of these foreign banks as of 31 December 1970 came to 1.2 per cent only of the combined total of Japanese 'city' banks, and accounted for 2.5 per cent of the loans (*JEJ*, no. 462, 2 November 1971, p. 20). The leading Japanese banks only recently organized themselves into two huge consortia, which are now active internationally in support of Japanese business: Associated Bank International (Nomura Securities; Mitsui Bank; Sanwa Bank; Nippon Kangyo Bank; Dai-Ichi Bank) and Japan International Bank (Fuji Bank; Mitsubishi Bank; Sumitomo Bank; Tokai Bank; Nikko Securities; Yamaichi Securities).

have played a big part, particularly in loans to the petroleum sector (in 1961, for example, half all loans were to this one sector). Second, the *relatively* low level of U.S. investment in Japan: in the mid-sixties Japan took only just over 1 per cent of total U.S. overseas investment, and about one fourth the sum which American companies had invested in West Germany at the same time. On the other hand, third, it must be stressed that American investment in Japan as of 1969 was equal to eight times the total Japanese investment in the U.S.A., including Alaska (see below).

There is, of course, also the special factor of Okinawa. From 1945 until May 1972 this was an American colony, governed by an American general, and using the dollar. During this period Japan had only 'residual sovereignty' over the Ryukyus Archipelago. American capital was able to invest in the area on extremely favourable terms, and use Okinawa as a base for getting round the various barriers on capital investment which applied to Japan proper. U.S. penetration via Okinawa was particularly important in the petroleum sector (this is detailed below: see the section on Okinawa).

JAPAN AND THE U.S.A. IN SOUTH-EAST ASIA: SOME GENERAL REMARKS

At any rate up until the mid-sixties, the U.S.A. actively promoted the expansion of the Japanese economy. American procurements and other military-associated expenditures covered some 20 per cent of Japanese imports over the period 1945–62. America also ensured that the World Bank and other puppet organizations lavished funds on Japan: Japan has been the second highest recipient of World Bank loans; as of 1964 it had received $500mill., exceeded only by India ($700mill.), a much poorer country with five times Japan's population.[1] To the beginning of 1971, Japan had received more than

1. T. F. M. Adams, *A Financial History of Modern Japan*, Tokyo, 1964, p. 298.

$850mill. from the World Bank, in addition to $150mill. in credits from the International Development Association (IDA), the Bank's 'soft loan' affiliate.

Back in the mid-fifties, under John Foster Dulles, the Americans had initiated a triangular programme to boost Japanese exports and make the Japanese economy self-sufficient. The U.S.A. put up funds for South-East Asian countries to purchase Japanese exports, in return giving these same South-East Asian countries 'privileges' in the American market: as Yanaga puts it; 'A major goal . . . was to develop markets for Japan in South-East Asia in order to counteract Communist trade efforts and to promote trade between Japan and South-East Asian countries.'[1] In retrospect, this looks one of the crazier of Dulles's many crazy schemes.

The scheme only makes sense in the light of America's comparative *weakness* in the area. In spite of the massive imperialist military activity in the area, South-East Asia has not been a major area for investment by the U.S.A.: in 1967 only 2.3 per cent of U.S. direct overseas investment was in South-East Asia.[2] From America's point of view, Japanese

1. Chitosh iYanaga, *Big Business in Japanese Politics*, New Haven and London, 1968, p. 266.

2. A more recent estimate is that 3.039 per cent ($2,145mill.) of American private investment was in the 'developing' countries of Asia (excluding the Middle East) in 1969 (Ashok Kapoor, 'The Understanding Gap', *FEER*, 16 September 1972, pp. 41–2, from his forthcoming book, *Foreign Investment in Asia*). It should be noted that official Japanese statistics sometimes include Japan under the heading 'South-East Asia': thus MITI, *Tsusho Hakusho* (*Trade White Paper*), *Soron* (*General Considerations*), 1971, p. 366 estimates that, as of the end of 1969, some 4.8 per cent ($3,363mill.) of total U.S. overseas investment ($70,762mill.) was in what it calls 'South-East Asia'. This included U.S. investment in Japan ($1,218mill. at the time) – well over one third the total, and much the fastest-growing component during the 1960s. Kawata Tadashi, 'South-East Asia and the Japanese Economic Thrust', *Sekai*, November 1971, pp. 193–207, states that U.S. investment in the area [presumably East Asia, including Japan] *fell* from $3,570mill. in 1967 to $3,160mill. in 1969. A September 1971 *Newsweek* calculation that 'direct U.S. economic investments in the region [South-East Asia] total more than $1·5 billion' (*Newsweek*, 27

capital was welcome in the area to help tie down reactionary regimes.

September 1971, p. 15) would seem a bit low, putting the American stake in the zone at around only 2 per cent of its overseas total (*The Times*, 20 January 1972 gives total U.S. foreign investment as $78,000 mill., or £31,200mill.). *Newsweek* quotes one American official as saying: 'I think it can be argued that these American oil wells and factories will offer a helluva lot better guarantee of long-term continued American interests in South-East Asia than an air base in Thailand.'

Chapter 2

JAPAN AND SOUTH-EAST ASIA

JAPAN'S IMPORT NEEDS

It is well known that Japan lacks many of the raw materials needed for industrial manufacturing. As of the early sixties, Japan had to import all its cotton, wool, natural rubber, bauxite, phosphate rock, nickel and abaca; more than 90 per cent of all its crude petroleum, tin ore, sugar and iron ore; more than half its consumption of soyabeans, wheat and salt.[1] Few of these items can be reduced more than negligibly; at the same time, most of them are widely and therefore fairly cheaply available.[2] The paradoxical element is that Japan gets most of its largest group of imports, primary products, from the United States.

If maximum diversification takes place in agriculture, Japan could lower its dependence on some food imports (see section on agriculture below). But as far as minerals and industrial raw materials are concerned, Japan is bound to continue being heavily dependent on imports. The October 1971 Report on Resources estimated that if current economic growth rates were maintained, Japan would, in ten years' time, be consuming 30 per cent of the world's total exports of raw materials, compared with 12 per cent today. And by 1980 the annual

1. Warren S. Hunsberger, *Japan and the United States in World Trade*, New York, 1964, p. 111; Hunsberger, although a complacent conservative, gives a very thorough background to both the economic and political relations involved in U.S.–Japanese trade.

2. ibid., pp. 113, 129–31; Hunsberger stresses the importance of Japan's 'traditional avoidance of unnecessary imports'.

TABLE FOUR Japan's Needs for Resources and Level of Overseas Dependence

Item	Unit	1963		
	1,000 Tons	Needs	Domestic Supply	Overseas Dependence (%)
Copper	,,	396	160	59.6
Lead	,,	141	69	51.1
Zinc	,,	328	221	32.6
Aluminium	,,	252	0	100
Nickel	,,	25	0	100
Iron Ore	,,	34,449	8,020	76.7
Coal	,,	22,260	11,820	46.9
Oil	1,000 Kilolitres	65,637	794	98.8
Natural Gas	Millions Cubic Litres	2,133	2,133	0
Uranium	Short Tons	—	—	—
Timber	1,000 Cubic Metres	67,761	51,119	24.5

Source: Hayashi Naomichi, 'The Economic Basis for the Revival of Japanese Militarism', citing the 1970 Report of the Research Committee on Resources of the Economic Council, a top-level consulta-

consumption of crude oil would rise to about 11 per cent of total world consumption.[1] Table 4 sets out the level of dependence, with the 1975 estimates.

As of 1971 Japan was estimated to be living with only something around twenty days' supply of most raw materials for industry available in the country. Oil supplies were enough for forty-five days – compared with an average sixty-day supply maintained by most other advanced capitalist economies. The government recently announced an official programme to build up the reserves to the sixty-day level.[2]

This extreme dependence on imports has had several consequences: the development of gigantic shipbuilding capacity

1. *The Times*, 8 October 1971.

2. *JEJ*, no. 474, 25 January 1972, p. 1. cf. Miyoshi Shuichi, 'Japan's Resources at a Turning Point', *JQ*, vol. 18, no. 3, 1971, p. 342.

1968			1975 Estimates			Average annual increase in require-ments 1968–75 %
Needs	Domestic Supply	Overseas Depend-ence (%)	Needs	Domestic Supply	Overseas Depend-ence (%)	
740	197	73.4	1,400	240	82.9	9.6
186	81	565	367	163	55.6	10.2
628	290	53.8	1,290	494	61.7	10.8
657	0	100	1,780	0	100	15.3
60	0	100	131	0	100	11.8
77,437	11,856	84.7	164,288	16,429	90	11.3
43,650	12,260	71.9	86,640	12,260	85.9	10.3
148,299	799	99.5	290,000	800	99.7	10.1
2,510	2,510	0	9,500	2,510	73.6	20.9
—	—	—	4,210	0	100	—
91,806	48,963	46.7	128,400	53,900–65,300	58–49.1	4.9

tive body under the Prime Minister, *The Resources Problem in a Period of Internationalization*.

and a large merchant fleet; an ever-widening search for more raw materials; and an increasing trend towards long-term investment in the actual extraction of these raw materials. The extent of European–American control over the world's mineral resources is given in Table 5. Japan's fears are not entirely groundless.

SHIPPING

Immediately after the war Japan was completely dependent on foreign (especially American) shipping. The first ship built in Japan for export was launched only in 1951. In 1971 Japan was by far the largest shipbuilding nation in the world, producing almost 12mill. gross tons (11,992,495 gross tons) – almost half the total for the capitalist world (24,859,701 tons). Japan's

TABLE FIVE European–American Capital Control over World Mineral Resources

Copper	10 companies	70.9% of world production
Nickel	4 ,,	74.5% ,, ,, ,,
Aluminium refining	6 ,,	82.8% ,, ,, ,,
Crude oil	8 ,,	64% ,, ,, ,,

In copper, aluminium and oil, the U.S.A. controls 40 per cent or more of world output.

Source: MITI, *Tsusho Hakusho, Soron*, 1971, p. 349.

total was 1.5mill. tons up on 1970, 55 per cent of the tonnage (6.5mill. tons) for export. The fleet is now the second largest in the world, after Liberia (a 'convenience'), having overtaken Britain in 1969. Japan's determination to control transport facilities has already paid dividends, as has the early move into mammoth ships. The world's increasing reliance on bulk carriers for ores and oil (particularly since the closing of the Suez Canal) has enormously benefited Japan, which now exports over half its total ship production each year. Big Japanese companies, like Ishikawajima-Harima (IHI), now have sizeable or controlling interests in shipbuilding in countries as diverse as Brazil, Peru, Taiwan, Australia, Turkey, Greece and Singapore.[1] In 1970 Japan doubled its exports of shipping tonnage over 1969, to $3,311mill. – 2.4 times the target set at the supreme foreign trade conference for 1970.[2]

Japan's economic relations with East and South-East Asia have had three waves of artificial stimulants: the Korean War (and American procurement); the 'reparations' programme; and the 'aid' programme.

1. *The Times*, 9 March 1971.

2. ibid., 8 April 1971. Up until 1971 world oil consumption had been growing at a steady 10 per cent per annum, and this increase was relatively independent of the rate of expansion of world trade as a whole. However, the severe slowdown in world trade in 1971 did affect global oil production more than had been envisaged (*The Times*, 4 January 1972).

REPARATIONS

Japan's 'reparations' programme was instigated by big business as a means of pumping taxpayers' money back into the hands of industry. It was specifically designed to bring Japanese exports back into most of the former Greater East Asia Co-Prosperity Sphere with which, naturally, it was coextensive (with the exceptions of the socialist states). The Korean War had, of course, been a great boon to Japanese business, but it also had its limitations, both geographically and product-wise.

It is important to note that Japan's so-called reparations programme was invented by business, and run by business, exclusively as a self-serving plan. In Yanaga's discreet phrase, 'Organized business was quick to see the connection between reparations payments and the revival of the nation's economy.'[1] Moreover, all the reparations negotiations were carried out not by Foreign Office officials, but by businessmen: 'The government actually preferred the services of businessmen to those of the officials of the Foreign Office, because it was essential

TABLE SIX Japanese Reparations Payments to South-East Asian Countries*

Country	Signed	Terms (Years)	Reparations (millions of dollars)	Loans (millions of dollars)
Burma I	5 Nov. 1954	10	200.0	50.0
Burma II	29 Mar. 1963	12	140.0	30.0
Philippines	9 May 1946	20	550.0	250.0
Indonesia	20 Jan. 1958	12	223.8	400.0
South Vietnam	15 May 1959	5	39.0	7.5

*Source: Yanaga, op. cit., p. 206. cf. Imagawa Eiichi, 'Inroads of the Japanese Economy in Asia', *Sekai*, no. 11, November 1970, pp. 77–86.

that the negotiations be based on realistic business arrangements (*sic*).'[2]

The total 'reparations' payments came to $1,152,800,000 in

1. Chitoshi Yanaga, *Big Business in Japanese Politics*, p. 202.
2. ibid., p. 204.

'damages', plus $737,500,000 in loans. The 'reparations' agreement which best reveals the real nature of the entire programme is that with South Vietnam. This arrangement was simply invented by big business to cash in on the benefits of the American involvement in Vietnam:

> After the fall of Dienbienphu . . . South Vietnam came under the protection of the United States. As a result, considerable amounts of aid money started flowing into the country. This new situation had the effect of revising the thinking of the Japanese government. Organized business, which had been feeling the effects of the termination of United States special procurements program in Japan for the Korean War, saw new opportunities . . .
>
> In order to derive sizeable profits from United States aid funds, both organized business and the government concluded that it would be best in the long run to make a fairly large reparations payment, which would over a period of time pay off handsomely . . . The payments were in fact a form of investment, promoted by business leaders close to the Prime Minister because they saw an excellent opportunity to realize profits while cooperating with the United States in its policy of resisting Communism in Southeast Asia.[1]

The Philippines programme exemplifies the two key traits of the whole affair: utter business dominance, and the self-serving nature of the actual content of the agreements. In the case of 'reparations' to the Philippines, the business leaders handling the negotiations came to an agreement among themselves on the sum to be advanced to the Philippines without even informing their own Finance Minister, Ichimada.[2]

The Philippines refused to enact an investment guarantee law (because of residual hostility to the Japanese, and under pressure from the American–Philippine lobby); Japanese

1. Yanaga, op. cit., pp. 225–6, 227; p. 228 gives a breakdown of the various Japanese figures involved in the South Vietnam deal, a list which is of use in attempting to descry the current divisions within the Japanese ruling class. Cambodia and Laos (see below) did not, apparently, ask for reparations, since their territories (like Vietnam itself) did not suffer great material damage during the Japanese occupation.

2. Yanaga, op. cit., p. 220.

interests therefore had to make themselves felt through their control of transport, licences, trained personnel, etc. A study of the effects of Japanese 'reparations' and 'aid' to the Philippines shows that these activities have been used to unload unwanted consumer goods onto the Philippines, to stifle local economic development, to take over Philippine concerns, bribe government officials, etc.[1] The culmination of the programme came when Japan exported a $6mill. bullet manufacturing plant to the Philippines – as war reparations![2]

NON-REPARATIONS

As part of the collusion between the Japanese and American ruling groups, concretized in the so-called Peace Settlement and its resulting operations, Japan never made any compensation to either China or the Democratic People's Republic of Korea. 'Directly or indirectly, the Japanese had killed an estimated eleven to fifteen million persons in China, left sixty million homeless, and caused damage estimated at $60 billion.'[3] In May 1960 the *People's Daily* re-asserted China's *right* to claim $50 billion in reparations, and demanded that the *issue* of compensation be settled to China's satisfaction as a precondition for entering into diplomatic relations with Tokyo. Subsequently China clarified its position as follows: Japan must pay full compensation in unequivocal apologies for its misdeeds, even though this compensation need not necessarily

1. Josefa M. Saniel, 'Japan's Future in the Philippines', in Masamichi Inoki, ed., *Japan's Future in Southeast Asia*, Kyoto, 1966. Although Inoki (a former commandant of the Japanese Defence Academy) is a dangerous reactionary, much pampered by Western imperialist writers, Saniel's essay is excellent.

2. The bullet plant was exported in 1969; in 1968 Japan was also building a gunpowder plant and military-related electrical facilities in the Philippines.

3. John Dower, 'Occupied Japan and the American Lake, 1945–1950', in Edward Friedman and Mark Selden, eds, *America's Asia: Dissenting Essays on Asian–American Relations*, New York, 1971, p. 188, from Chang Hsin-hai, 'The Treaty with Japan: A Chinese View', *Foreign Affairs*, vol. 26, no. 3, April 1948, p. 506.

take the form of cash and commodities, or industrial plant (as had originally been planned at the end of the war in 1945). For a long time the question of reparations to China played quite a big part in Japanese domestic and foreign policy: Kishi and his group in the pro-Taiwan lobby repeatedly adduced the fact that the Chiang regime had renounced reparations as an excellent reason for supporting Taipei rather than recognize the People's Republic. More recently the problem seems to have evaporated: the Chinese have let it be known that they will not demand financial reparations;[1] Foreign Minister Fukuda formally stated that Japan should apologize to China for the 'trouble' Japanese troops caused the Chinese people.[2]

A further case of non-reparations by Japan involves Micronesia. Many of the islands in this vast area suffered terribly under both Japanese and, later, American rule. Being widely scattered, and receiving little support from other peoples, the inhabitants of these islands have been subjected to repeated occupations, bombings and ultimately the atomic bomb itself; Micronesia has laid a claim against Japan for $1 billion (and against the U.S.A. for $2 billion). Japan has laid a counterclaim against Micronesia for $100mill. The U.S.A. and Japan have colluded in a nauseating deal to make a $10mill. 'ex gratia' payment ($5mill. each) to the islands, a negligible pittance in the light of the devastation wreaked on this beautiful area, and the callous inactivity shown by both occupying powers.[3]

1. This was formally made clear via ex-Foreign Minister Fujiyama in October 1971 (*v. FEER* no. 42, 1971, p. 4). Fujiyama was formerly Foreign Minister for a time under Kishi, who was Prime Minister from 1957 to 1960. Kishi, a major cabinet minister under Tojo, was later condemned as a Class A war criminal. He is still powerful on the right wing.

2. *The Times*, 17 December 1971, reporting Fukuda's statement in the Diet; cf. Fukuda's interview with *The Times*, 16 December 1971.

3. For details on Micronesia, see *The Young Micronesian*, vol. I, no. 5, May 1971, esp. pp. 10–11. For a recent American report on the stagnation of the area under U.S.A. domination, see C. L. Sulzberger, 'Haphazard Empire', *International Herald Tribune*, 17 March 1972. It should be noted that, quite apart from the atom bomb explosion on Bikini, the U.S.A. has also used Micronesia as a dumping ground for poison gases and other noxious weapons moved from Okinawa.

AID

Although Japan furnishes loans, it takes back with its other hand, as if by magic, almost twice the amount that it provides.
Tunku Abdul Rahman at Expo '70[1]

Japanese 'aid' has been in line with its 'reparations' policy. All imperialist 'aid' is, of course, only disguised investment or export credits. Given the *essential* mendacity of the terminology, which is designed to deceive and confuse, it is rather hard to re-categorize the information, and it is therefore here presented, critically, under its imperialist headings.

Japanese aid by area is given in Table 7. Japanese aid to Asia by country is given in Table 8.

In 1969, the official Japanese figure for 'aid' (combined private and governmental resource transfer to the developing countries) was $1,263mill. (0.76 per cent of GNP) and in 1970 this increased to $1,824.3mill. (0.94 per cent of GNP) – a 44 per cent increase.[2]

According to official Japanese statistics, in 1969 Asia received 83.3 per cent of Japan's total bilateral aid flows and 79.9 per cent of the total transfer of private capital funds from Japan.[3]

As of the end of September 1970, the accumulated total of governmental loans, $1,963.7mill. on the commitment basis, was distributed among South-East Asian countries as given in Table 9.

Although subsequent data are incomplete, it would seem that one of the main trends since the publication of this White Paper has been an acceleration of loan funds to Indonesia.

1. Quoted in *The Times*, 29 April 1971.

2. Hiroshi Kitamura, 'Japan's Economic Policy Towards Southeast Asia', *Asian Affairs*, vol. 59, part I, February 1972, p. 51 (from *Nihon Keizai Shimbun*, May 1971). In 1970 Japan's official development assistance actually declined from the 1969 figure in terms of GNP. Japan likes to proclaim that it is the second largest capitalist 'aid' donor, but in terms of 'quality' it is way down the list (*JER*, vol. 3, no. 8, August 1971, p. 20).

3. Kitamura, op. cit.

TABLE SEVEN Japanese Aid by Area (in $mill.)

	Total	Asia (excl. Mid. East) Total	S.E. Asia	Mid. East	Africa	South America	Pacific	Europe	Int. Organ-izations
1960 ('59) –'63	(1,413.9) 1,218.3	52 631.1	36 434.8	11 139.7	4 44.6	26 322.3	* 2.4	3 41.2	3 36.6
'64	360.7	69 248.2	38 137.9	3 11.4	21 76.0	2 7.3	* 0.7	2 6.8	3 10.3
'65	600.8	53 320.8	28 167.2	2 11.5	22 134.8	13 80.4	* 0.2	6 35.4	3 17.7
'66	669.0	58 384.8	21 143.5	5 31.1	91 124.8	8 54.7	* 1.4	4 23.7	7 48.4
'67	855.3	58 500.2	25 215.8	8 69.3	23 199.7	5 44.9	* *	* 4.2	5 45.4
'68	1,049.3	53 559.0	21 218.8	9 89.5	7 70.6	10 102.6	* 0.2	5 51.5	17 176.3
'64–'68	3,535.1	57 2,013.0	25 883.2	6 212.8	17 605.9	8 289.9	1 2.1	3 113.2	8 298.1
'60 ('59) –'68	(4,949.0) 4,753.4	56 2,644.1	28 1,318.0	7 352.5	14 650.5	13 612.2	1 4.5	3 154.4	7 334.7

Source: *Chosa Geppo* (Research Monthly) published by the Cabinet Research Office, vol. 14, no. 12, December 1969, p. 14.

The upper offset figures are the percentage aid to a given area of the whole.

* negligible.

TABLE EIGHT Japanese Aid to Asia by Country (in $mill.)

	Korea	Tai-wan	Burma	Philip-pines	Indo-nesia	Thai-land	S. Viet-nam	India	Pakis-tan	Ceylon	Asia (excl. Mid. East)
1959–'63	5.5	0.1	105.4	79.4	104.4	7.0	40.8	86.6	13.1	0.5	450.7
	7.7	10.4	105.7	122.7	162.7	37.8	40.8	131.8	21.2	1.3	631.1
'64	0.2	0.2	16.8	21.4	15.0	3.5	5.9	35.5	16.2	0.2	116.5
	2.3	2.3	16.7	34.5	42.6	34.3	5.9	81.0	18.5	0.4	248.2
'65	45.9	0.3	11.8	35.3	21.5	3.9	0.7	53.2	32.7	0.1	205.5
	50.7	4.7	12.9	65.3	59.8	22.1	1.3	67.4	25.8	*	320.8
'66	31.2	8.8	10.3	30.5	50.6	3.7	0.6	49.4	21.3	6.9	216.0
	126.2	17.9	10.1	46.7	43.1	22.6	0.6	58.6	14.6	7.1	384.8
'67	53.6	30.7	6.5	61.5	112.9	4.1	0.5	40.3	26.4	2.4	343.3
	115.5	69.4	14.1	116.0	73.4	6.5	1.8	69.1	20.6	8.5	500.2
'68	44.0	23.6	10.4	27.8	83.7	4.9	0.5	64.7	41.7	5.1	311.4
	140.0	78.3	20.4	85.3	69.2	37.0	1.3	75.1	42.9	8.1	559.0
'64–'68	174.9	63.6	55.8	176.5	283.7	20.1	3.6	243.1	138.3	14.7	1,192.7
	434.2	172.6	74.2	347.8	288.1	122.5	3.5	351.2	122.4	24.1	2,013.0
'59–'68	180.4	63.7	161.2	255.9	388.1	27.1	44.4	329.7	151.4	15.2	1,643.4
	441.9	183.0	179.9	470.5	450.8	160.3	44.3	483.0	143.6	25.4	2,644.1

Source: ibid., December 1969, p. 15.

The upper figure gives government aid only, the lower figure is both government and private aid.
* negligible

Japan has also extended a very large yen loan to Burma: $71mill.[1] An important Mitsubishi group toured India at the end of 1971 to investigate investment and loan possibilities, and this mission reportedly also undertook a survey of the

TABLE NINE Accumulated Governmental Yen Loans to South-East Asian Countries as of the end of September 1970 (in U.S. $ mill.)

Country	Amount	Percentage of total
India	549.5	28.0
Indonesia	388.6	19.8
Pakistan	255.0	13.0
South Korea	200.0	10.2
Taiwan	150.0	7.6
Thailand	60.0	3.1
Malaysia	50.0	2.5
Burma	30.0	1.5
Philippines	30.0	1.5
Ceylon	25.0	1.3
South Vietnam	7.5	0.4
Cambodia	4.2	0.2
Afghanistan	2.0	0.1
Nepal	1.0	0.1

Source: MITI, *Keizai Kyoryoku no Genjo to Mondaiten* (White Paper on Economic Co-operation), 1970, p. 140.

Bangladesh scene.[2] Japan, which was surprisingly swift to recognize Bangladesh, at once announced that it was going to re-negotiate the distribution of its outstanding credits to what was Pakistan: these totalled just under £100mill., of which 60 per cent was earmarked for the East.[3] Japan is also lending money to the Democratic Republic of Vietnam (D.R.V.), at fairly low interest (3–5 per cent).[4]

Japan overtook the U.K. as 'aid' giver in 1969, and West Germany in 1970, to become second only to the U.S.A. Japan

1. *FEER*, no. 51, 1971, p. 4.
2. *FEER*, no. 50, 1971, p. 70.
3. *Le Monde*, 11 February 1972: the total given there is 1,135mill. francs.
4. *FEER*, no. 50, 1971, p. 64: where the U.S.S.R. is reportedly charging 2.5 per cent, and France was asking 6 per cent.

was the number one 'aid' source for Taiwan, the Philippines, Singapore and Burma; the number two for South Korea and Malaysia; the number three for Thailand and Laos.[1]

As a percentage of GNP, Japan's 1969 'aid' figure is around the capitalist average. But even by the degraded measurements used in this field, Japan had a rotten record: only one third of the 1969 figure (0.26 per cent of GNP) was official development assistance; and nearly 50 per cent of the 'aid' total can be considered as out-and-out trade promotion of one kind or another.[2] As of the end of 1969, the outstanding balance of Japan's export credits totalled $2,898mill. – of which South-East Asia took about $1,080mill. In the year 1969, however, South-East Asia took only 28 per cent of the total of that year's deferred payment credits (58 per cent went to Africa, whose total of outstanding export credits from Japan as of the end of 1969 was almost exactly the same as that of South-East Asia – $1,080mill.).[3]

Table 10 gives Japanese export credits, along with Japanese overseas investment up to the end of 1969.

Several comments must be added: Japanese interest rates have, on the whole, been high: $4\frac{3}{4}$–$5\frac{3}{4}$ per cent on ordinary loans, whereas the capitalist European average has been around 3 per cent. The signs are that Japan is now lowering its percentage somewhat.[4] The average terms on Japanese

1. Hayashi Naomichi, 'The Economic Basis for the Revival of Japanese Militarism', *Gendai to Shiso* 1, October 1970, p. 255.

2. Dick Wilson, 'Putting the Screw on Scrooge', *FEER*, no. 50, 12 December 1970, p. 45. Other information from *The Times*, 14 and 15 September 1970 and 29 April 1971.

3. Kitamura, op cit.

4. According to the *Asahi Journal*, 23 April 1971, the 1970 conditions of twenty-year loans at 3.5 per cent were 'improved' in 1971 to twenty-five years (including seven years' deferment) at 3 per cent. The *FEER* recently reported that 'the practice of giving tied loans to developing nations is expected to be totally discontinued by 1 April 1972' (*FEER*, no. 29, 1971, p. 31). One may doubt this. Japan's loans policy, as the case of South Korea so starkly shows, is sure to be determined by the criterion of how fast Japan can get a profit back from the loan.

loans in 1970 were: 3.7 per cent interest; repayment over 21.4 years; 6.7 years deferment (i.e. allowed before repayment begins). The DAC (Development Assistance Committee) average in the same years was: 2.7 per cent interest; 29.7 years repayment; and 7.5 years deferment.[1]

If loans go through the Export–Import Bank, the interest rate is 6½ per cent. By the end of 1970 Japan had not reached the OECD (Organization for Economic Co-operation and Development) target for *1965* for softening loans. In addition, repayment schedules have been tighter than the capitalist average, and deferment periods about equally tough. Moreover, even by capitalist standards, a very big proportion of Japan's loans have been tied to the purchase of Japanese goods: at least 90 per cent (and nearly 80 per cent of all official bilateral loans) have been tied in the same way.

At a world capitalist conference on 'aid' convened by OECD in Tokyo in September 1970, Japan committed itself to meeting the target of 1 per cent of GNP for 'aid' by 1975. At the same time, the Tokyo regime implicitly announced that it would refuse to allot anything like 70 per cent of this figure to official 'aid'. (One per cent of GNP in 1975 would be about $3,940mill.)[2]

Japan may soon hit the 1 per cent figure. As the *FEER* puts it:

> Foreign aid is a most stable and profit-assured business. Where in the Sixties there was 'no business like reparations business', the slogan today is 'no business like the foreign aid business'. As long as foreign aid is profit motivated it will be difficult for Japan to correct its present image – removing more with the left hand than is given with the right.[3]

The most striking example of Japanese 'aid' is provided by Malaysia: according to *The Times*, Malaysia was 'unable to

1. Kawata Tadashi, 'Southeast Asia and the Japanese Economic Thrust', *Sekai*, November 1971, pp. 193–207.
2. Wilson, *FEER*, no. 50, 1970, op. cit.
3. Koji Nakamura, 'The Okinawa Payoff', *FEER*, no. 34, 21 August 1971, p. 38.

use' a Japanese loan of $50mill. which Japan had been offering for five years; the terms involved, as even the Tunku noticed, made it better not to have the loan at all . . .[1]

JAPANESE INVESTMENT IN SOUTH-EAST ASIA

Until very recently Japan had invested very little capital overseas, in comparison with the other major capitalist countries. Table 10 gives the picture in the years 1965–9.

It is important to stress that in recent years world capital flows have been growing much faster than those of world trade. In addition, until the mid-sixties Japan had a continual deficit in its current account, only just balanced by the inflow of foreign money into Japan. Since then, Japan has converted the deficit into a huge surplus. As is described in a later section on South Korea and Taiwan, Japanese capitalism has its own good reasons for investing abroad and these have, by and large, coincided with recent strong American pressure, both monetary and political, on Japan to invest in South-East Asia and the Pacific rim area.

South-East Asia has not been a major investment area for imperialism: at the end of 1969 the U.S.A. only had some 3 per cent of its total direct overseas investment there. In 1968 Japan still had only just over half as much capital invested in the region as it did in Latin America (14 per cent and 26 per cent of its total overseas investment, respectively). Table 11 gives the relative picture up to the end of 1969. Table 13 gives the breakdown of Japanese investment by sector and region.

A general assessment made in May 1971[2] was that of Japan's then total $3 billion overseas investment, only one fifth was in Asia (including the Middle East) – and of that one fifth, only a minor part involved the building of manufacturing facilities.

1. *The Times*, 29 April 1971.

2. *Wall Street Journal*, 5 May 1971, p. 62. Embassy of Japan, London, *Japan Information Bulletin*, 12 December 1971, states that: 'As of the end of fiscal 1970, the cumulative total of Japan's investments stood at $3,600 million. Of this $1,770 million was invested in the developing countries.'

TABLE TEN Japanese Overseas Investment and Export Credits 1965–9 (in $mill.)

	1965		1966		1967		1968		1969	
	Investments	Credits	Investments	Credits	Investments	Credits	Investments	Credits	Investments	Credits
Europe	0.4			48.3		21.1		84.0	0.5	103.3
Latin America	45.2		44.5	41.9	34.5	77.5	23.5	152.1	51.9	102.4
Africa	1.9		3.7	180.6	2.5	279.9	42.9	34.1	17.1	46.3
S.E. Asia	34.2		32.0	243.5	42.6	267.0	50.7	363.6	109.1	621.8
Middle East	13.0		22.9	10.9	19.3	53.6	21.8	76.1	43.0	78.3
Pacific	0.2		1.6		0.2		0.1		0.4	
Total	94.4		104.7	525.2	99.1	699.2	139.0	931.7*	222.0	952.0
Overall Total (Investments and Export Credits)	94.4		629.9		798.3		1,070.7		1,174.0	

*The total export credits figure for 1968 includes an unspecified 'other' of 221.8.

Source: *Keizai Kyoryoku Kankei Shiryo* (Materials on Economic Co-operation), Foreign Office, Tokyo, 1970, pp. 26–7.

TABLE ELEVEN Outstanding Overseas Direct Investment of Major Countries (in $mill.)

	end 1966	end 1969					1966–9
	total	total	% in Developed countries	% of GNP	% of exports	$ per capita	average % increase rate
U.S.A.	54,562	70,763	60.9	7.5	189.0	348	9.0
U.K.	16,002	18,655	16.0	20.0	110.5	336	5.2
France	4,000	4,779	4.1	3.7	32.4	95	6.1
W. Germany	2,500	4,814	4.1	2.9	16.6	79	24.4
Canada	3,238	3,806	3.3	5.2	27.7	180	5.5
Japan	1,000	2,683	2.3	1.6	16.7	26	31.4
DAC total	89,583	116,246	100.0	6.3	69.2	187	9.1

Source: MITI, *Tsusho Hakusho, Soron*, 1971, p. 365.

FEER, 28 August 1971, gives Japan's total in March 1971 as $3,594mill. and estimates Japan's total by 1980 as $25,700mill.

However, equally important, it was estimated that over $1.2 billion of the $3 billion total had been invested in the previous two years.

Put crudely, three determinants have operated on this development: the domestic needs of Japanese industry; the

TABLE TWELVE U.S., W. German and Japanese Outstanding Overseas Direct Investment by Sector and Region (in $mill to the end of 1969)

	U.S.A.	W. Germany	Japan	
Total	70,763	4,814	2,683	
Mining	5,635	4,200	892	(mining and oil)
Petroleum	19,985	102		
Manufacturing	29,450	3,558	722	
Other	15,693	954	1,070	
W. Europe	21,554	2,675	303	
N. America	21,075	799	720	(27%)
Latin America	13,811	896	513	(19%)
S.E. Asia	3,363	103	604	(22%)
Middle East	1,829	29	306	
Africa	2,970	259	79	
Oceania	3,099	53	158	
Unclassified	3,061	—	—	

Note: 40 per cent of the Japanese total is accounted for by the years 1968–9.

Source: MITI, *Tsusho Hakusho, Soron*, 1971, p. 366.

big shift in Japan's trade balance and the reserves; and America's political pressure on Japan to take a greater role, as 'ring-master', in East Asia.

As regards the last point: the watershed year was 1965. At this point the U.S.A. was bogged down in Vietnam, and cuts in foreign 'aid' to countries like South Korea were being mooted to protect the dollar. Considerable pressure was put on Japan to share the costs of policing the area. Washington began talks with Tokyo about the return of Okinawa. Johnson forced a speed-up in the Tokyo–Seoul 'normalization' talks which had been limping along for *thirteen* years. Sukarno was

TABLE THIRTEEN The Structure of Japanese Overseas Investment by Sector and Region to the end of 1969

	North America	Latin America	South-East Asia	Middle East	Europe	Africa	Oceania	Total
Development Enterprises	129	96	266	302	1	57	108	959
Manufacturing	160	249	233		39		41	722
Commerce	431	168	105	small	287	small		1,003
% of total	26.9	19.1	22.5					

Note: Development Enterprises: mining, forestry, fisheries . . .

Source: MITI, *Tsusho Hakusho*, *Soron*, 1971, p. 374.

brought down and replaced by a coalition of Japanese-trained generals, led by Suharto, and U.S.-trained technocrats, known collectively as 'the Berkeley mafia'.[1] Tokyo had, of course, had relatively good relations with Sukarno (based on their wartime 'alliance', and on the mediation of Sukarno's Japanese wife); but it was only after his downfall that Japanese money moved into Indonesia in a big way. It was, moreover, Tokyo, with its good political connections, which co-ordinated the 'rehabilitation' of the Indonesian economic scene after the Suharto putsch.[2]

The rapid evolution in the situation can best be illustrated by reference to the number one target of plunder in the area – Indonesia. Table 14 gives the bare outlines.

The main point about Japanese investment in Indonesia hardly needs commenting on: Japan's total of over $100mill., just in the first four months of 1971, outpaces the total of all the other countries of the world combined, and is equal to almost two thirds of Japan's total investment in the country in the previous four years. (The Hong Kong figure is also striking: more investment in January–April 1971 than in the previous four-year period.)

It goes without saying that Indonesia is the richest prize in the area: immense resources in oil, rubber, tin, bauxite, copper, timber, etc. The big rush started in 1967, after Japan and America together had rallied Indonesia's capitalist creditors to stabilize the Suharto group.[3] U.S. capital won the race: it has grabbed the most promising oil areas, rubber areas, copper and bauxite mines. Japan, for its part, has got some oil rights, forests (see section on Lumber below), fishing rights and nickel. In general, Japan is way behind, and the weakness of Japanese capitalism (to date) can be seen from this failure to

1. On this, see David Ranson, 'The Berkeley Mafia and the Indonesian Massacre', in B. Garrett and K. Barkeley, *Two, Three Many Vietnams*, San Francisco, 1970.

2. No author, 'Japanese Aid to Indonesia', *JQ*, vol. 15, no. 4, 1968, pp. 407–13. cf. David Conde, *Eastern Horizon*, vol. 9, no. 6, 1970.

3. Imagawa Eiichi, 'Inroads of the Japanese Economy in Asia', *Sekai*, November 1970.

TABLE FOURTEEN Foreign Capital Investment in Indonesia

	Jan. 1967–Dec. 1970		Jan. 1971–April 1971		Total	
	Projects	Capital ($)	Projects	Capital ($)	Projects	Capital ($)
U.S.A.	53	516,020,000	5	12,130,000	58	528,150,000
Philippines	13	261,500,000				
Japan	53	156,620,000	12	101,938,419	65	258,558,419
South Korea	4	53,400,000				
Canada	3	77,660,000				
Hong Kong	41	43,890,000	8	44,600,000	49	88,490,000
Singapore	26	37,520,000	2	16,300,000	28	53,820,000
Britain	27	28,240,000	1	1,150,000	28	29,740,000
Australia	10	12,450,000	4	3,710,000	14	16,160,000
All countries of the world	335	1,339,360,000	42	188,726,419	377	1,528,086,419

Source: *FEER*, no. 35, 1971, p. 62.

The Philippines figure is presumably disguised American capital. Virtually the entire Korean figure is accounted for by lumber investment: Robert Coats ('Indonesian Timber', *PR & WET* vol. 2, no. 4, May–June 1971) indicates that this is reported by different sources as being either South Korean government investment or American money. Some of the Hong Kong, Singapore, Panama, and Bahaman money can also be assumed to be American or Japanese.

dominate this key, rich, source of vital raw materials close to home. What seems to have happened is that while the U.S.A. develops the key resources in Indonesia, Japan is active in manufacturing, transport, communications, electrical power and in funding the actual regime. The Chairman of the Indonesian Government Investment Committee, Sadli, was recently quoted as saying: 'Japan and the U.S. already control the Indonesian economy. The U.S. has seized the natural resources and Japan the manufacturing industry.'[1]

Japan's biggest investment in Thailand will be in the huge petrochemical complex planned some sixty miles from Bangkok, on the Gulf of Thailand: this will be the biggest petrochemical installation in the whole of South-East Asia. Tokyo and Bangkok have been discussing building a big industrial harbour and steelworks there, and laying a pipeline across the Kra Isthmus. The Japanese companies involved in putting up the $120mill. needed for the petrochemical plant are: Mitsubishi Trading, Mitsubishi Oil and Fats, Mitsui Trading, Mitsui Petrochemicals, Mitsui High Tension and Teijin. Petroleum subsidiary products would be used for the chemical works, manufacturing various items, including man-made fibres. The harbour could accommodate 200,000-tonners. Another Japanese giant, Marubeni Corporation, has presented a pipeline plan to the Thai government. Japan is to refine oil in Thailand, as well as control shipbuilding and automobile plants. There were already more than 200 Japanese companies in Bangkok in 1971. Naturally, the big American bases in the area may be an attraction to Japanese investors. The question is: with so much Japanese money around, who controls what?

The difficulties of assessing Japanese investment are brought out by every study. The June 1970 issue of the prestigious *Chuo Koron* attempted a survey. It came up with a figure of almost $300mill. for aggregate Japanese direct investment in East and South-East Asia, as of the end of 1969.

Table 15 sets out the relative position of major investing

1. Ogiso Misao, 'Intangible Economic Empire', *Chuo Koron*, no. 6, 1970, pp. 164–73.

countries in five South-East Asian countries as of the end of 1969. However, the position has changed a good deal since then. In the case of Thailand, by mid-1971 Japan had further increased its lead over the U.S.A.; whereas the U.S.A. had \$4mill. in solely-owned projects and \$18.7mill. in joint ventures, Japan had, respectively, sums of \$10mill. and \$31mill. Taiwan had just over \$19mill., almost entirely in joint projects, followed by the U.K. with \$6½mill.[1] In Malaysia, Japan had already moved up from number five to number four by early 1971, and the *Wall Street Journal* was predicting that it would soon be the primary foreign investor in Malaysia.[2]

The situation in Singapore, as is well known, has been moving very fast. Japanese investment there more than doubled between 1965 and 1970 – from U.S. \$27mill. to \$61mill. (and \$68mill. by a year later) – putting Japan third in the overall league, behind only the U.S.A. and Britain. Japan is Singapore's number one source of imports, and the close relationship seems bound to continue. The Japanese ship-building giant, IHI, has a joint enterprise with the Singapore government, the Jurong Shipyard. Further joint enterprises for a total of Sing.\$1 billion are planned between Japanese interests and bureaucratic comprador capital – half over the next five years.[3]

The situation in Hong Kong is not completely clear. Two recent estimates quoted are as follows: 'While the U.S. remains the prime source of foreign investment with 44 per cent of the total, Britain has slipped into third place behind Japan with 23 per cent.' And: 'U.S. investment in Hong Kong factories amounts to half the foreign investment. The United Kingdom and Japan follow with 24 per cent and 19 per cent respectively.'[4]

1. *FEER*, no. 35, 1971, p. 59.
2. *WSJ*, 5 May 1971.
3. *FEER*, March 1972, p. 65 (the 1971 figure is from Takeuchi Ikuo, *Asahi Journal*, 14 January 1972).
4. The first statement is from *FEER*, no. 35, 1971, p. 42: in context, it *implies* that it is referring only to recent capital. Certainly if property and suchlike is taken into account, it would seem improbable that

TABLE FIFTEEN Foreign Capital in South-East Asia to the end of 1969 (in $mill.)

	Country	Amount	% share
a. *Thailand*	Japan	32	31.8
	U.S.A.	16	16.1
	Taiwan	14	14.5
	Others	37	37.6
	Total	99	100.0
b. *Taiwan*	U.S.A.	174	41.3
	Overseas Chinese	134	31.8
	Japan	61	14.4
	Others	53	12.5
	Total	422	100.0
c. *S. Korea*	U.S.A.	81	60.9
	Japan	38	28.2
	W. Germany	1	0.6
	Others	14	10.3
	Total	134	100.0
d. *Malaysia*	U.K.	23	22.6
	U.S.A.	22	22.0
	Singapore	21	20.8
	Hong Kong	11	10.8
	Japan	11	10.5
	Others	13	13.3
	Total	100	100.0
e. *Indonesia*	U.S.A.	441	40.3
	Philippines	259	23.7
	Japan	119	10.9
	Canada	77	7.4
	Others	197	17.7
	Total	1,093	100.0

Source: MITI, *Tsusho Hakusho, Soron*, 1971, p. 385.

Britain is not the *real* leading foreign owner of assets in Hong Kong: many of these are registered at their nominal value. The second estimate is by an American businessman based in Hong Kong, quoting an official Hong Kong survey up to May 1970: this statement is explicitly limited to *factories* (*FEER*, no. 39, 1971, p .47). Cf. *FEER*, no. 10, 1972, p. 56.

The Philippines is another different case. Because of anti-Japanese feeling arising out of the wartime occupation, the Philippines refused to enact an investment guarantee law for Japanese capital. A lot of Japanese money flowed into the Philippines, but fairly little of it was recorded as direct investment: a 1971 estimate by the *Wall Street Journal*[1] was that, whereas the figure for Japanese equity investment was only $10–12mill., there was something like $350mill. of private unrecorded Japanese loans floating around – all ready to be converted into investment at short notice, and in terms of real power probably acting as such already. A more recent Chinese estimate is that 60 per cent of all recent investment in the Philippines was Japanese.[2]

All this raises the question of the form which Japanese financial power and control take. The Philippines is one case of extremity. Another, for different reasons, is South Korea, which has had vast quantities of Japanese capital in the form of loans, but until recently very little as direct investment. India and Pakistan also fall into this group: they have received very little Japanese private capital, but Japan has been important in the imperialist consortia propping up the ruling cliques in both Islamabad and New Delhi: in the case of Pakistan, Japan has been among the four main contributors,

1. *WSJ*, 5 May 1971. The Japanese government puts out fairly accurate figures for officially approved investment overseas: it is on these that such widely used estimates as those of the June 1970 *Chuo Koron* estimate (up to end 1969) are based. The well-informed Japanese economist, Kitamura Hiroshi, has suggested that a more or less standard multiplier should be used on all such official approval figures: thus, the official figure for Japanese investment in the Philippines should be multiplied by 3.5 to give the correct figure; in Thailand by 2.3 times; in Malaysia and Singapore by about twice; and in Indonesia by about 1½ times (Kitamura, op. cit., p. 55).

2. *PR*, no. 41, 1971. The U.S.A. is still by far the biggest foreign investor in the Philippines. But since the Philippines Investment Incentives Act came into effect in 1968 Japan accounted for 58 per cent ($262mill.) of all new foreign capital up to April 1971, far outdistancing the U.S.A. (14 per cent: $52mill.) (*FEER*, no. 42, 1971, p. 65).

along with the U.K., the U.S.A. and West Germany. The same goes for the broken-down economies and currencies of Indo-China (see below).

To revert to the balance of power between Japan and the U.S.A. in South-East Asia, one must consider both the ratio of foreign investment and the output by foreign subsidiaries. The figures in Table 11 show that Japan's investment, to GNP ratio, was extremely low: 1.0 per cent in 1966 and 1.1 per cent in 1968. By the end of March 1970, Japan's accumulated foreign investment (on the approval basis) came to $2,083mill. or 1.4 per cent of the current GNP – whereas the comparative percentage for the U.S.A. was 7.5, and for West Germany 2.5.[1]

As for the output of foreign subsidiaries, in Japan's case this is only a little over 30 per cent of Japan's annual exports – whereas in the case of the U.S.A. it is nearly four times as much as U.S.A. exports. To assess the relative strengths, one must consider a country's total exports plus total sale of foreign subsidiaries (minus transactions between the mother country and its foreign subsidiaries). Taking each country's share of the combined total of the world's four main trading countries, the U.S.A., the U.K., West Germany and Japan (exports and 'foreign sales'), the comparison between Japan and the U.S.A. shapes up as follows:

	1968	
Country	Exports*	Total 'foreign sales'
U.S.A.	39.2	63.3
Japan	15	7.1

*as a percentage of the combined exports to the world

Even in South-East Asia, where Japan's exports have just overtaken those from the U.S.A., by a small margin, Japan's share in terms of 'foreign sales' was only 26.4 per cent, as compared with the U.S.A.'s share of 42.7 per cent. Japan's

1. Kitamura, *Japan's Economic Policy Towards South-East Asia*, p. 53

economic influence in the South-East Asia region (as of late 1969) was thus only about 60 per cent that of the United States.[1]

Changes have been coming so fast in the last year or so, including revaluation of the currencies involved, that it is impossible to give an exact overall position as of this moment (early 1972). By the end of 1971 Japan's reserves had risen to $15,235mill., thus greatly enlarging Japan's possibilities of overseas investment and loans; the whole anti-pollution campaign has acquired increased strength, accelerating pressures on business to export its 'dirtier' processes out of Japan; and much of imperialism's anti-China policy is in disarray, with important political and economic effects on Japan's policies. Projections made in early 1971 by the Industrial Structure Council, an advisory body to MITI, indicate that Japanese overseas investment will reach a total of $11,500mill. by the end of 1975, and somewhere around $26,000mill. by 1980. This would mean an increase of 4.3 times over the five years 1971–5, and put Japan's overseas stake at close to 3 per cent of GNP (i.e. slightly higher than the current West German percentage, but still less than half the U.S.A. figure). The total increase over the decade would be nearly ten times. All previous predictions have underestimated the rate of expansion of Japanese investment.

As Table 16 shows, Japan had a very high percentage of its investment in the Third World – more than 60 per cent (incomparably higher than other capitalist countries). Relative to trade, the two areas where investment was still extremely low in 1968 were Europe and South-East Asia. It is still hard to draw any precise correlation between trade and investment in Japan's case.

1. Kitamura, op. cit., pp. 53–4. Hayashi Naomichi, 'The Economic Basis for the Revival of Japanese Militarism', p. 247, gives Japan as the origin of 6.2 per cent of the capitalist world's exports in 1968 (6.6 in 1969), compared with 16.2 per cent from the U.S.A. in the same year (15.0 in 1969).

TABLE SIXTEEN Levels of Japan's Outstanding Investment and Annual Investment Flows Relative to Japan's Foreign Trade

	Investment Level Relative to Exports		Investment Level Relative to Imports	
	Accumulated Investment	*Investment Flow, Average 1966–8*	*Accumulated Investment*	*Investment Flow, Average 1966–8*
Developed Areas	0.79	1.03	0.78	1.02
North America	0.99	1.25	1.02	1.28
Europe	0.21	0.21	0.27	0.28
Oceania	1.00	1.95	0.48	0.93
Developing Areas	1.35	1.08	1.42	1.14
South-East Asia	0.70	0.66	1.26	1.17
Latin America	4.02	2.84	3.01	2.13
Middle East	3.61	2.07	1.10	0.63
Africa	0.48	0.81	0.59	1.00

Note: Figures are derived from the formula:

$$\frac{\text{Each region's share of investment total or flows}}{\text{Each region's share of exports or imports}}$$

Outstanding investment balance relates to 1968.
Source: Government of Japan, Economic Planning Agency, *Nenji Keizai Hokoku* (Economic Survey of Japan), 1970, p. 118.

The Politics of Japanese Investment and Loans

It is quite possible to show the extent of Japan's political involvement in a number of South-East Asian countries. The *Japan Quarterly* study of Japan's relations with Indonesia (cited above) made no bones about the objective of Tokyo's economic policy: to prop up the Suharto regime. As early as July 1966 Japan had pledged the then very large sum of $300mill. emergency aid to the new regime in Djakarta, under strong prompting from business leaders.[1] The Keidanren (Federation of Economic Organizations) studies on 'postwar' South Vietnam are blatantly designed to prop up an anti-

1. Hayashi Naomichi, *Gendai to Shiso*, p. 259.

Communist regime in Saigon.[1] The cases of Taiwan and South Korea are discussed below. The loans policy to India and Pakistan follows the same pattern. So do the exports of bullet manufacturing plants to South Vietnam and the Philippines (the latter explicitly requested by the Manila regime to combat the revolution).

A rather interesting recent case of Japan's role in the general counter-revolution has been its participation in imperialist groups to 'underwrite' the Laotian kip and the Cambodian riel.[2] The cost of 'supporting' the Laotian kip runs to some $30mill. p.a., and is covered by a fund backed by the U.S.A., the U.K., Japan, France and Australia. The latest news of the now thoroughly enfeebled kip was a devaluation against the dollar of more than 16 per cent (from 500 to 600 kip to the dollar) in November 1971.[3]

The cost of supporting the riel (currently fluctuating as much as 30 per cent in the space of a few hours, and overall inflated 700 per cent since the start of the war in Cambodia) is conservatively calculated at about $75mill. (c. £30mill.) p.a. The U.S.A. has stitched together a group consisting of itself, the U.K., France, Australia, Japan, Taiwan and South Korea![4] The fund provides hard currency backing for worthless, unbacked paper money (kip and riel).

> The most conspicuous aspect of such funds is an influx of foreign consumer goods . . . The technique may seem paradoxical but it is not. Available foreign currency soaks up local currency. Money spent on foreign goods reduces demand for

1. *Interim Report* by Liaison Committee for Cooperation with Viet-Nam, April 1970: reprinted in full in *Looking Back*, no. 3, 1971.
2. T. D. Allman, 'Purchase of a Nation', *FEER*, no. 32, 1971, pp. 61–2.
3. *The Times*, 8 November 1971.
4. The participation of the South Korean regime, whose own currency is subject to spiralling inflation (14.4 per cent in 1970) and has twice been devalued since 1969, can only be some kind of corrupt sop to the Seoul junta. Presumably, it covers looting by Pak (Pak Jung Hi, President of South Korea) operatives in Vientiane and Phnom Penh.

locally-produced items . . . Unfortunately, the foreign purchases tend to foster foreign economic dependence and fail to encourage local development.

The local currency is simply taken out of circulation.

Stabilization funds, therefore, act as giveaway programmes – sponsored for political reasons rather than return on investment in local development.[1]

The U.S.A. was then reported to be trying to get the fund working in time for the Cambodian rice crop.

The fund, however, will not be an economic step forward but a sign of Cambodia's maturing 'client' relationship with the U.S. With the fund, the Cambodian riel – like the survival of the Lon Nol regime itself – becomes dependent on the priorities of foreigners. Besides the loss of economic independence, stabilization accustoms a country to a standard of living it cannot afford. For all their cosmetic effects such funds are the most habit-forming narcotics in the entire arsenal of economic imperialism.[2]

In late 1971 the riel was devalued by the large (but virtually meaningless) figure of 60 per cent.[3]

As well as the level of straightforward plundering of raw materials, there is this other level – currency manipulation, a powerful narcotic of imperialism – in which Japan is a leading partner of the U.S.A.

Not surprisingly the corruption effect has worked at both ends. A report released by the U.S. Congress House Government Operations Committee in early December 1971 stated flatly that the kip fund 'promoted rather than discouraged fraud, corruption and dishonesty'.[4]

1. Allman, op. cit.
2. ibid.
3. *The Times*, 1 November 1971. For Britain's part in the riel operation, see T. D. Allman in the *Guardian*, 8 November 1971.
4. *FEER*, no. 51, 1971, p. 4.

Vietnam Investment

Japan has derived enormous profits from the Vietnam war, yet it was not until 1969 that economic aid was first furnished to Saigon. In 1971 the total amounted to some $30mill., with the Vietnamese hoping for another $50mill. in 1972. This was partly a move to offset the decline in trade resulting from the 1970 ruling, part of the dollar defence measures, that American aid monies could not henceforth be used to finance imports from Japan. Since that time many Japanese firms have moved into South Vietnam and set up joint ventures with local interests. In a very short time the Japanese have established themselves as the country with the greatest economic stake in Vietnam. A recent Saigon offer seems to have been particularly attractive to the Japanese: any foreign firm willing to establish an assembly plant in the country is now granted a monopoly of exports of the readymade products to South Vietnam until the plant is ready to operate, which usually means for two years.[1]

The key point for Japanese involvement in Vietnam came in 1970. At the Sato–Nixon talks of late 1970 Sato agreed to give due consideration and take a 'forward looking stance' on the U.S.A. request for $150mill. in aid for Thieu, a request, in other words, for Japanese government underwriting for a large scale operation by Japanese industry to go into Vietnam as it had in Korea and Taiwan.[2] Commitment to Vietnam was the third specific direction of Japanese policy as spelt out in the Sato–Nixon communique of the previous year, it will be remembered. (See Appendix III and section below on the military.) In 1969–70, first a Keidanren group, and later a government-sponsored 'Vietnam Economic Co-operation Group' toured Vietnam.[3] The Japanese appear to have

1. *FEER*, 4 March 1972, pp. 66–7.

2. Yasushi Hara, *Asahi Evening News*, 24 October 1970.

3. The Keidanren mission was headed by Senga Tetsuya, longtime head of Keidanren's Defence Production Committee, and was thought likely, among other things, to have looked into the prospects for Japanese arms sales to Vietnam (Akagi Shoichi, *Nihon No Boei*

accepted Nixon's request and the level of their activity subsequently showed a marked increase. Even in the absence of precise overall figures there are any number of indices of the new Japanese push: the opening of yen credits for infrastructural items, such as the Saigon power plant ($4.5mill. in August 1970), the Can Tho thermal powerhouse ($16mill. in June 1971), the Phan Rang irrigation project ($9mill., under consideration still in June 1971), and the Saigon telephone and waterworks improvement scheme ($6mill., also under consideration); the establishment of joint industrial ventures, such as Vikyno and Farmassin agricultural machinery factories (the latter 49 per cent Mitsubishi group);[1] and the formation of even more monopolistic export consortia, such as the joint Sony/National/Sanyo home electrical linkup reported in March 1971.[2]

A recent report speaks of the 'optimism' in Binh Dinh province arising from the plans of Japanese businessmen for the development of its considerable natural resources. 'Japanese engineers have surveyed the An Khe area in the hills

Sangyo [*Japan's Defence Production*], Tokyo, 1969, pp. 207–10). On the government mission see Wada Haruki, *Asahi Journal*, 7 May 1971, pp. 97–101.

1. Yasushi Hara, op. cit; *Japan Times*, 26 March, 20 June 1971; *Mainichi Daily News*, 21 April 1971; *FEER*, 4 March 1972, pp. 66–7. Till the Sato–Nixon 1969 meeting, incidentally, Japanese aid had been largely restricted to 'humanitarian' aid – hospitals and the like. The major exception to this was the export in the late 1950s of a bullet manufacturing plant to South Vietnam – which became the subject of a major scandal in Japan.

Mitsubishi's 49 per cent participation in establishing a factory in South Vietnam to build and market agricultural machines and diesel engines merits close attention: Mitsubishi have gone into this venture with the South Vietnamese puppet trade union federation, the CVT. This is a particularly Japanese move, since American business in Vietnam (like Bunker and the U.S. embassy) is not friendly to the CVT. Yet Mitsubishi's decision to join with the CVT in trying to demobilize rural discontent has to be seen as part of Japanese imperialism's plan to strengthen the counter-revolution in South-East Asia, in its own specific way (see *FEER*, no. 19, 1971, p. 28).

2. *Asahi Shimbun*, 1 March 1971.

thirty-six miles northwest of Qui Nhon. Construction has begun on a hydro-electric power plant capable of generating 160,000 kilowatts and irrigating 50,000 hectares of land. It will provide power for a proposed industrial centre clustered around the port of Qui Nhon.' The same area seems marked by the Japanese also for its timber and grazing potential, and as a site for a Toyota plant and textile mill.[1] The war has already produced a cheap, concentrated and depressed labour force which, added to the natural riches of the area, make it a most attractive investment proposition.

One of the objects of the Laird visit to Japan in July 1971 was reported to have been to request further Japanese aid for Vietnam;[2] on 24 August the Japanese Foreign Ministry announced it had decided to grant an annual $10mill. loan to the Thieu administration, under eased loan conditions, etc., and this just nine days after the 10 per cent cuts in U.S. foreign aid announced as part of the dollar defence moves.[3] Again, at the U.S.A.–Japan Ministerial Conference of 9 September 1971, Secretary Rogers for the U.S.A. side is reported to have asked for '. . . substantial, indeed dramatic, increase' in Japanese official assistance to developing countries, especially Indochina.[4]

THE WORLD BANK AND THE ASIAN DEVELOPMENT BANK

As noted elsewhere, Japan was a major recipient of World Bank funds throughout the postwar period. In 1966 a special Asian bank, the Asian Development Bank (ADB) was set up, largely to systematize the U.S.A.–Japanese investment relationship in the area.

When the ADB was originally set up there was a much-

1. *FEER*, 14 August 1971, p. 21.
2. *Mainichi Shimbun*, 10 July 1971.
3. Hagiwara Yoshiyuki, 'Relations with Asia at a Crossroad', *Asahi Journal*, 15 October 1971, pp. 10–13.
4. *The Times*, 10 September 1971.

publicized tug-of-war between America and Japan about the siting of the Bank's HQ: Japan wanted Tokyo, the U.S.A. wanted Manila. Eventually it was located in the latter, with a Japanese head, Watanabe. It was then widely stated that Japan had little real influence in the Bank. This was a false assumption. That Japan was extremely important in the Bank right from the start is well documented in a recent study on regional development banks.[1]

After a few years of fairly low profile, both the World Bank and the ADB have recently stepped up their activities in Asia. The World Bank opened an office in Tokyo only in November 1970, but this has already become the HQ for its entire Asian operations. The Bank has already borrowed $450mill. from Japan, and in fiscal 1970 Japan supplied more than one third of all funds collected by the Bank. The first foreign bonds ever floated in Japan were those of the ADB (December 1970). A more recent World Bank flotation is said to be the largest publicly subscribed issue in the history of Japan's bond market.[2]

It is not hard to see why Japan is mobilizing itself. These allegedly international organizations have played a vanguard role in crippling the economies of the borrowing countries: the case of South Korea is exemplary. But it is only an extreme case, for the external debts of the developing countries already totalled $65,000mill. by mid-1971, and they are increasing by 15 per cent per year.[3] Annual payments on these debts

1. John White, *Regional Development Banks*, London, 1971, chapter on the ADB. White, a standard liberal, criticizes the ADB as being neither regional nor a 'development' bank.

2. This information and all the quotes in this section are taken from John G. Roberts, 'The American Zaibatsu', *FEER*, no. 30, 24 July 1971, pp. 49–51. This is an extremely useful analysis of the World Bank and its relationship to Japan; the article also contains an excellent breakdown of the particular American interests which both dominate the World Bank and structured Japan's postwar relationship with the U.S.A. (John Foster Dulles, John J. McCloy and Eugene Black being the three key figures).

3. This is an official estimate by Robert McNamara. UN figures prepared for UNCTAD, however, showed that the foreign debts of

amount to nearly twice as much as the World Bank's total input.

In view of the chasms of poverty to be filled, it appears that the best to be expected is to keep friendly governments afloat and alleviate some of their most pressing problems to stave off insurrection.

Indeed, it is hard to imagine that the World Bank, the International Development Association and ADB really expect their pittances to substantially relieve Asian poverty. It is much more credible that they are attempting to create and preserve a climate favourable to foreign investment while building up an infrastructure that will facilitate the exploitation of Asian resources.[1]

In the words of Sir Denis Rickett, Vice-President of the World Bank, since the poor countries of Asia are important suppliers of raw materials to Japan, Japan 'has a vital interest' in political stability in them: 'While development is no guarantee of stability, there is today little chance of ensuring stability without development.'

'In this context,' notes Roberts, 'the word "stability" itself takes on a rather sinister connotation.' Roberts sees the U.S.A. manipulating the World Bank, using European bankers to speak for it in Asia, while McNamara and the big American oil interests operate behind the scenes. The shape of the future would seem to be gigantic American investments in the area, often in partnership with Japan, and particularly in oil. In 1970 David Rockefeller predicted that big oil interests would invest a total of $30,000mill. in and around Singapore during the next twelve years – a staggering total. Since the World Bank is largely under the control of the Rockefeller–Chase Manhattan–Standard Oil group, this prediction is likely to

---

eighty developing countries nearly tripled between 1961 and 1969, when they reached $59,000mill. With a 15 per cent annual increase, this would give something like a total of $80 billion by the end of 1971 (*The Times*, 2 December 1971).

1. Roberts, op. cit.

become reality, and the Bank will presumably play quite a large part in it.

Roberts concludes his study thus:

> U.S. business and financial giants seem to be making plans for transforming the 'Pacific Basin' into a Japanese–American Co-prosperity Sphere that will outshine the original version.
>
> Japan, on the basis of its experience and talent, has been built up into the industrial base, the international entrepreneur and the raw-materials consumer that will, hopefully, make the region economically viable and enable U.S. investments to pay off handsomely. In the process, Japan's economic strength is being harnessed to development organizations, and it is expected that Tokyo will eventually become the principal money market for Asia. It is with such grand strategy in mind that ADB and World Bank have floated their yen bond issues and will presumably come back for more.[1]

Roberts notes, however, that Japan may not be entirely happy with the relationship, given America's rotten reputation throughout Asia. Furthermore, as he puts it, 'the Pacific rim countries are only the crust of the Asian loaf'.

But the big international institutions like the World Bank and the ADB are rather important for Japan, particularly since big Japanese business has not participated in the multinational corporations to the same extent as other major capitalist economies have (see below). And the international organizations may also provide a forum for Japan to lean slightly on the Americans in the current political and monetary turmoil, since the American role in them is very much posited on an integral 'partnership' with Japan – against the peoples of Asia.

JAPAN'S TRADE WITH SOUTH-EAST ASIA

Japan's top ten trading partners both ways are given in Table 17 from which the overall world situation is clear: among South-East Asian countries only Indonesia, the Philippines and

1. The second yen-based issuance of the ADB was signed in Japan later in 1971 and a third early in 1972.

TABLE SEVENTEEN Japan's Trading Patterns: Top Ten Trading Partners, 1970 (in $mill.)

Exports		Imports	
U.S.A.	5,939.8	U.S.A.	5,559.6
S. Korea	818.2	Australia	1,507.7
Taiwan	700.4	Iran	995.3
Hong Kong	700.3	Canada	928.6
Australia	589.0	Indonesia	636.6
Liberia	587.6	W. Germany	617.0
China	568.9	Philippines	535.5
Canada	563.3	U.S.S.R.	481.0
W. Germany	550.2	Saudi Arabia	435.1
U.K.	479.9	Malaysia	418.9

Source: MITI, *Tsusho Hakusho, Soron*, 1971, p. 113.

Malaysia figure in the top ten exporters to Japan. The top ten items are given in Table 18.

As a percentage of its total trade, Japan's trade with South-East Asia has been declining: Japan's exports to the area dropped from 35.8 per cent of total exports in 1955 to 27.8 per cent in 1969 and to 25.4 per cent in 1970, while imports fell from 26.3 per cent of the total to only 15.8 per cent in 1970.[1]

TABLE EIGHTEEN Japan's Exports and Imports, 1970. The Ten Major Items (in $mill.)

Exports	Value	Imports	Value
Iron and steel	2,843.7	Crude oil	2,535.6
Textiles	2,407.5	Timber	1,572.1
Machines	2,006.2	Iron ore	1,208.2
Ships	1,409.6	Non-ferrous ores	1,064.1
Cars	1,337.4	Coal	1,010.1
Metal products	713.7	Non-ferrous metals	944.8
Radio receivers	694.9	Fodder	671.1
Foodstuffs	647.0	Petroleum products	549.9
Precision machines	628.0	Oil and fats	542.0
Plastics	426.6	Grains (non fodder)	513.9

Source: ibid.

1. Except where otherwise stated, information in this section is taken from Kitamura, op. cit.

Japan's share of the region's total imports, however, rose from 10 per cent in 1955 to 23.2 per cent in 1968, surpassing that of the U.S.A. Also, the relative importance of Japan as a market for South-East Asia's exports grew from 8.3 per cent in 1955 to 14.6 per cent in 1963. There is a heavy imbalance between imports and exports – as can be seen from Table 19. Official statistics show that Japan's export surplus with the South-East Asian region increased from $550mill. in 1960 to $1,664.2mill. in 1968, and $1,888mill. in 1970.[1]

There are two general points of note: first, that Japan's trade with the area is exceptionally lop-sided; and, second, that Japan continues to buy an exceedingly small amount of its raw materials from the poor countries. Japan's import needs have been growing extremely fast: between 1964 and 1968 the increase in Japan's annual imports of primary products from the developing countries – $786mill. – was the largest among the main developed countries. And Japan is now *the largest resources-importing country in the world*, taking 18.2 per cent of the total resources imports of the OECD countries and surpassing the U.S.A. in terms of the value of raw material imports. But most of these imports – *some 60 per cent* – come from the other rich countries. Japan clearly does not want to continue to run such an imbalance with the region, and is therefore taking steps to build up what Kitamura rather ominously refers to as 'deliberately complementary productive capacities' – i.e. economies subordinate to Japan. Despite this the whole trend is speeding up, rather than slowing down. Between 1965 and 1968 Japan's exports to the region were expanding at the annual rate of 18 per cent, whereas its imports from South-East Asia were only growing at 10.4 per cent p.a.[2] A Japan Economic Research Centre projection for 1975 envisages Japanese exports taking as much as 40 per cent of

1. MITI, *Tsusho Hakusho, Kakuron* (*Detailed Exposition*), 1971, p. 110.

2. This was about in line with the general rate of increase in Japan's exports (18.6 per cent p.a. 1964–9; cf. U.K.: 6.5; U.S.A.: 7.3; France: 10.8; West Germany: 12.4; and Italy: 16.6 per cent over the same period).

TABLE NINETEEN Japan–South-East Asian Trade 1967–70 (in $mill.)

	Exports (from Japan)				Imports (to Japan)			
	1967	1968	1969	1970	1967	1968	1969	1970
S. Korea	406.9	602.6	761.6	818.1	92.3	101.6	133.9	228.9
Okinawa	266.8	226.1	312.4	368.9	76.1	87.9	93.5	100.9
Hong Kong	348.9	367.5	614.5	700.2	53.4	54.0	68.1	91.8
Taiwan	328.1	471.6	606.3	700.4	137.0	150.7	180.5	250.7
Cambodia	15.3	20.2	23.5	10.7	7.0	6.5	7.3	5.9
S. Vietnam	174.5	198.8	223.1	146.0	4.5	2.7	3.3	4.5
Thailand	340.9	365.4	433.8	449.1	160.0	147.0	167.4	189.5
Malaysia	87.3	104.4	133.4	166.4	334.4	343.3	406.7	418.8
Singapore	160.1	209.2	312.5	423.0	36.0	61.7	65.9	86.5
Philippines	362.9	411.0	475.6	453.7	473.4	397.4	468.0	433.4
Indonesia	155.3	147.2	237.2	315.7	196.6	253.5	398.8	636.5
Burma	26.3	39.2	37.1	38.7	12.0	12.3	12.9	12.5
India	137.9	139.3	95.8	103.1	258.8	293.0	321.1	390.0
Pakistan	81.7	116.0	106.5	138.4	37.6	56.8	37.5	42.3
Ceylon	18.4	24.6	35.7	24.9	12.6	12.3	12.6	17.3
Total	2,930.8	3,612.5	4,447.9	4,901.8	1,794.9	1,948.3	2,380.9	3,013.2

Total also includes small amounts from Laos, Maldive Islands, Macao, Timor, Afghanistan, Nepal, Bhutan and Brunei, of which details are here omitted.

Source: MITI, *Tsusho Hakusho, Kakuron*, 1970, p. 277; 1971, p. 300.

the import markets of South-East Asia and exceeding Japanese imports from the area by as much as $5,800mill. It is difficult to see what transfers could make up a gap of this size; the case of one of the local 'success stories', South Korea, is hardly encouraging: the burden of debts involved as a result of the massive transfusion of imperialist loans now threatens to cripple the entire economy, as well as having driven it into a state of total vassalage to the U.S.A., Japan, and their puppet agencies.

Trade: some examples

1. *Hong Kong*. In 1970, Japan's exports to the colony amounted to U.S.A. $698mill., while its imports from Hong Kong came to only U.S.A. $82mill. Japan was the number one exporter to Hong Kong, and also the number one importer of goods re-exported from Hong Kong (Japan's total: U.S. $97mill.).[1] In one typical sector, cameras, Japanese still cameras increased their share of the Hong Kong market from 73 per cent to 87 per cent.[2]

2. *South Vietnam*. Japanese exports to South Vietnam rose from $37mill. in 1965 to a peak of $223mill. in 1969.[3] The colossal imbalance in trade between the two areas is shown by the 1968 figures: imports from Japan came to $200mill., while exports to Japan totalled a mere $2.7mill.[4] In early 1971 Japan

1. *FEER*, no. 26, 1971, p. 46.

2. *FEER*, no. 30, 1971, p. 25. In another significant sector, Japan ousted Britain as the leading source of motor car imports into the colony for the first time in 1971, in spite of the 'preferential tax' operating in Britain's favour: Japanese exports for the first eight months of 1971 were 7,345 cars – nearly 1,000 more than the British total of 6,371 (*Ta Kung Pao*, 2 December 1971, p. 15).

3. *Newsweek*, 15 February 1971. Statistics relating to South Vietnam are particularly hard to check, mainly because of smuggling. The Economist Intelligence Unit study, *The Economic Effects of the Vietnamese War in East and Southeast Asia*, London, 1968, p. 21, shows Japanese exports to South Vietnam in 1967 as $173mill. (recorded in Japan) and Vietnam's imports from Japan as $139.5mill. (recorded in Vietnam).

4. *Asahi Journal*, 15 January 1971, pp. 116–19.

TABLE TWENTY Commodity Trade and Resources Flows between Individual South-East Asian Countries and Japan, 1968 (in $mill.)

	Flows from Japan	Japan's share of exports (%)		Japan's share of imports (%)		Commodity Trade to Japan	Commodity Trade from Japan	Balance
		1960	1968	1960	1968			
Taiwan	78.3	37.5	16.1	35.4	40.4	127.6	361.6	−234.0
S. Korea	140.0	63.7	21.9	20.2	42.5	99.7	624.5	−524.4
Burma	20.4	5.1	8.9	22.6	23.6	9.9	25.2	−15.3
Indonesia*	69.2	15.0	23.9	21.3	25.4	175.5	170.7	4.8
Malaysia*	1.1	15.6	31.2	7.2	13.8	301.1	96.6	204.5
Philippines	85.3	24.0	33.4	23.3	27.5	283.3	351.7	−68.4
Thailand*	37.0	18.0	21.6	26.1	36.1	147.6	382.2	−234.6
Ceylon	8.1	3.1	2.8	8.4	5.4	9.2	19.6	−10.4
India	75.1	5.3	11.5	5.4	6.6	201.5	166.2	35.3
Pakistan	42.9	7.2	6.1	8.6	11.0	50.4	109.4	−59.0

*All trade figures under 1968 relate to the year 1967.

Source: MITI, *Tsusho Hakusho*, 1970, p. 351.

was accounting for 48.7 per cent of all non-tied South Vietnamese imports.[1] Japan also has a virtually unassailable marketing network in certain consumer goods: in 1967, for example, 60,000 Hondas were sold per month (the best year), for a distribution rate reckoned by the *Asahi Journal* to be 200 per cent in Saigon.[2] Imports from Japan declined, however, to $160mill. in 1970, and to just under $100mill. in 1971, as U.S.-imposed restrictions on the use of aid dollars to buy goods in Japan began to bite. The fact that Japan's aid to South Vietnam began in the year in which its trade began to fall off underlines the trend already noted above in connection with reparations: as the directly war-related export boom eases off for one reason or another the government moves to subsidize Japanese industry by instituting an aid programme to the area concerned.

3. *Singapore.* In 1970 Japan overtook Malaysia as the number one source of Singapore's imports: U.S. $486mill., equivalent to 19.4 per cent of Singapore's total. This was a jump of more than $150mill. over 1969, and some $225mill. over 1968.[3] Singapore's exports to Japan totalled only $120mill. (7.6 per cent of total exports of $1,535mill.); Japan was the number three market, after West Malaysia (14.5 per cent) and the U.S.A. (11.1 per cent).

4. *Thailand.* This is another apparently doomed 'partner'. Already by 1965 Japan was accounting for more than half Thailand's large trading deficit, $138.9mill., as compared with $124.6mill. with all other trading partners. By 1970 the trade imbalance had grown to a whopping $316.8mill. just between Thailand and Japan: this accounted for over half the entire Thai trading deficit, even though only one third of overall trade was with Japan.[4]

1. *Newsweek*, 15 February 1971.
2. *Asahi Journal*, 15 January 1971.
3. *FEER*, no. 32, 1971, p. 46.
4. *FEER*, no. 46, 1971, p. 39.

A survey by the Thai motor industry showed that in 1969 50 per cent of all cars and 98 per cent of the trucks on the road at that time were Japanese, and 72 per cent of the monthly sales of 4,000 cars were Japanese.[1]

Two Commodities

Oil

At present Japan consumes 180mill. tons of oil per annum, which requires 700 tanker calls annually. About 90 per cent of Japan's oil comes from the Middle East, and therefore passes through the Straits of Malacca, between Singapore and Indonesia; this has been the main argument behind business calls for stationing Japanese forces on the Straits. Although Japan has invested sizeable sums in the Middle East, it does not control its sources there to any large extent, and its political leverage in the zone is rather small (although not negligible in Saudi Arabia, Kuwait and certain areas of the Gulf). Japan has recently committed itself to several very large deals with oil-producing Middle Eastern countries which go further to meet the interests of the producing countries than any previously concluded. In Saudi Arabia two Japanese companies (Mitsubishi Corporation and Chiyoda Chemical Engineering) signed a contract with Petromin (the Saudi state body) to buy $127mill. worth of Saudi crude oil in return for building oil refineries in Saudi Arabia – the first time the Saudis have been able to achieve their current goal of breaking through the international oil wall and reaching the position where the producing company will sell direct to the consumer.[2]

1. Cited by Shibata Toshiharu, 'The Real Nature of Views of Japan', *Asahi Journal*, 11 October 1970, pp. 102–5.

2. *JEJ*, 9 November 1971. This followed on the important state visit by King Faisal to Japan in May 1971, which greatly strengthened Saudi–Japanese ties. In Iran, with which Japan also has close links, four Japanese companies (three Mitsui firms plus Toyo Soda) have agreed to join the National Iranian Oil Company in a $358mill. petrochemical deal at the port of Bandar Shahpur (*Newsweek*, 1 November 1971). The Japanese companies will put up $258mill. initially: the

However, Middle East oil has recently risen quite a lot in price, and it is not all of low sulphur content (like Siberian and Indonesian oil), which is becoming an increasingly important consideration in pollution-conscious Japan. One of the biggest Japanese oil companies, Arabian Oil, which has been having great difficulty unloading its high-sulphur-content crude oil from the underseas Khafji field, held onto its ties with Taiwan until late 1971, as this was a convenient captive market.[1]

The October 1971 White Paper on raw materials stressed Japan's heavy dependence on oil imports controlled by the other major capitalist powers: it estimated that American capital alone controlled the supply of 80 per cent of Japanese imports of crude oil. It is now state policy to lower this dependence consistently.

Of the 10 per cent of Japan's current supply that is developed by Japanese companies, almost all (19mill. of the 20mill. kilolitres) is developed by Arabian Oil Co., and the rest by the North Sumatra Oil Development Company.[2] MITI has also been making strenuous efforts to strengthen the all-Japanese company, Kyodo Oil, to increase domestic control over refining[3] (the largest refiner at present, Nippon Oil, is a joint U.S.–Japanese company; the second largest, Idemitsu Kosan, is all-Japanese).

Up to the end of 1970 Japanese promoters had sunk about ¥150 billion (about $487mill.) into overseas oil development projects – which was equivalent to about 50 per cent of Japan's outstanding balance of funds in the development of major natural resources.[4] And in the last couple of years the Japanese

---

plant, when complete, will make Iran a major manufacturer of ethylene (300,000 tons p.a.), as well as other products. This deal followed only a week after two Japanese firms (Toyo Engineering Co. and C. Itoh) had signed a $93mill. deal with Algeria for supplying a petrochemical plant capable of producing 200,000 tons of ethylene per year (*Newsweek*, 25 October 1971).

1. *JEJ*, 9 November 1971.
2. *JEJ*, no. 475, p. 20 (a very useful survey).
3. *JEJ*, no. 477, p. 11: this MITI support is likely to increase.
4. *JEJ*, no. 476, p. 20.

have made even more prodigious efforts to diversify their sources of oil: Japanese companies formed a consortium to bid for concessions on the North Slope of Alaska in February 1970. In Indonesia, where Japan already takes a large proportion of the country's output,[1] Japanese interests have been active from Sumatra to East Kalimantan: and it is here, in the Attaka oilfield, that Japan (Japex, together with Union Oil) has had its only big successful find to date – with extremely low sulphur-content oil. Japan has also invested heavily in Brunei gas and oil.[2] Four big Japanese companies formed a consortium in July 1971 to exploit Iran's Lurestan oil fields, reportedly one of the world's most promising untapped areas. A ten-company Japanese group was formed in August 1971 to undertake oil prospecting in Western Australia; and in January 1972 Mitsubishi announced a $119mill. investment plan for oil development in Australia. Japanese interests have also been scouring New Guinea. In October 1971 a group of three Japanese companies (Teijin Ltd, Teikoku Oil Co. and Mitsui Oil Exploration Co.) accepted a deal with Nigeria for a joint venture in oil allowing Nigeria a 51 per cent share: this was the first time that Japan had accepted less than 50 per cent in any overseas oil development with a producing country, and the arrangement was at once heavily criticized by Nippon Oil, Arabian Oil and Idemitsu Kosan Ltd as having dangerous implications for the future.[3]

Rather, the Nigeria deal reflects the urgency felt by Japanese industry to diversify its sources of supply and make concessions

1. *FEER*, no. 33, 1971, p. 40, states that in 1970 Japan took 37 per cent of Indonesia's oil *exports*; Keith Buchanan, 'Japan and the Pacific Rim Strategy', *Indochina* (London), no. 15, June 1971, p. 5, quoting from *Petroleum News Service* of February 1971, writes that: 'By early 1971 Japan was taking seven-tenths of Indonesia's daily output of 850,000 barrels (mostly from U.S.-controlled fields).'

2. Mitsubishi, in association with Shell, had originally planned to take 3½–4 million tons of liquefied natural gas (LNG) a year from Brunei for Japan (Buchanan, op. cit.). In early 1972 Japan contracted for a further 1,490,000 tons of LNG, bringing the total to over five million (*JEJ*, no. 478, p. 7).

3. *JEJ*, 2 November 1971.

in order to be sure of actually being supplied: going in with the producing country clearly seems attractive insurance to some. For, apart from the successful Attaka find, Japan's oil exploration, particularly in the South-East Asia area, has been conspicuously negative. The October 1971 White Paper stated that out of a total of twenty-one projects in which some $220mill. had been invested to date, only one (Arabian Oil) was in full commercial production.[1] Hence also the attractiveness of the Siberian deal offered by the U.S.S.R. (see below).[2] The extent of Japan's future demand is projected as follows: from the fiscal 1969 figure of 2.9 million barrels of oil per day, import needs by 1985 have been calculated at 8.6 million barrels daily – almost exactly three times the 1969 total.

Two main locations along the Asian Pacific rim are currently the focus of Japanese government and business interests – one in the Yellow Sea/East China Sea area of the Chinese continental shelf and the other off the coast of Vietnam. In both the oil, in so far as any is found, may well turn out to have some of the properties of dynamite.

Tiaoyu Islands. These, known as Senkaku to the Japanese, are a small, long, uninhabited group, a 'scattering of poppy seeds' on the East China Sea about 125 miles north-west of Irieomote island of the Yaeyama group in the Ryukyus and 100 miles north-east of Taiwan. Till they became the centre of an inter-

1. *The Times*, 8 October 1971. *Newsweek* of 29 November 1971 carries a useful survey of the South-East Asian oil hunt stressing Japanese timidity – and the high cost of drilling dry holes: $800,000 a time. As the *Newsweek* survey stresses, however, the Japanese market remains the big lure and largely determines not only prospecting, but also the location of refining (see, for example, *FEER*, no. 51, 1971, p. 73 for the case of Hong Kong). Japan has also been heavily involved in recent attempts to reinvigorate the flagging Burmese oil scene (as has West Germany), and is already involved in a big naphtha deal with Burma (*FEER*, no. 51, 1971, p. 74). *JEJ*, nos. 475, 476, February 1972, give two Japanese oil ventures as actually producing; six others have struck oil, of which three have drilled.

2. Also of interest is the 1972 tie-up between the big trading company, C. Itoh and the Italian ENI, which is already involved in China oil (*JEJ*, no. 477, p. 1).

national oil scramble their history was inconsequential. For about 500 years they served as little more than a navigational aid for shipping on the route between Naha in Okinawa and Foochow in China, during the period when Okinawa stood in a tributary relationship towards China. No doubt they also on occasion provided shelter to parties of Chinese fishermen, and there are references in Chinese texts relating to the Tiaoyu Islands from at least the early fifteenth century.[1]

On the Japanese side the islands were unknown until the early Meiji period (from 1868). In 1884 a certain Koga Tatsushiro of Fukuoka in southern Japan began to operate a business collecting albatross feathers and tortoiseshell in the area, and Japanese habitation there dates from this time.[2] With Japan's victory in the Sino-Japanese war of 1894–5 and the conquest of Taiwan the Japanese Cabinet decided also to incorporate these islands as part of Okinawa prefecture, which had itself only been absorbed into the Meiji state in 1879. Since the wealth of the area was unsuspected, and since China was involved in territorial disputes with Japan going to the heart of her territory, the status of the Tiaoyu group rested there until the end of the Pacific war. Then, by the Proclamation No. 27 of 25 October 1953, determining the geographical limits of the Ruykyus, the U.S. administration held that the islands were part of their jurisdiction, and in 1958, for example, awarded $5,763.92 to a descendant of the old albatross feather merchant who had first settled there, as rent for the use of one of the Tiaoyu group as a gunnery range.[3]

The UN's Economic Commission for Asia and the Far East began in 1965 to show interest in the resources of the

1. Chung-wu Kung, 'A New May Fourth Movement', *BCAS*, vol. 3, nos. 3 and 4, summer and fall 1971, pp. 61–72. The most thorough research on the historical background to the Tiaoyu question is by Inoue Kiyoshi, 'History of the Tiaoyu Islands and the Problem of Title to them', *Rekishigaku Kenkyu*, February 1972; an abbreviated version of this in English is in *PR*, no. 19, 12 May 1972.

2. 'The Senkaku Island Problem and its Background', *Sekai*, September 1971, pp. 133–6.

3. ibid.

Asian Pacific area generally, with the setting up of a 'Committee for Co-ordination of Joint Prospecting for Mineral Resources in Asian Offshore Areas'. Japan, Taiwan, South Korea and the Philippines were members, and the U.S.A., Britain, France and West Germany participated in an advisory capacity in this committee. Little seems to have happened till 1967, when another ECAFE committee, this time entitled the Committee for Far Eastern Underseas Resources, commenced exploratory survey work. In 1969 the first announcements were made of the discovery of oil in the sea in the Tiaoyu area.

Extremely rich deposits were predicted and were thought to lie over an area of approximately 200,000 square miles centring on the Tiaoyu Islands. In June and July of 1969 Japan's Tokai University was commissioned by the Prime Minister's Office (Special Liaison Bureau – now the Okinawan Northern Policy Agency) to carry out further surveys. These confirmed the ECAFE optimism on the extent of the finds, and excitement began to mount in anticipation of a real bonanza.[1] *Fortune* magazine reported that '... the shallow sea floor between Japan and Taiwan might contain one of the most prolific oil and gas reservoirs in the world, possibly comparing favorably with the Persian Gulf area'.[2]

The rush by governments of the area to lay claim to the field and by international oil consortia to win concessions in it then followed. The question of sovereignty, however, raised obvious and acute problems, both within what might be called the Japanese bloc – Japan/Taiwan/South Korea – and between it and China and the D.P.R.K. (North Korea). During much of 1970 the utmost confusion reigned as Japanese, European, and American consortia applied for or were granted overlapping rights around Tiaoyu. Between Japan and Taiwan, in particular, acrimony ran high. During the most active period on

1. ibid. and also 'Machinations of the Japan/ROK/ROC Committee: On the Beginnings of Continental Shelf Development', *Asahi Journal*, 29 November 1970, pp. 105–6, and John Gittings, the *Guardian*, 18 December 1970.

2. *Fortune*, March 1970.

Taiwan, newspapers and magazines, including the party organ, *Chung-yang jih-pao*, published detailed discussions of the dispute and denunciation of Japan. The tone of debates in the Legislative Yuan was similar, and on 21 August 1970 the Taiwan Administration ratified the Continental Shelf Treaty, which had been signed in 1958, and thereafter based its claims to the area on International Law. As the islands are a natural extension of the mainland continent and the sea depth between coast and islands nowhere exceeds 200 metres a Chinese claim would be difficult to rebut under this treaty. Furthermore, in September 1970 a party of journalists and marines from Taiwan hoisted the Nationalist flag on the islands, amid a mounting press campaign.[1]

However, given the subordinate economic and political status of Taiwan and also of South Korea, which had also been issuing concessions to oil companies in the area, and given the U.S.A.'s continued support of Japanese claims through the negotiations over the 'return' of Okinawa, the objections of the Chiang and Pak cliques could not long be sustained. The Ryukyu authorities, clearly under instructions from Tokyo, sent an armed coastguard force to tear down the Chinese flag and to chase away Chinese fishing boats in the area at gunpoint.[2] The dual dependence of the Taiwan authorities on Washington and Tokyo meant that they had no room at all to manoeuvre and no alternative but to back down.

The need to deal with these embarrassing differences was an important factor behind the formation in November 1970 of the Co-ordinating Committee of Japan–Republic of China–Republic of Korea Co-operation Committees (on which see also the chapter on the Tokyo–Taipei–Seoul nexus). One of the first fruits of this new stage of co-operation was the formation in Tokyo in December of a joint 'Ocean Development Corporation', in which the question of sovereignty was supposed to be shelved for the time being.[3] However, the *Wall*

1. *Sekai*, op. cit.
2. Chung-wu Kung; also Gittings, op. cit.
3. 'Machinations of the ...', *Asahi Journal*, op. cit.

Street Journal (24 August 1971) reported an officially sponsored demonstration in Taiwan against the handing over of the islands to Japan which was attended by some 1,000 people. Also, despite this understanding, the island group has already been incorporated within the jurisdiction of the Japanese navy's '11th Maritime Safety District' for armed patrol, also in Japan's 'Air defence identification zone', and some preliminary work on 'exploiting' the sea bed resources was reported to have been begun by Japan on 15 October 1971.[1]

Meanwhile, Peking has made it perfectly clear that it is well aware of what has been going on and is resolved not to tolerate it. 'There are indeed,' it said, 'rich oil, mineral gas, and other mineral resources on the sea floor in the water areas around China's Taiwan province and its attendant islands and in the shallow water areas close to China and Korea. The resources of the sea bed and subsoil of the seas around these islands, and of the shallow seas adjacent to other parts of China, all belong to China, their rightful owner, and we will never permit others to put their fingers on them.'[2]

As the *raison d'être* of the Co-ordinating Committee of Co-operation Committees, as first set out in the Taiwan paper *Lien-ho-pao* in April 1970, was '... the promotion of a north-east Asian alliance and the smashing of all the various plots and threats of the Mao communists in this area',[3] it seems unlikely that Chinese protests would cut much ice there. As part of the thaw in U.S.–Chinese relations, however, in the spring of 1971 the U.S. State Department announced that because of the 'problems' in the area it was 'undesirable for

1. *Sekai*, op. cit.; and on the commencement of work see *Yomiuri Shimbun*, 29 October 1971.

2. *People's Daily*, cited Gittings, op. cit.; also *Hsinhua*, 4 December 1970. For a more recent statement of Chinese views see *PR*, no. 1, 7 January 1972; for support from Western sources for the Chinese view cf. Robert E. King of the Woods Hole Oceanographic Institution: 'If they [the Tiaoyu] are parts of a sedimentary basin, they presumably belong to China, which was awarded them after World War II.' (*Oil and Gas Journal*, 27 April 1970.)

3. *Lien-ho-pao*, 27 April 1970, cited in 'Machinations of the ...', op. cit.

U.S. enterprises to participate in underwater oil field development in the East China Sea and Yellow Sea area', and thereafter Pacific Gulf for one cancelled its planned activity there.[1]

No doubt more will be heard of this tiny island group, and while the questions it poses will obviously be part of the overall China policy rethinking now going on in Tokyo, there has to date been no sign of any Japanese willingness to reconsider the issue of sovereignty over Tiaoyu; on the contrary, every effort now seems to be being made to commit Japan militarily to its defence.

Vietnam Oil

As for the second major field – the oil fields thought to lie along the coast of South Vietnam – Japanese capital has been linked with Gulf Oil in the hope of obtaining concessions. On the Japanese side the Ocean Development Company was formed in March 1971, with the participation of the Petroleum Development Corporation (50 per cent), the five major trading companies — Mitsui, Mitsubishi, Nissho-Iwai, Marubeni and C. Itoh – plus Alaska Oil, Idemitsu Kosan and Toyota Motor Sales. The tie-up was effected in response to the South Vietnamese move of dividing up the Mekong Estuary area into eighteen blocks for the award of concessions, and the Japanese side anticipated an expenditure of approximately $55.5mill. within five years of exploration work if their bid was successful.[2] Should the exigencies of a new China policy lead to back-pedaling on claims in the Chinese continental shelf area the consequence may be a much greater thrust of Japanese attention to the South-East Asian fields, where Japanese capital is much more closely integrated with U.S.A. and European interests.

Buchanan sums up the overall strategy:

The pattern which is emerging is that of a multinational

1. 'The Senkaku island problem and its background', *Sekai*, (translation back from the Japanese).

2. *The Financial Times*, 11 March 1971; Wada Haruki, *Asahi Journal*, 7 May 1971, pp. 97–101.

drive, spearheaded by the U.S. to control the potential oil wealth of offshore Asia; this is designed to assure U.S. oil needs, to provide economic living-space and resources for a rapidly expanding Japan (within the framework of the Pacific Rim strategy), and to open up new and profitable fields for the capital and technology of the developed nations . . . By 1970 pro-western regimes had been established in all the countries margining the major offshore oil deposits of South-East Asia and around the great oil and gas reservoir of the Chinese continental shelf.[1]

And, as Malcolm Caldwell concludes:

Sooner or later, if South East Asia is to industrialize, the countries will require, in the absence of major coal resources, every drop of oil they can lay their hands on. Supposing by the year 2000 South East Asia had attained the 1968 Japanese level of per capita oil consumption . . . no estimate [of South-East Asian total reserves] known to me has ever suggested that South East Asia can achieve local industrialization and sell oil at the same time.

The contradiction between the needs of U.S. imperialism and the needs of the peoples of (South) East Asia is, therefore, absolute. No compromise is possible.[2]

The oil discovery off the Vietnam coast has led to a land-grab quite similar to the Japanese seizure of the Tiaoyu Islands. Both Taiwan and the Philippines recently landed forces on the Nansha (Spratley) Islands in the South China Sea. Apart from China, the Chiang group, the Philippines, South Vietnam, France and Holland all lay claim to the islands.[3]

In addition to its activity off China and Vietnam, Tokyo has been promoting oil searches nearer home. A big search is being made off the southern shore of Honshu (the main island

1. Keith Buchanan, 'Japan and the Pacific Rim Strategy', *Indo-china*, no. 15, June 1971.

2. Malcolm Caldwell, 'Oil and Imperialism in East Asia', *JCA*, vol. I, no. 3, 1971, p. 31.

3. See *FEER*, no. 29, 1971, p. 4 for Taiwan forces on Itu Abu and for China and the Paracels; *FEER*, no. 30, 1971, p. 4 for South Vietnam and the Spratleys.

of Japan).[1] And the regime recently took the unprecedented step of setting up a $1 billion fund to guarantee private prospecting for essential supplies: this is obviously a huge pork-barrel, amongst other things; but the novelty of the fund is that, provided there is government approval (and no one in their right mind in Japan would move without it), the government guarantees to reimburse in full any losses incurred by a Japanese company prospecting.

The other aspect of the oil situation is that Japanese industry's thirst for the commodity is being manipulated by a very powerful group inside Japan to bring down the last barrier against monopoly: the old postwar provision against the formation of holding companies. The group pushing for a special holding company for the development of overseas oil resources is so powerful and so well-placed within the Japanese ruling class that it is impossible to think it will not succeed – and thus some twenty large and very large companies will be grouped together into what may well be the world's largest economic combine.[2] A recent study of this move ominously concludes that if the holding company is formed it will provide an unprecedented breakthrough for the re-cartelization of the Japanese economy (already beyond its prewar level of concentration).[3]

Lumber

Sitting in the middle of a West European or North American city, it is only too easy to forget what an important item wood is in the economics of the world. Wood is now Japan's second largest import, after oil. In 1970 42 million cubic metres of timber were imported at a cost of $1,572mill. – which represented an increase of over 16 per cent on the previous year's demand.[4] There is no reason to expect any slackening of this

1. *Time*, 15 March 1971.
2. John G. Roberts, 'The Final Barrier', *FEER*, no. 31, 1971, pp. 53–4.
3. Roberts's list (ibid.) gives a good idea of the strength of the inner hard core of the big business right as of mid-1971.
4. MITI, *Tsusho Hakusho, Kakuron*, 1970, p. 215; 1971, p. 233.

demand in the foreseeable future. What is particularly important about lumber is that the pillaging of South-East Asia's forests has a devastating effect on the lives of millions of poor peasants throughout the area, and utterly negative, and often irreversible, effects on the whole ecology. One of the biggest uprisings in Taiwan in the early period of Japan's occupation there, was triggered off by Mitsui's devastation of huge forest areas on the island.

Japan consumes more wood than any other nation on earth – because of its huge paper consumption, and because so many Japanese houses, and their contents, are still made of wood. Japan's timber requirements increased by 5–10 per cent per annum during the 1960s. And, although the U.S.A. remains the single most important source, South-East Asia as an area provides more wood to Japan than does the U.S.A. (including Alaska) – 42.8 per cent and 40.1 per cent of Japan's imports in 1970 – and is becoming more and more crucial (see Table 21). Both the U.S.A. and Canada are becoming more restrictive in their timber export policies. This has accelerated moves in the direction of both South-East Asia and the U.S.S.R.[1] Having already worked their way through many of the forests of Korea and Taiwan, Japanese lumber interests are now concentrating on the Philippines, Malaysia, and Indonesia.[2] In August 1970 the Philippines instituted a ban on the export of Mindanao mangrove.

Lumber has also been one of the bases of the warm relationship between Tokyo and Moscow in recent years. In August 1968 Nikolai Patolichev, Soviet Foreign Trade Minister, visited Tokyo to sign a $160mill. lumber agreement – the first joint Russo-Japanese venture in Siberia, for which the Japanese were able to sell the Russians a lot of forestry equipment.[3]

1. *The Times*, 12 September 1968; see Appendix I on Japan and the Soviet Union.

2. Robert Coats, 'Indonesian Timber', *PR & WET*, vol. 2, no. 4, May–June 1971; an extremely valuable study, containing a mass of interesting and up-to-date material.

3. See Appendix I.

TABLE TWENTY-ONE

Major Sources of Japan's Timber Imports (by Region) 1967–70

	1967		1968		1969		1970	
	tons	$mill.	tons	$mill.	tons	$mill.	tons	$mill.
S.E. Asia	13,768	434.5	14,864	457.5	17,752	555.7	20,439	673.5
N. America	8,435	355.5	11,183	490.8	9,784	489.7	12,511	631.1
Africa	150	1.9	30	2.1	92	3.6	48	4.2
Oceania	810	20.6	1,614	44.2	2,015	53.4	2,264	63.0
Communist	5,082	119.9	5,869	164.4	6,158	170.5	7,097	197.9
Other	6	1.7	6	1.8	6	1.8		

Source: MITI, *Tsusho Hakusho, Kakuron*, 1970, p. 224; 1971, p. 243.

Major Sources of Japan's Timber Imports (by Country) 1968–70

	1968		1969		1970		
	tons	$mill.	tons	$mill.	tons	$mill.	
U.S.A.	9,301	405.8	8,604	426.2	10,262	517.7	(32.9%)
Philippines	7,437	235.3	8,320	263.0	7,079	264.8	(16.8%)
U.S.S.R.	5,861	164.0	6,151	170.1	7,095	197.7	(12.6%)
Malaysia	6,078	166.7	6,420	178.5	6,290	188.8	(12.0%)
Indonesia	1,092	30.6	2,734	79.6	4,942	176.4	(11.2%)
Canada	1,882	84.9	1,180	63.5	2,249	113.3	(7.2%)
New Zealand	1,378	38.4	1,708	45.9	1,770	50.1	

Source: ibid., pp. 233, 243.

TARIFF-FREE ZONES

As an urgent measure to attempt to deal with the problems of chronic balance of payments deficits, inflation and mass urban unemployment – with the peasantry being driven into over-crowded cities either by bombing or by deliberate policies undertaken to foster consumer-urbanization – many Asian countries have, in recent years, set up what are known as 'tax-free zones'. Recent reductions in official, largely U.S., government aid, and in 'special procurement' orders, have also accentuated the need to attract private foreign investment on the best of possible terms. While the unrestricted opening of East and South-East Asian countries to foreign investment might be the most attractive business proposition, some concession to nationalist sentiment and desire to protect and foster the growth of indigenous industry on the part of the 'developing' countries has operated in the devising of the system by which a special area is marked off from the domestic market within which export goods are to be manufactured or assembled. The exported goods can thus enjoy the benefits of preferential tariffs applied to the manufactured or semi-manufactured goods of the 'developing' by the 'developed' countries. The foreign capital investor benefits three ways: from the cheap and plentiful labour supply that is available; from tax exemption in the country where he establishes his enterprise; and from further tax privileges in the country to which the finished goods are exported. He can almost certainly count on the host country restraining any form of industrial or political activity on the part of his work force, and he will have little or no labour legislation to bother about. His advantages greatly outweigh those accruing to the host country as a whole (as distinct from the ruling comprador elite): advanced industrialization, technical experience for the work force, and expanded exports, the latter being largely notional since profits accrue almost entirely to the foreign investor. However, there is a further general consideration that is almost certainly operative and that is the defence one: the desire on the part of the ruling cliques in the countries concerned to involve as much foreign capital as possible in order to secure the commitment of the capitalist powers to the defence of a satisfactory and profitable status quo.

The first of such zones was set up at Kaohsiung in Taiwan (December 1966) followed rapidly by others in Cambodia, the Philippines, Singapore, India, Indonesia and Korea, while Thailand and Vietnam (the Cam Ranh Bay area) are likely to follow suit. The Keidanren Liaison Committee for Co-operation with Vietnam interim report of April 1970 was particularly enthusiastic about the prospects of such a zone in the Cam Ranh Bay area, reckoning it to be 'the best site for a free port in South-East Asia, considering various conditions favourable to it, such as port, electric power and labour supply source centring on workers at the local military base'.[1]

A characteristic free zone scheme is the one in Korea at Masan, sixty kilometres west of Pusan, a site of 430 acres which is planned to accommodate 100 enterprises whose total export value should be $100mill., and to specialize in precision instruments, optical instruments and electronic products.[2] Of the sixteen applicants so far approved or outstanding for setting up at Masan, fourteen are Japanese. A second such zone in South Korea is being mooted. Its location would be on the west coast of the country, at the point closest to China's Shanghai–Nanking commercial and industrial area – with the idea of it serving as a 'logistics base' for U.S. and other manufacturers with an eye on the future China market possibilities.[3]

These zones, modern treaty ports, are likely to proliferate in the future, and increasing Japanese investment in manufacturing industry throughout the area is an important element in this trend. In places like Taiwan and South Korea, however,

1. See this report, reprinted in full in *Looking Back*, no. 3, July 1971.

2. Nakagawa Nobuo, 'Japanese–Korean Economic Co-operation in the 1970s', *Sekai*, November 1970.

3. *FEER*, no. 35, 28 August 1971.

it should also be remembered that even outside these specialized 'export processing zones' investment in manufacturing industry may be up to 100 per cent foreign, and profits may be remitted in full. The export zones simply offer even greater facilities and privileges than elsewhere.[1]

THE INFRASTRUCTURE OF INFLUENCE AND PRESENCE

As a coda to Japan's relations with South-East Asia a few disparate items connected with the 'infrastructure' should be noted.

First: South-East Asia has been by far the biggest recipient of Japanese technical 'assistance' experts: in 1966 62.5 per cent of these went to the region.[2]

Second: the training of foreign students in Japan, which is particularly important as an index because of the language problems which have impeded Japan's advance on many occasions. Compared with other advanced capitalist countries, Japan has taken in very few foreign students. Of those admitted as of 1966, no less than 86.5 per cent had come from the South-East Asia area plus India.[3] On the whole, students who

1. In Taiwan (Kaohsiung), for example, the government has built huge dormitories for unmarried girls who form the bulk of the 40,000 strong labour force there (Louis Kraar, 'Taiwan's Strategy for Survival', *Fortune*, November 1971, p. 131). Despite such official 'generosity' the situation in Taiwan seems very bad: see 'Taiwan's White Elephants', *FEER*, no. 36, 1971, p 35.

2. Marshall E. Dimock, *The Japanese Technocracy*, New York and Tokyo, 1968, p. 164. Over the fifteen years up to 1970 1,600 Japanese technical experts had been sent to Asia and Africa – ranging from economic advisers to Suharto to the Chief of the Fisheries Section in the Thailand government, as well as to Iran, Cambodia, South Vietnam, etc.; in Africa, Japan has supplied the Bureau Chiefs of both the Domestic Commerce and Foreign Trade sections in the Uganda government; see Yü Yi-ch'ien, *Jih-pen chen-hsiang*, Hong Kong, 1971, translated into Japanese by Arai Takeo as *Nihon no Razo* (*Japan Unmasked*), Tokyo, 1971, pp. 210–11.

3. Dimock, op. cit. cf. table 22 for comparative figures on Japan's overall exchanges up to 1969.

TABLE TWENTY-TWO Educational and Technical Assistance Projects of Major Advanced Countries (to 1969)

	Students Admitted	Trainees Admitted	TOTAL	No. of field Instructors Sent Out	No. of Advisers Sent Out	No. of Education-alists Sent Out	'Peace Corps' Volunteers	Specialists Sent Out
Japan	563	1,614	2,177	—	1,124	50	472	1,646
U.S.A.	11,511	7,741	19,292	—	9,159	1,559	15,101	25,819
W. Germany	7,174	9,201	16,375	731	693	2,473	2,061	5,963
France	—	—	15,836	—	—	—	—	47,562
U.K.	6,490	4,399	10,899	9,195	498	6,851	2,157	18,701
Italy	1,103	234	1,337	242	37	1,126	—	1,405
TOTAL (16 DAC Countries)	43,013	35,301	78,314	20,153	18,885	48,716	23,876	111,630

Blank spaces indicate either not available or none.
Source: MITI, *Tsusho Hakusho, Kakuron*, 1971, p. 820 (from DAC sources)

go to Japan are 'second class'; top students who go abroad still go to the U.S.A. and Western Europe. The new King of Nepal is one of the few Asian leaders to have studied in Japan (other than militarily). Furthermore, foreign students who come to Japan frequently become fairly hostile to the society, and the longer they stay the more anti-Japanese they become.

Third: hotels, which are always an indicator of business presence. Up to now many Japanese businessmen have had to languish in alien surroundings and have apparently suffered greatly abroad. New Japanese hotels in many South-East Asian cities now form the core of Japanese exile life. And by summer 1971 Tokyo Express had finalized arrangements to extend its hotel chain from Bangkok to Fiji, via Kuala Lumpur and Djakarta.

Fourth: culture. Again, Japan has been rather backward in this field, partly because of negative wartime memories, partly because of language difficulties, and partly because of the general bankruptcy of contemporary Japanese capitalist culture. However,

Worried about Japan's uncomplimentary image in Asia, the Japanese Foreign Office has decided to send a six-man cultural mission to Thailand, Malaysia, Singapore, the Philippines and Indonesia.

Headed by the former parliamentary vice-foreign minister, Rokosuke Tanaka, the mission included a University of Tokyo Professor, the president of Ushio Electric Co., the president of Seibu Department stores, a novelist and the managing director of the Kansai Gakuyukai centre for Asian students . . .

According to a Foreign Office spokesman, the mission will try to 'eradicate wrong impressions peoples in the region may have about Japan, such as a feeling that the Japanese are interested only in money and that Japan may want to become a military power to dominate the region'.[1]

1. *FEER*, no. 29, 17 July 1971, p. 31.

Chapter 3

THE MILITARY

THE ARMED FORCES

Postwar Revival

At the time of the Japanese surrender in 1945, the armed forces were officially disbanded. In fact two important groups of the Japanese military were kept in existence: an intelligence sector headed by Lt.-Gen. Arisue Seizo, former Chief of Military Intelligence for the General Staff; and a group headed by Col. Hattori Takushiro, former secretary to Premier Tojo and Chief of the First Section of the General Staff's Operations Division.[1]

Arisue, like Gehlen in Germany, had latterly been in charge of intelligence operations to do with the Soviet Union, and he was early picked out as a key figure for preservation and exemption from the scheduled purge, like Gehlen. Indeed, when the advance party of the American occupation forces landed at Atsugi Air Base on 28 August 1945, the officer who came forward to greet them was none other than Arisue.[2] He was thus the very first Japanese to initiate on-the-spot liaison with the American forces. Arisue and the core of his intelligence staff (about fifteen) were immediately put back to work, and exempted from the official purge.

Hattori and his group were put in charge of the Demobiliza-

1. John Dower, 'The Eye of the Beholder: Background Notes on the U.S.–Japan Military Relationship', *BCAS*, vol. 2, no. 1, October 1969, p. 16.
2. John Toland, *The Rising Sun*, New York, 1970, p. 864.

tion Boards. They thus were able to build up a filing system on the entire Japanese army and navy as they were demobbed; the information covered some 4 million troops and some 70,000 officers. But it went further than 'pure' information: the Hattori group were also able to collect numerous IOUs from former military for whom they found jobs and, of course, they were also often able to put old colleagues in touch with each other.

When the Korean War broke out in June 1950 MacArthur took two steps. He authorized the formation of a 'National Police Reserve' (Keisatsu Yobitai) of 75,000 men, explicitly to ensure military security in Japan on the sudden departure of American occupation troops to Korea. And he arranged for some thousands of former Japanese troops who were well acquainted with the terrain to be transferred back to Korea, where they served in the 'United Nations' command.[1]

Throughout this period, the Japanese government, headed by the crusty old imperialist Yoshida, was being 'advised' by a military career officer, General Tatsumi Teruichi, who had been military attaché to Yoshida at the time the latter was ambassador in London in the 1930s. Tatsumi sat on the military group which 'discussed' the arrangements for the restoration of

1. Robert Murphy, *Diplomat Among Warriors*, London, 1964, p. 424. See also Walter G. Hermes, *Truce Tent and Fighting Front, U.S. Army in the Korean War*, Washington, D.C., 1966 (the official U.S. army history), p. 348. Japanese troops had, of course, been heavily engaged in fighting after the August 1945 surrender in Korea when they were re-armed by the Americans and sent out under U.S. command to try to suppress the new independent Korean government, the People's Republic. Other Japanese troops fought extensively under British officers in Indonesia and in Vietnam in 1945–6 (see Laurens Van Der Post, the *Observer*, 23 February 1969 for Indonesia; and George Rosie, *The British in Vietnam*, 1970, for Vietnam).

It is worth stressing that Yoshida, who was premier for most of the critical period 1946–54, was not at all an 'anti-imperialist' prior to 1945, as he has consistently been presented by Western sources. He was an important agent of Japanese expansionism, particularly in China. See David Conde, 'Who was Yoshida's Ghost-writer?', *Eastern Horizon*, vol. 10, no. 4, 1971, and David Bergamini, *Japan's Imperial Conspiracy*, New York and London, 1971, for much useful information on Yoshida.

formal sovereignty to Japan in the years 1950–51, as well as acting as spokesman for military interests on general strategic issues.[1]

After formal sovereignty was restored, the 'Police Reserve' was renamed the Safety Force (Hoantai), in 1952, and a navy was officially restarted. In 1954, the Hoantai became the Jieitai or Self-Defense Force (the name it still has) and a start was made on an air force.

The Korean War was extremely important in moulding postwar industrial development. Early in the occupation the Americans had shown marked reluctance to proceed with designated confiscations, particularly in the armaments industry. Most of the productive capacity in this sector was still intact at the beginning of 1951 and was switched into full production to meet U.S. orders for the war against the Korean people.[2]

Growth of Armed Forces

The authorized strength of the forces rose from 75,000 in 1950 (land only) to 152,110 by the end of Yoshida's term in office, in late 1954. During the Hatoyama period (end 1954 to end 1956) there was a more rapid rise – to 214,182. In 1955 Hatoyama, an old-style 'nationalist', undertook a full-scale streamlining of the forces. In 1957, under Premier Kishi, the Japanese-American Committee on Security was set up (renamed the Security Consultative Committee in 1960). Kishi was also the first premier to discuss publicly the possibility of Japan acquiring nuclear weapons. In 1957 he proclaimed:

> Not all nuclear weapons can be considered as falling within the purview of this prohibition (Article 9 of the Constitution). If there is a nuclear weapon that can be considered as solely a

1. Martin E. Weinstein, *Japan's Postwar Defence Policy, 1947–1968*, New York and London, 1971, pp. 54 ff.

2. Takahashi Ryozo, 'Full Picture of the Defence Production Plan', *Chuo Koron*, April 1953, p. 78. Yanaga (*Big Business in Japanese Politics*, op. cit., p. 255) cites Takahashi as his reference for the statement that in January 1951 '72 per cent of [Japan's] production capacity was directly engaged in the manufacture of weapons'. Takahashi does not say this, and it certainly is incorrect.

defensive weapon, then it is not outside the realm of possibility for Japan to possess it.[1]

As is well known, Kishi fell in a major political upheaval over the revision of the so-called Security Treaty in 1960. One of the main features of the revised 1960 Treaty was that its sphere was extended to the 'Far East'. Earlier, in 1955, Dulles had tried to expand the sphere from Japan proper to the 'Western Pacific', but the proposal was blocked by the uproar in Japan. Both the Americans and Kishi refused to specify the area covered by the term the 'Far East'; Kishi gave two quite different interpretations of the area, and his second definition (8 February 1960) included the islands of Habomai and Shikotan off the north of Japan, and the islands of Jinmen and Matsu off the coast of China and held by the Kuomintang; Kishi said he was not certain if the 'Far East' included Korea *north* of the 38th parallel.[2]

Under the 1960 Treaty specific reference to the United States' responsibility for the defence of Japan in case of internal disturbances was dropped; yet responsibility in the last resort still remained with the U.S.A. forces under the terms of the general clause relating to 'direct or indirect' aggression. The Japanese forces, it should be noted, were entirely headed by veterans of earlier wars of aggression. The Chief of Staff in the years 1959–62 was General Genda Minoru, the main planner of Pearl Harbor and key adviser to Yamamoto (he figures prominently in the film *Tora! Tora! Tora!*).

By 1962 the authorized strength of the armed forces was up to 243,923 men, by which time the army had thirteen divisions (145,000 men), the navy 469 vessels totalling 128,000 tons and the air force 1,100 planes. In the decade 1953–63 defence expenditure rose from ¥1,231mill. to ¥2,412mill.

Since 1945 the Japanese military has been treated with wholly unscientific charity by Western writers. The military budget has consistently been estimated by the most flattering

1. Quoted by Wolf Mendl, 'Japan's Defence Problems', *Yearbook of World Affairs*, 1968, p. 155.

2. Yanaga, op. cit., pp. 279–80; cf. Weinstein, op. cit., pp. 79–80.

criteria, which have in fact been used to mask the speed of Japan's military growth and, above all, the specific characteristics of the Japanese forces. Before going on to look at Japan's military plans and the question of overseas action and expansionism, these characteristics must be outlined.

First, Japan has attained a degree of self-sufficiency in munitions manufacture which is unparalleled among the Western powers, with the possible exception of the U.S.A. By the end of 1969, Japan was making 97 per cent of its own ammunition and 84 per cent of its aircraft, tanks, guns, naval craft and other military equipment.[1] As of mid-1970 munitions production accounted for 12 per cent of all machine-building production.[2]

Japan has fought doggedly to ensure a high degree of self-reliance: during the visits of Laird and Connally to Japan in the latter half of 1971, intense pressure was applied to oblige Tokyo to buy more of its planes in the U.S.A. – both as part of a package to prop up the U.S. dollar, and to enforce Japanese dependence on America. The Japanese Defence Agency and arms industry, headed by Mitsubishi Heavy Industries (MHI), successfully staved off this demand. The new defence budget published in January 1972 shows that Japan is to start building at once twenty supersonic jet trainer-fighters, and to build some 200 over the next five years, even though these could be bought much cheaper in the U.S.A. Likewise, MHI has obtained a licence to manufacture the McDonnell Douglas F-4EJ Phantom fighter aircraft (which will replace the F-86 over the next few years), even though this, too, could have been obtained both much more rapidly and much cheaper from the U.S.A.[3] MITI had vigorously opposed the Defence Agency/

1. Swadesh R. de Roy, 'Japan: A Nation Rearms', *FEER*, no. 51; 1969, p. 600. *The Times* of 15 January 1972 gives the much lower figure of 'about 50 per cent', which, it says, is expected to rise to about 80 per cent during the next five years. Robert Guillain, *Le Monde Diplomatique*, July 1971, gives figures of 45 per cent self-sufficiency at the end of the 3rd Plan (end 1967) rising to 80 per cent by the end of the 4th Plan (end 1971).
2. *PR*, no. 30, 1970, p. 18.
3. *The Times*, 15 January 1972.

MHI proposals,[1] both on the grounds of actual cost (particularly as the Mitsubishi prototype had already risen from about ¥1 billion to nearly ¥1½ billion – some $3.8mill. – largely due to the collapse of Rolls Royce) and on the grounds that it would make it harder to come to an overall agreement with the U.S.A. on the dollar-yen and trade problems.[2] The government was able to infiltrate the plane decision into the new budget as part of an overall plan to boost the domestic economy in the wake of the Nixon shocks.[3]

Second, in the important area of technology, Japan is among the leading handful of countries in the world: it was the fourth to launch a space satellite, after only the U.S.A., the U.S.S.R., and France. Research on nuclear energy has been extensive: there has been what one American authority calls 'technological preparedness for nuclear developments'.[4] In hardware, too, Japan has not exactly been lagging: already by 1967 it had the latest Type-61 tanks, heavy artillery, transport helicopters, F-104 supersonic jet fighters, Nike Hercules anti-aircraft missiles, and destroyer and destroyer escorts specially equipped for anti-submarine warfare.[5]

Third, all three branches of the forces are heavily over-officered, which means they could be expanded at very short notice by perhaps four to five times; many of these officers, like the NCOs (also a big surplus), are battle-hardened veterans of the Pacific and Asian wars. There is no conscription in Japan (mainly because business is hostile to a draft while the manpower shortage continues), but the military would like a larger pool of trained personnel than is available at the moment – hence a number of moves which merit attention. One of these is the idea of a 'homeland defence corps' of about one million men. Another is the increased military activity in universities,

1. *The Times*, 25 October 1971.
2. *JEJ*, 2 November 1971, pp. 2, 8.
3. *The Times*, 13 January 1972.
4. M. B. Jansen, 'The United States and Japan in the 1970s', in Gerald L. Curtis, ed., *Japanese–American Relations in the 1970s*, Washington, 1970, p. 36.
5. Weinstein, op. cit., p. 110.

and the armed forces' 'Open house' programmes under which students and ordinary Japanese can camp, spend their holidays, and train in military establishments at government expense.[1]

Fourth, although Japan's armed forces are not – proportionate to population – on the scale of those of South Korea or Taiwan, they are not inconsiderable: they are already the seventh strongest in the world. They are approaching a point of maximum effectiveness and power, short of a leap to a full-scale offensive nuclear strategy.

The methods by which Western writers have computed the Japanese defence budget have to be criticized. As a percentage of GNP it is true that Japan expenditure on its armed forces comes out lower than that of Britain or France. But:

> Relating Japanese military expenditures to percentage of GNP has little relevance in a country where annual economic growth rates are over 10 per cent. Annual military expenditures have been increasing at a high rate despite a decrease in the percentage of GNP allocated to them. An increase in military expenditures to two per cent would provide more money than can rationally be used unless Japan undertakes an ambitious nuclear weapons development programme.[2]

The total defence budget for fiscal 1970 came to ¥569,354 mill. ($1,600mill.): this was about 7 per cent of the general account budget, but this was a 17.7 per cent increase over the 1969 defence appropriations, and rate of increase, in a moving situation, is the critical criterion. In April 1971 *The Times* correspondent wrote: 'The fourth defence programme, run-

1. On expandability, see de Roy, op. cit.; for the 'homeland defence corps', *The Times*, 11 August 1969; for the army's open training programmes, *The Times*, 17 March 1969 ('Japan Army Trains Right-Wing Group'); for military funding of 'research' in universities, see Herbert P. Bix, 'The Security Treaty System and the Japanese Military–Industrial Complex', *BCAS*, vol. 2, no. 2, January 1970, p. 40: military infiltration into universities has been a big issue in Japan for many years.

2. Gerald L. Curtis, 'American Policy Toward Japan in the Seventies: The Need for Disengagement', Curtis, ed., op. cit., p. 170.

ning from 1972 to 1976, will cost from £6,000mill. upwards – and the operative word is "upwards".'[1]

The new defence budget unveiled in February 1972 ran to ¥802,000mill. (about £1 billion) – a 19.6 per cent increase over the previous year – i.e., an even faster rate of increase than previously.[2] This was the first annual budget under the new 4th Defence Build-Up Programme: like the whole programme, it was greeted with considerable anxiety. And, at the time of writing, the outcome of the fluctuating situation inside the ruling group in Tokyo was not clear. In October 1971 the then Defence Minister Nishimura got Sato's approval to a cut of about ¥500 billion in the original ¥5,800 billion estimate (a cut of about 8.6 per cent) – of which ¥300 billion related to helicopter carrier cruisers, submarines, Phantom jets and tanks.[3] But this seems only to have been an interim decision. A short time later, the *Sunday Times*'s Peter Wilsher wrote (under the subhead 'Cutting back on Armaments') that 'all the aggressive new equipment . . . [has] now been chopped out, leaving the emphasis wholly on replacing existing equipment', which, Wilsher implied, is out-of-date.[4] But at least one of the items Wilsher claimed had been chopped – the F-4EJ – is very much in production. It may be that various proposals have been floated to test popular and international reaction; it is also probable that there are genuine differences of opinion. The report on the October 1971 cut by Nishimura suggested it was a temporary measure, and the December economic shocks may well have provided the excuse to restore the projected cuts.

In view of the importance of the issue, it is perhaps worth giving some details about the debate over the 1972 Defence budget. Popular hostility to the 4th Defence Build-Up Programme when it was announced was much greater than most

1. *The Times*, 29 April 1971.
2. *The Times*, 8 February 1972.
3. 'How the 4th Defence Build-Up Changed Course', *Asahi Journal*, 14 January 1972, pp. 110–11.
4. The *Sunday Times*, 12 December 1971, p. 55.

of the Western press reported. All three major Japanese dailies, the *Asahi*, *Yomiuri* and *Mainichi*, came out with strong editorials against the draft programme. The *Asahi*, noting that big changes had taken place in East Asia, pointed out that the programme was making people frightened of Japan right through the area, and not just in China: 'It is clearly evident that the original plan is excessively large . . . We also gravely doubt the Defence Agency's continued adherence to the thinking on which its original draft is based.' The *Yomiuri* wrote: 'We hereby warn that the trend to build up military might on a *fait accompli* basis is tantamount to turning one's back towards the Japanese people.' Moreover, wrote the *Yomiuri*, there can be no justification on grounds of 'filling a vacuum', since there is no 'vacuum' to be filled. And even the *Mainichi*, hitherto the least hostile, came out with strong criticism of the programme.[1]

Presumably largely because of mass hostility, the Sato government failed to clear the 1972 defence budget through the National Defence Council (NDC), which it is statutorily obliged to do: when challenged, the government stated that it failed to do this 'because of inadvertency'. After further Opposition attacks, the government tried to infiltrate the defence budget into the general budget retroactively and extremely abstractly. This 'improvised and rash rhetoric', in the words of the *Nihon Keizai Shimbun*, angered many. The Opposition demanded the restoration of civilian control over the military budget, as well as a reduction in the actual arms budget. The civilian staff of the NDC were also reported (rare thing in Japan) to be extremely angry with the Defence Agency for drafting the programme without proper reference to the NDC. The Opposition succeeded in preventing the passage of Sato's concocted budget, and the government had to agree to an unprecedented revision of the fiscal 1972 budget (April 1972 to March 1973). The Sato government, wrote the *Nihon Keizai*, 'must assume grave political responsibility' for this

1. Quoted in a survey of press reactions in *JQ*, vol. 14, no. 1, January–March 1972, pp. 89–90.

behaviour;[1] and on 23 February the *Mainichi* reported that Sato's resignation would probably be moved forward, with this as the primary reason. On 26 February 1972, the Diet unanimously approved a cut in the 1972 defence budget, after eighteen days paralysis of the Diet.[2] It is worth insisting on this episode to stress the utterly autocratic methods of the ruling Liberal Democratic Party (LDP).

Furthermore, the usual method of computing Japan's forces all in one lump is extremely misleading: as far back as 1967, while Japan stood only in twenty-second place as far as ground troops were concerned, it had the seventh strongest navy in the world and the sixth strongest air force:

> The level of defence spending is about seventh in the world, as is Japan's population ... even the present rate of defence spending ... will make Japan a significant military power. Not, to be sure, in land forces, where the lack of conscription and insular security, combined with the naval weakness of her neighbors, make it unnecessary. But in the more expensive aspects of naval and air armament, Japan's technological superiority and economic potential over her Asian neighbours will give her maximum advantage.[3]

It is obvious that Japan's huge industrial potential makes purely static comparisons unsound.

To resume: to state that Japan has the seventh strongest armed forces in the world is too vague, as it stands. Japan has concentrated on the two key arms – the navy and the air force, in which it has vast technological superiority over all its neighbours, except the U.S.S.R. The armed forces have now grown to the point of *maximum* advantage, and further expansion of the land army is *unnecessary* (Jansen's assessment). All three forces could be expanded very fast, given the high proportion of officers and NCOs; the situation is very similar to that of the German army after Versailles, which was also highly over-officered and readily expandable. The army is highly mechan-

1. As given in *JEJ*, no. 477, 15 February 1972.
2. *FEER*, no. 10, 4 March 1972, p. 4.
3. Jansen in Curtis, ed., op. cit., p. 36.

ized for a land force, with one vehicle for every five men (as of 1968).

The 1970 White Paper on Defence

What have these armed forces been doing up to now, and what are they designed to accomplish (in both existing and future plans)? Until quite recently, at any rate, the army has been distributed within Japan primarily to prevent a domestic insurrection. 'The Self-Defense Forces, in particular the Ground Self-Defense Force, have been equipped, deployed, and trained to maintain internal security.'[1] Domestic repression ('security') was, of course, the main task of the so-called National Police Reserve during the Korean War. In 1968 nine of the thirteen army divisions were stationed in Honshu and Kyushu close to the big towns and industrial complexes,

> where they could better counter the internal threat ... The Self-Defense Forces are the Government's last resort in a showdown with the anti-parliamentary opposition. For the Ground Self-Defense Forces, in particular, the maintenance of internal security remains the basic mission.[2]

At that time (1968), the remaining four divisions were all stationed on the northern island Hokkaido, facing the U.S.S.R., although the proportional deployment of the army (less than one third stationed opposite the country which, in theory, was the main threat to Japan) gives an excellent indication that external 'aggression' was not seen as a very real danger. This has recently been confirmed in striking fashion by *Le Monde*: 'The military pressure exercised on northern Japan by the Soviet bases in the Kuriles has been somewhat eased, and part of the (Japanese) defence forces ... have been moved towards the South, nearer Korea and China.'[3] As part of the anti-Chinese rapprochement between Japan and the Soviet Union, a Japanese military delegation was recently greeted in Siberia,

1. Martin Weinstein, *Japan's Postwar Defence Policy, 1947–1968*, New York and London, 1971, p. 121.
2. ibid.
3. *Le Monde*, 17 July 1971.

where it was allowed to tour Soviet military installations – presumably to ensure the Japanese military that the U.S.S.R. could be relied on not to make any move if Japan wished to redeploy more of its troops and hardware down to the coast opposite Korea and China.

Apart from Japan's designs on Korea, always the main focus of interest for the Japanese armed forces (see below), Korea figures largely – or *is made to figure* largely – in the general plans for domestic repression within Japan. Weinstein quotes a secret Self-Defense Force (SDF) policy paper of 1966 which sees a new war in Korea as the most likely detonator of 'large-scale internal disorders':

> Ever since 1960, the Defense Agency and the Self-Defense Forces have shown a renewed awareness of the internal threat and have been preparing to deal with it . . . The war in Vietnam has led the defense planners to turn their attention from 1960-style disorders . . . to the problem of dealing with an insurrection in the form of a protracted guerrilla war . . . It is anticipated that such a war of national liberation would be likely to accompany the renewal of war in Korea.[1]

In October 1970 the Japanese government issued a highly important White Paper on defence. This appeared only four months after the renewal of the Security Treaty with America: formally, this was merely an extension of the 1960 Treaty, but *de facto* it included the *revised* terms agreed on by Nixon and Sato in their crucial discussions in late 1969, which were partly embodied in the now notorious Sato-Nixon communiqué of November 1969. Because of the importance of this communiqué, and the fact that the English text of it is not readily available elsewhere, we have included all relevant sections of it in Appendix III.

The difficulty about trying to interpret American–Japanese strategic relations is that the basic information is concealed. Well before the 1970 White Paper was issued, and before the 1969 Sato–Nixon talks, Japan had probably taken over responsibility for its external as well as internal defence (as Weinstein

1. Weinstein, op. cit., p. 117.

hints). But this has not been made explicit. The further stage is outlined in the 1969–70 documents: Japan's sphere of influence is extended to include both Taiwan and Korea. The latter is called 'essential to the security of Japan', and the then Director-General of the Defence Agency (i.e., Minister of Defence), Nakasone, has referred to Korea as 'Japan's advance stronghold'.

As of the end of 1970 the total strength of the SDF was 230,000 men, 1,564 planes, 709 tanks and 206 naval vessels, (totalling 137,000 tons). Under the official published plan Japan aims by 1975 to have armed forces made up as follows: the overall total of all the forces combined will be about 336,000 men, with some 66,000 reservists. The army will grow 1.9 times, and total spending on it will come to $5,000mill.; it will then, in Nakasone's words, be 'essentially complete' at 180,000 men, 1,000 tanks and eight Hawk missile battalions – plus surplus mobility. The navy will grow from 138,000 tons to 240–250,000 tons (and perhaps 300,000 tons thereafter); spending at $3,700mill. will be up 2.3 times over the previous five-year period. The air force will grow 2.8 times, and spending will rise to $4,000mill., although the actual number of planes will remain roughly the same.

Per capita defence spending will be up from $12 in 1969 to about $30 in 1975: 'in terms of total spending, Japan eventually will compare with the U.K., France and West Germany and, in the non-nuclear area, will outrank France, the U.K. and China'.[1] By 1975 Japan will be the mightiest non-nuclear power in the world, if it is still non-nuclear.

1. Koji Nakamura, 'The Mightiest Non-Nuclear', *FEER*, no. 45, 1970. Cf. Harada Makoto, 'The SDF and Overseas Military Co-operation', *Sekai*, August 1971, pp. 96–9. *The Times* of 8 February 1972 gives 'present' figures as follows: GSDF:* 179,000 men (to rise to 180,000 during the coming fiscal year); MSDF:* 38,323 (to rise to 40,204); ASDF: 42,300 (to rise to 43,676). Kubo Ayazo, 'Fourth Defence Build-Up: Re-establishment of Control over Asia Aimed At', *Asahi Journal*, 3 November 1970, pp. 18–22; the *Sunday Times*, 12 December 1971.

* GSDF: Ground SDF (army); MSDF: Maritime SDF (navy); ASDF: Air SDF (air force).

The new programme, in the words of the *Far Eastern Economic Review*'s correspondent, 'involves a "strategic change" – Japan's military set-up clearly is becoming "offensive" as well as defensive in potential. Japan's defence efforts will now be designed to place sea and air space surrounding the nation under its control.'[1] As is obvious from past experience in the Far East and elsewhere, such a change tends to carry with it its own dynamic. In the first place, equipment spending is scheduled to rise vertiginously: from $2,400 mill. under the last programme (1967–71) to about $7,000mill. under the 1972–6 plan. The oligopolic trend in the arms industry is perhaps the most worrying tendency of all (see section on Military–Industrial Complex). Furthermore, there is the factor of the political climate. This may sometimes be hard to pin down, but it is nevertheless something real. It is particularly important in considering the status of the armed forces, the position of the Emperor, and revision of the Constitution.

It can reasonably be assumed that the vast majority (and perhaps the totality) of the ex-Imperial officer corps, as well as the NCOs who are frequently more bellicose than their superiors, are more or less opposed to Article 9[2] of the Japanese Constitution. In 1969 the Chairman of the Joint Staff Council, Admiral Itaya, voiced his version of this sentiment in characteristic terms:

The state does not exist because there is a Constitution. There is a constitution because there is a state . . . If it is absolutely

1. Nakamura, op. cit.

2. Article 9 of the 1947 Constitution states: 'Aspiring sincerely to an international peace based on justice and order, the Japanese people forever renounce war as a sovereign right of the nation and the threat or use of force as a means of settling international disputes. In order to accomplish the aim of the preceding paragraph, land, sea and air forces, as well as other war potential, will never be maintained. The right of belligerency of the state will not be recognized.' It should be noted that the preamble to the 1960 United States–Japan Treaty of Mutual Co-operation and Security is specifically written to circumvent Article 9 in a particularly pernicious way; it states that: 'Recognizing that they [the U.S.A. and Japan] have the inherent right of individual or collective self-defense as affirmed in the Charter of the United Nations . . .'.

necessary for the survival of the state, the Constitution should be interpreted accordingly. If that cannot be done, the Constitution should be revised.[1]

Itaya is here voicing with undiplomatic clarity the two options open to the Japanese ruling group: either to revise the Constitution, or to stretch it, perhaps indefinitely (the option favoured up to now).

The future strength and objectives of the Japanese military are intimately bound up with Constitutional revision. Back in 1953 a Committee on the Constitution was set up, chaired by Kishi Nobusuke, a cabinet minister under Tojo and a Class A war criminal (who is also Sato's elder brother). The LDP right has concentrated its fire on two aspects: Article 9, banning all armed forces and armaments; and the status of the Emperor. Apart from the LDP Committee, Kishi heads his own organization, the 'League for an Autonomous Constitution', which recently was reported to have the support of 264 out of a total of 440 LDP Dietmen, and also to have reached an agreement with the official LDP body for a review of the Constitution. The visit of the Japanese Emperor, himself a war criminal (although not tried by the War Crimes Tribunal), to Western Europe in autumn 1971, formed a central part of this overall plan of the right wing to revise the Constitution and eliminate the meagre quotient of 'popular' sovereignty enshrined in the postwar Constitution. The Emperor, as a willing tool of his own reactionary fellow-countrymen, is actively complicit with this scheme. The trip, however, was not a success.

In assessing the general climate in Japan, it is important to note the active role of both old and new right. Mishima's ludicrous little private army, the Shield Society (Tate no Kai) was often written off in the West as some completely *marginal* institution – but this is quite wrong. The Self-Defence forces did not just tolerate Mishima and his group, they actively assisted them, allowing them to train in military installations with official equipment. The Tate no Kai was accepted as a

1. Quoted by Swadesh R. de Roy, 'Japan: A Nation Rearms', *FEER*, no. 51, 1969, p. 600.

semi-autonomous detachment of the armed forces, *slightly* to the right of the official line. In Mishima's own words:

Our *Tate no Kai* was nurtured by the Self-Defense Forces. In fact, one could say the Self-Defense Forces has (*sic*) been a father and an elder brother to us . . . We have been treated within the Self-Defense Forces as quasi-members . . . and we have received training without any strings attached.[1]

The same sort of connection between 'official' and 'unofficial' lines (where the latter functions as a kind of outrider for the former) can be seen in the relationship between Nakasone and Kodama, the legendary rightist who built up a fortune in China during the Japanese occupation, was condemned as a war criminal, and has bankrolled many of the leading right-wing nationalist politicians in postwar Japan. Kodama now 'is back as a top rightist leader closely aligned with the political and economic leadership' (in the words of the *Far Eastern Economic Review*); he was recently quoted by the leading Japanese daily, the *Asahi*, as saying that he would assassinate, or help to assassinate, premier Sato if he felt it was 'good for the country'.[2]

Kodama has, of course, been rather powerful for quite a time. But one must take note of a situation where a powerful backer of a leading cabinet minister can once again openly talk about assassinating the premier – of that same cabinet! Particularly since the emergence of Nakasone into the spotlight, and the advent of Nixon and his 'doctrine' of making Asians fight Asians, there has been a significant shift in the climate in Japan. Nakamura writes:

There is a growing preference for an 'independent' defence structure, tightening of internal 'security' against liberal and

1. Mishima Yukio, 'An Appeal', *JI*, vol. 7, no. 1, winter 1971, p. 7; for an extremely stimulating and provocative discussion of the whole Mishima affair, in its political context, see Muto Ichiyo, 'Mishima and the Transition from Postwar Democracy to Democratic Fascism', *Ampo*, no. 9–10, pp. 34–50.

2. Cited by Koji Nakamura, 'The Red Rag', *FEER*, no. 37, 1970; on Kodama see also the evocative article by David Conde, 'Let the Sad Music Begin Again', *Eastern Horizon*, vol. 10, no. 1, 1971.

anti-war movements, an ever-increasing number of rightist organizations and an enlarging of the rightist shadow over the political and economic structures.[1]

A reference to the Constitution (indicating resigned acceptance) in the draft of the 1970 White Paper was deleted by Nakasone in the final version, which now only appeals for 'the settling of the decision that the SDF is in accordance with the Constitution'. The final version also contains a jingoistic appeal for 'rousing the patriotic spirits of the people of the nation'.[2] This was accompanied by what has been called 'a rousing message to the troops' from Nakasone, calling strongly for better pay and conditions for all the armed forces. The outline of defence spending produced by the National Defence Council in February 1972 indicates that forces pay will be lavishly increased as an inducement to new recruits: in 1970, while 28,484 people signed on, 14,000 resigned, with bad pay and conditions as a major reason.[3]

Nuclear Weapons?

Much of the discussion of Japan's military posture is dominated by the nuclear issue. It should be said at once that Japan is at present constructing a military force quite capable of infiltration into positions outside Japan without the use of nuclear weapons. Its armed forces are also tightly designed for a swift switch to nuclear arms. Japan has signed the Moscow Partial Nuclear Test Ban Treaty. But at least three qualifications should be attached to this at once: first of all, the treaty is, as its correct name states, only partial (indeed, it is rigorously referred to in Japanese left circles as the *P*NTBT); second, although Japan has signed the Moscow treaty, it has not yet ratified it (this is a common dodge in capitalist countries designed to fool gullible and ill-informed onlookers); third,

1. Nakamura, 'The Red Flag'.
2. Kubo Ayazo, *Asahi Journal*, 3 November 1970, pp. 18–22.
3. *The Times*, 8 February 1972; the *Sunday Times*, 12 December 1971.

nuclear weapons, *like all weapons*, are already strictly banned by Japan's Constitution.

The only way to approach the issue is to realize that Japan will arm itself with nuclear weapons when it wants to, and decides the time is opportune, as Kishi implicitly stated back in 1957. The ability to construct such an arsenal is already there: Japan is outdistanced only by the U.S.A. and the U.K. in the number of nuclear power plants, either in operation, or being built. Japan now has arrangements to mine and import uranium (from Niger), and to process it (with Australia). Japan has nuclear co-operation pacts with the U.S.A., Britain, Canada and France, as well as with Australia. Although these agreements are formally confined to peaceful uses, there is little reason to think this could not be stretched if so desired. It has been reliably estimated that the conversion programme, including putting nuclear weapons onto Japan's missile system, could be carried out in less than one year.

Up until now, although there has been a certain autonomous Japanese pressure for nuclear arms, the question could only be located within the context of Japan's essentially subordinate military relationship with the U.S.A. In the past two years or so, particularly since the major events of the summer of 1971, this relationship has undergone some real changes.

In late 1970 Nakasone visited the U.S.A., and stated it as his policy that Japan should be an absolutely equal partner with the U.S.A. in nuclear technology. The U.S.A., he said, should supply Japan with the know-how and techniques for producing enriched uranium, in a joint scheme with Canada – 'for peaceful purposes only' naturally. A meeting with Laird immediately afterwards, scheduled for twenty minutes, lasted two-and-a-half hours.[1] Nakasone's statements in the U.S.A. (in September) followed shortly after the long visit made by Laird to Japan and Korea in early July that same year, the longest visit ever made by a U.S. Defence Secretary to

1. Nihon Kokusai Boeki Shinko Kyokai (Japan Association for the Promotion of International Trade), *Atarashii Nihon Gunkokushugi* (*New Japanese Militarism*), Tokyo, 1971, p. 23.

the zone. During this visit Laird made a detailed survey of the Japanese military scene; he expressed himself distressed at the 'outdatedness' of much of the SDF's conventional armaments, and pressured Japan to buy more modern equipment from the U.S.A.; he also urged Japan to take over more of the American role in East Asia, and in this context the nuclear issue was extensively scrutinized. In background briefings during the Laird visit Japanese authorities gave assurances that Japan would probably have nuclear weapons (probably meaning an ABM system) in the 1980s.[1] This was subsequently publicly denied by the Defence Agency. However, even from the public statements made by Laird it was not unreasonable to deduce that a fairly firm arrangement had been made about Japan going nuclear, with the U.S.A. assisting it in this objective in return for Japan taking over more air and naval work, particularly from the 7th Fleet: after citing Secretary Laird, the *Guardian* wrote: 'Mr Laird . . . clearly seemed to imply that he could foresee a Japanese ABM in "the 1970s and beyond".'[2]

1. Murakami Kaoru, 'From Support Status to Full Nuclear Armament', *Asahi Journal*, 23 July 1971, pp. 21–4. The 'nuclearization' of Japan had been publicly aired by Defence Agency circles back in 1966. A special issue of the magazine *Ushio* (spring 1966) carried an article by Kazumaro Makoto entitled 'The Defence Policy of a Middle Ranking Non-Nuclear', which was an obvious plant. 'What should Japan as a middle ranking non-nuclear do in the event of the U.S.A.'s ability to respond to a Chinese nuclear attack becoming greatly less reliable?' asked Kazumaro. 'There are two ways: one would be to abandon the non-nuclear policy, and the other would be normally non-nuclear but adopting the way of "gradual emergency nuclear availability" (*sic* in English) – and this is to be recommended.' Against the time they may be needed, he went on, Japan should prepare systems appropriate to either – delivery, transport, air-to-air, ground-to-air missiles, submarine delivery. It should then warn China of the consequences of continuing its tests and publish a U.S.A.–Japan '. . . system agreement' but not sign it, just train personnel and keep the equipment, leaving its options open. If the Chinese threats become military, then at once sign the deal with the U.S.A. and import nuclear heads . . .

2. The *Guardian*, 15 July 1971. Cf. Selig Harrison, 'Nuclear Weapons by Beginning of 80s', *Washington Post*, 8 July 1971. *Jane's Weapons Systems 1971–2* is quoted in *The Times*, 18 November 1971,

About a month after the White Paper was issued, Nakasone made a major speech in Tokyo in which he announced that Japan would not acquire nuclear weapons as long as the American deterrent remained 'credible'. This was not considered very reassuring by many observers, including the editor of the *Far Eastern Economic Review*, who noted that this meant that Japan would only remain non-nuclear 'as long as it was considered strategically advisable'.[1]

An official spokesman rapidly 'clarified' Nakasone's remarks: Japan, he said, would remain non-nuclear as long as the treaty with the U.S.A. was 'in force'. But there is no reason to think Nakasone did not mean what he said, particularly in the light of the murky dealings over the reversion of Okinawa (see section on Okinawa). At any rate, Nakasone has mapped out a possible scenario for Japan to 'justify' arming itself with its own nuclear weapons. However, it should be stated that there does not appear to be unanimity in the Japanese military establishment about nuclear policy. Since Nakasone left the Defence Agency in the summer of 1971 there has been a veritable cascade of incumbents in the job: resignations have been ascribed to marginal events such as an 'indiscretion' about the United Nations, but the swift changes seem to reflect underlying conflicts. Moreover, the powerful head of Mitsubishi Heavy Industries, Mr Kono, has suggested that Japan should rent U.S.A. nuclear protection; this way, he argued, Japan could (a) stay non-nuclear in theory; (b) pay the U.S.A. large sums in 'rent' to assist the American balance of payments; and (c) thus leave Japan free to manufacture most of the other weapons it wants.[2]

---

to the effect that India may go nuclear 'because of the fear that Japan [will]'. However vague and fluid the Japanese scene may be, its wider effects must not be underestimated.

1. Derek Davies, 'The Challenge of Japan', *FEER*, no. 1, 1971, p. 71.

2. *The Times*, 15 January 1972.

Korea and Taiwan

Japan's seizure of the Tiaoyu islands in the winter of 1970–71 went almost unnoticed, and scandalously misreported, in the Western press, which still panderingly refers to the islands by their Japanese name, the Senkaku. The seizure is closely related to the discovery of oil in the area (see above). It is particularly worrying since it is the first open act of aggression by Japan since 1945 – and, as to be expected, directed against China. Because of its geographical location, and its geopolitical implications, it contains more than enough dynamite to cause a major explosion in the future.

As of now, though, the key area of Japanese expansion(ism) is, as it always has been, Korea. Korea was one of Japan's first colonies (it was seized *de facto* in 1895) and its inhabitants have consistently been treated with malignant callousness by Japan, both in Korea and throughout the Japanese empire, as well as in Japan itself, where many Koreans were exploited, in conditions tantamount to slavery, in the mines and other work (including building the Japanese Diet!). Japan fought its first imperialist war, with China in 1894–5, largely over (*and in*) Korea, and Korea has uninterruptedly been the number one target of all Japanese expansionists, particularly because of its *strategic* importance.

Japan took only a clandestine part in the 1950–53 war against the Korean people. But since the revision of the Security Treaty in 1960, Japanese military planning has increasingly encroached on Korea. In 1965 it emerged that, at least since 1963, a plan had been in operation which would involve Japan in the occupation of both Korea and North-East China (Manchuria), as well as the blockade of China and virtual martial law within Japan. This plan, the 'Three Arrows' (Mitsuya) plan, was designed simultaneously: (1) to occupy South Korea; (2) to invade North Korea; and (3) to suppress any revolution within Japan.[1] The plan was further developed in

1. On the plan, see Herbert P. Bix, 'The Security Treaty System and the Japanese Military–Industrial Complex', *BCAS*, vol. 2, no. 2,

1964 in the operation 'Flying Dragon', and then in operation 'Bull Run'. In March 1969 the scenario was still a renewal of the Korean war and, in the exercise 'Focus Retina', the entire U.S. 82nd Airborne Division was airlifted from the U.S.A. to South Korea via Okinawa to engage in war games with South Korean troops which the *Asahi Shimbun* correspondent observing described as obviously a simulated attack north across the 38th parallel.[1]

In 1970 once again it was operation 'Golden Dragon', basically a joint U.S.–South Korean exercise involving the participation of various units stationed in Japan and Okinawa in naval movement through the Taiwan straits followed by four-day landing manoeuvres on the Korean peninsula.[2] Operation 'Freedom Vault', conducted from 3 to 6 March 1971, was slightly different in emphasis and designed to demonstrate to Koreans the speed with which U.S. troops could be flown from home bases to meet any emergency on the peninsula and thus to silence any arguments against continuing reductions in the U.S. forces garrisoned in Korea.[3] The Air Force's C5A Galaxy, which has a capacity of 120 tons, is actually capable, given ninety planes, of transporting the entire U.S. Korean forces from home bases in the States to Korea. It is therefore strategically feasible to keep soldiers and equipment within the continental U.S.A., where they can spend their dollars in the U.S. economy, not antagonize foreign populations, can still be called out to suppress uprisings of students and blacks, and yet send them out in no time to trouble spots anywhere in the world.

'Freedom Vault', involving extensive use of base and communications facilities in Japan and Okinawa, is the most recent

---

January 1970, pp. 32–3; T. Matsueda and G. Moore, 'Japan's Shifting Attitudes Toward the Military: *Mitsuya Kenkyu* and the Self-Defense Force', *Asian Survey*, July 1967, pp. 614–25.

1. *Asahi Shimbun*, 19 March 1969, cited in *Ampo*, no. 7–8, p. 36.
2. *Ampo*, no. 9–10, p. 66.
3. ibid; Nakagawa Nobuo, 'Political-Economics of the Japan–Korea Unification', *Sekai*, May 1971.

example of a co-ordinated U.S./South Korean military operation and shows clearly the primary direction of the Security Treaty's military thrust – against Korea. The degree of military co-ordination between the U.S.A. and Japan was nicely brought home in the April 1970 incident when radical Japanese students hijacked a JAL plane to Pyongyang, since it was then revealed that Japan was totally dependent on U.S. aerial reconnaissance – meaning that the whole apparatus might be scrambled into action in some future *Pueblo* situation.[1]

Finally, there are several indications in recent exercises that Japanese military planning is moving towards a much more active role in future operations than the one adhered to hitherto of rear support. Among them are the Japanese participation in joint exercises with U.S. and Korean troops in Okinawa in June 1971 (see section on Okinawa), and participation by Maritime Self Defence Frigates with the U.S. nuclear submarine, *Snook*, in joint manoeuvres coinciding with the 'Freedom Vault' exercise.[2]

Although Korea was savagely oppressed by the Japanese during their fifty-year colonial rule, a small group of Koreans collaborated with the Japanese: among these were the two generals who staged the 1961 putsch – Chang and Pak, the present dictator of South Korea. As in Indonesia and several other South-East Asian countries, much of the ruling group in Seoul is Japanese-trained, with close ties to both the Japanese military and certain big business interests. In 1967 the Japanese government appointed as its new military attaché in Seoul one Tsukamoto Shoichi, who had been a class-mate of Pak and of several of the Korean leaders in the wartime Japanese Imperial Military Academy. Mitsubishi Heavy Industries, which was deeply involved in the Pohang Steel Works (see below) was also active in supplying funds to ensure Pak's illegal 'election' to a third term in office as President.

1. See Gavan McCormack in *NLR*, no. 65, 1971, on the JAL (Japan Air Lines) hijacking incident. The *Pueblo* was an American spy-ship seized by North Korea in 1968.

2. *Ampo*, no. 9–10, p. 66.

Within the last couple of years, particularly since the Nakasone White Paper, Japan has intensified its military tie-up with South Korea. The following steps have been taken: Japan has established a naval and air repair network in Korea, manned by Japanese technicians; an exchange of servicemen on training exercises has been started (1971); and the entire top group of the Japanese military has toured Korean facilities at least once in the past year. In addition, the vital Shimonoseki–Pusan ferry (the main sea link between Japan and South Korea) has been placed under navy control, through technically demobilized officers (in the same way as the RAF operates in Oman and Dhofar through allegedly unofficial personnel). This ferry, which was first opened in September 1905 to help cement Japanese control over Korea, links up with a new six-lane highway which runs from Pusan to Seoul, which was heavily funded by the Japanese. It is now only twelve hours from Japan to the 38th Parallel, via ferry and highway. The ceremonial opening of this ultra-modern communications link on 19 June 1970 was attended by the entire leading core of the big Japanese right: Kaya, Kishi and Yatsugi.[1]

At the time of the revelation of the 'Three Arrows' Plan in 1965 the Japanese government, assiduously backed by Western imperialist pundits, denied any intention of sending troops to Korea. But several facts undermine this contention: first, the plans themselves, which were far more than mere 'contingency' plans (whatever that may mean); second, the repair, maintenance and exchange agreements with Seoul necessitate the stationing of sizeable numbers of Japanese troops on Korean soil; and, third, there are a number of statements from authoritative sources indicating Japan's likely role in any new Korean conflagration. William Bundy, then U.S. Assistant Secretary of State, is on record as saying that if activity broke out again on the 38th Parallel, 'this time the Japanese army goes'. And the then R.O.K. Premier, Chong Il-kwon, has

1. Yü Yi-ch'ien, *Jih-pen chen-hsiang*, Hong Kong, 1971, translated into Japanese by Arai Takeo as *Nihon no Razo* (*Japan Unmasked*), Tokyo, 1971, pp. 102–7.

stated: 'I believe that Japan, as a UN member, must, under the command of the UN Headquarters in Korea, make an immediate response to any renewed Communist aggression here.'[1] (One may note the ready availability of the UN trickery to cover a Japanese move.)

Prior to the announcement of the Nixon visit to Peking and the Yen-dollar crisis, the situation appeared to be as follows: the U.S.A. had decided to let Japan have a fairly free hand in South Korea economically, and the Seoul clique had indicated their acceptance of this, although with a suitably cacophonous display of bellicose resentment; part of this resentment may well be genuine, reasoning that Japan might be more likely than the U.S.A. to sell South Korea out in return for improved relations with China. The Nixon regime has announced that it is withdrawing 20,000 U.S. troops from Korea, including the American guard on the Seoul sector of the frontier with the D.P.R.K. – largely to stem the dollar haemorrhage, although the 'counterpart' for Seoul is an extra 1½ billion dollars in military funds. Seoul, while howling in dismay at the troop withdrawals, has formally asked the U.S.A. to give a guarantee that Okinawa will effectively remain an American nuclear base after reversion; this appeal, although made public, has not been publicly answered by Washington (Seoul is the only American client to have made such a request).[2]

As part of the U.S.A.–Japan–R.O.K. alliance, Japan has clearly been prepared to move into the 'gap' created by the limited American withdrawal. In effect, now, Japan and South Korea form a strategic unit, with a unified air warning system and suchlike (apparently still under American control). Leading Japanese interests have openly announced that Japan would move into Korea to protect its now sizeable investment stake there. The situation is thus more than ripe. At this stage, though, it is impossible to state with absolute precision what

1. Quoted by Obata Misao, *JQ*, vol. 9, no. 2, 1968, p. 255.

2. In its desperation, the Pak clique even offered the U.S.A. Cheju-do, the large island off Korea's south coast as a replacement for Okinawa (*FEER*, no. 28, 1971, p. 6).

arrangement the Americans are making with Tokyo about Korea. The Laird visit in July 1971 was immediately preceded by the joint U.S.–Japanese–Korean manoeuvres on Okinawa in June, and by a week's tour of South Korea (and Taiwan) by forty trainee SDF officers 'to understand the real situation in neighbouring countries and to help in understanding the problems of national defence'.[1] The real details on the Japan–Korea arrangement worked out by Laird have not yet become clear. And it would be mistaken to think that there is not some genuine confusion in Seoul about which unreliable ally, Washington or Tokyo, to rely on.[2]

In the 1969 Sato–Nixon communiqué, Taiwan is treated in very much the same way as Korea: whereas Korea is described as 'essential to Japan's security', Taiwan is called a 'most important factor for the security of Japan'.

So far, Japan's military tie-up with Taiwan would appear to be less than with South Korea. However, it must be remembered that after the Japanese surrender in 1945, a number of leading Japanese officers and military strategists, including General Okamura, moved over to the Kuomintang (KMT)

1. Harada, op. cit.

2. From mid-1971 the Seoul regime began showing acute signs of panic. It proclaimed its willingness to make a formal renunciation of an alliance with Japan (including Japanese military 'protection') in return for recognition by China, in which case it (Seoul) would settle for a 'two Koreas' arrangement, including separate seats at the UN (Alain Bouc, *Le Monde*, 10 September 1971). It has also agreed, with repeated backtracking, to D.P.R.K. proposals to discuss means of allowing communication between divided families (i.e. involving virtually the entire population) inside Korea – a proposal it had stolidly blocked ever since the Korean war. Seoul also began withdrawal of some of its 48,000-man force from Vietnam. This move was both to bolster the ferocious repression at home, and to assuage Vietnamese opinion. In July 1972 came the announcement of the preliminary Pyongyang–Seoul agreements. In September 1972 South Korea announced that it would withdraw its entire 37,000-man force from Vietnam by June 1973. Immediately after this Seoul newspapers published what they alleged to be the transcripts of recent Congressional hearings at which Laird stated that all American troops would be withdrawn from South Korea by 1975–6.

side[1] and, after advising them in the civil war, migrated with Chiang to Taiwan.

With Japan's seizure of the Tiaoyu Islands (with the reluctant complicity of Taipei), and the reversion of Okinawa, the Japanese are now much closer to the shores of Taiwan than they are even to Korea. The Japanese navy has visited Taiwan and carried out joint manoeuvres with the Chiang navy. SDF trainee officers have visited Taiwan (see above), and Kuomintang military have studied in Japan. One of Sato's last acts as premier was to invite Kuomintang warships to Japan for the first time in June 1972.

Rest of Asia

In his above-mentioned speech of 1 December 1970 Nakasone spoke of Japan's defence as covering 'offshore areas and their peripheries'. This is a phrase open to limitless expansion, since a 'periphery' can always be claimed to be under 'threat'. In the famous case of the Korean war of 1950–53, those who held that America's 'defensive perimeter' actually ran *between* Japan and Korea were still prepared to stand up and wail that this 'perimeter' was 'threatened' by events in Korea.

The Foreign Office spokesman who 'clarified' Nakasone's remarks, indicated that Japan's 'security' area *might* include Vietnam, as well as Korea and Taiwan of course.[2] In Japanese strategic thinking East Asia is divided up into an 'inner ring' of Korea and Taiwan, and an 'outer ring' stretching from Thailand in the west to Indonesia in the south. In trying to estimate how Japan will behave in the future it is not good

1. These included perhaps the most brilliant of all the strategists from the Imperial Army, Tsuji Masanobu, who planned the victories at Bataan and Singapore. Tsuji disappeared on a visit to Laos in 1961. Many of the Japanese who went over to the Kuomintang belonged to the 'Asianist' wing of the Japanese political spectrum. Another group of 'Asianists' migrated to Ethiopia to advise the Haile Selassie regime (a tie-up from the days of the Asianists' anti-European colonialism in the thirties).

2. Gregory Clark, 'Japan: Flexing Nuclear Muscles', *FEER*, no. 50, 1970, p. 8.

enough simply to fall back on Japanese behaviour up to 1945 – although it is vitally important to stress the continuity in policy and personnel through the surrender. It is also important to note that Japan has played an active supporting role in both the major wars of U.S. imperialism in Asia since the victory of the Chinese revolution: in Korea, the Americans 'would have had difficulty' in not being thrown off the peninsula had it not been for Japanese assistance, according to Robert Murphy.[1] And in Vietnam, as well as serving as a rear base for supplies and repairs of every kind, Japan has also provided the personnel for about half the LSTs (Landing Ship Tanks) operating along the Vietnam coast up to the time they were discovered by a vigilant *Asahi* reporter in 1967.[2] According to the captain of one of these vessels, a former colonel in the Imperial Navy, the main task was transporting napalm (of which a reported 90 per cent was made in Japan)[3] and artillery shells, since the roads were unusable. The Japanese government actually recruited the sailors involved (some 1,400), and the vessels, although flying the American flag, were completely run by Japanese.

Apart from this 'training' in Vietnam, the main area of Japanese naval interest has been the Straits of Malacca, and Singapore. The first overseas cruise by Japanese naval vessels was a joint operation held in 1969 with Malaysia and Australia,

1. Murphy, *Diplomat Among Warriors*, London, 1964, p. 424.

2. *Asahi Shimbun*, evening edition, 22 April 1967, quoted in *No More Hiroshimas*, vol. 16, no. 2, June 1969, p. 13.

3. The Japanese have not officially acknowledged their interest in napalm production, and the first report of Japanese napalm being used in Vietnam came from Hsinhua in April 1966. More than half Japan's output of sulphur comes from five mines in Gunma Prefecture: in August 1965 these mines greatly increased output and advertised for labour in the middle of a general slump. In the Korean War it was Nihon Yushi (Japan Oil and Fats) which manufactured the basic crude oil for napalm bombs, and now it is the same company again stepping up production and buying sulphur: there is little doubt it is for the same purpose. (See Japan Peace Council, *Japan Black Book*, cited by Akagi Shoichi, *Nihon no Boei Sangyo* (*Japan's Defence Production*), Tokyo, 1969, pp. 207–10.

when Japanese destroyers went through the Straits for the first time since 1945. Japanese business has been prolific in its ranting about the Straits being 'Japan's lifeline', particularly for oil, and big business has openly called for the stationing of Japanese navy and repair facilities in the area. One of the big Japanese shipbuilding firms, Ishikawajima-Harima Heavy Industries (IHI), is engaged in dock construction in Singapore. Since about the time of the joint manoeuvres with Malaysia and Australia in 1969, Japanese hydrographic ships have been active in the Straits. There is also a 'Malacca Straits Council' in Tokyo, co-ordinating Japanese activities in the area. In July 1971 Japan officially called for the 'internationalization of the Straits of Malacca'; in November 1971 a joint statement was issued by Malaysia, Singapore and Indonesia announcing their joint management of the Straits and officially rejecting the Japanese idea of 'internationalization'.[1]

Even where pro-Japanese leaderships are in power, as in Seoul and Taipei, it would be quite a big step, in any normal circumstances, to move in large numbers of Japanese troops: during the 1950–53 Korean War the Japanese forces ran into a lot of local opposition, even from the (anti-Japanese) Korean right. It is therefore not surprising to find the Japanese Defence Minister, Nishimura, suggesting in October 1971 that the best way to infiltrate Japanese troops would be on some 'charity' operation. Speaking to the Tokyo Foreign Correspondents Club, Nishimura stated that: 'In such a situation as that of a great natural disaster in Asia, if the Japanese people agreed, and if there was no legal problem about it, we would like to send in Self-Defence Forces and use them as a technical force.'[2] Coming only a matter of months after the revelation in

1. *TKP*, 2 December 1971; *FEER*, no. 50, 1971, p. 69 indicates that Singapore is not happy with the new plan; both Malaysia and Indonesia have grandiose plans for alternative ports to Singapore (Port Klang and Tjilatjap, respectively) and Japanese money may be available for these.

2. Cited in 'The Logic of Unimpeded Transfer of Responsibility in Military Affairs', *Asahi Journal*, 17 December 1971, pp. 36–41, by the editorial staff of the *Asahi Journal*. In spite of the uproar created

the *Pentagon Papers* that Maxwell Taylor's original idea for inserting large numbers of U.S. troops into Vietnam in 1961 was under the guise of 'flood relief operations', Nishimura's suggestion is extremely ominous.

In the meantime, the SDF is training officers from several Asian countries (Thailand, Taiwan and Indonesia) at the GSDF Officer School and the Defence University. On 3 May 1971 Reuters carried an Antara (Indonesian government) report that 'Japan had suggested co-operation in training the Indonesian Army' and was prepared to send military instructors and to have officer cadets partake in training with the SDF. The proposals, denied in Japan, were reported to have come from a top SDF echelon to the Indonesian Army Chief of Staff on the latter's visit to Japan.[1]

Japan has a very strong network of protégés throughout South-East Asia. This ranges from many of the military officers in power in Seoul and Djakarta (including both President Pak and President Suharto) to civilian leaders like Prime Minister Lee Kuan Yew of Singapore (who worked for the Japanese during their occupation of Singapore) and ex-premier Tunku Abdul Rahman of Malaysia who deposed his father as ruler of Kedah at the time of the Japanese invasion of Malaya. Many of the ruling group round Ne Win in Rangoon were closely involved with the Japanese during the latters' occupation of Burma. And Thailand has traditionally had very good relations with Tokyo. American puppets in Saigon, Vientiane and

---

by his remarks, Nishimura did not have to resign until 3 December ostensibly because he had said the UN was becoming like a 'rural credit union' (or, alternatively, that the UN was engaging in 'parish pump politics') after the China vote in October. Nishimura was replaced by Ezaki Masumi, the fourth man to hold the job in 1971.

1. Harada, *Sekai*, op. cit. It should also be noted that the U.S.A. Army Intelligence School on Okinawa had trained 3,670 people from sixteen countries up to the end of 1970, with a big increase in the years 1967–70 in the number of trainees from Vietnam and Laos (House Foreign Relations Committee, *Hearings on Military Assistance Training in Asia*, February 1971): it is not known what Japanese connections there were with this programme. The School was scheduled for withdrawal by the time of reversion in May 1972.

Phnom Penh can always be bought, where necessary – witness the spectacular multiplication of local generals on the boards of successful Japanese companies in these client states. As the case of Indonesia detailed above (p. 36) shows, it is not correct to assume that Japan is all-powerful, or even necessarily the dominant power. But ties of history, money and firepower do count for quite a lot. The length of Japan's reach, and the power of its accumulated assets, were neatly shown in 1967 when a group of Israeli officers travelled to Japan to study the diversionary plans for the 1941 attack on Pearl Harbor.

MILITARY–INDUSTRIAL COMPLEX

Realization has begun to emerge in Japan within the past couple of years of the existence of a powerful element within the reconstituted *zaibatsu* which is working to speed the re-militarization of the country and whose profits have come increasingly to depend on it. Given the increasing pressure of competition for markets abroad, and the approaching saturation of some domestic ones, it is not really surprising that industrialists have openly identified defence as a key growth industry of the future and have been working to secure and increase the demand for their military hardware. Public attention to the issue was long lulled by belief that Japan was subject to a 'peace constitution', and by the misleading consideration that defence expenditure amounted to no more than 1 per cent of GNP. Yet the coincidence of ruling business, industrial and military elites, has in fact already produced a more powerful and concentrated lobby than exists even in the United States. From the structural concentration already effected even more rapid growth may be expected in the future.

Weapons for use in the Korean and Vietnam wars played a crucial part in Japan's postwar economic recovery and growth. U.S. military procurements in Japan between 1951 and 1960 amounted to 6 billion dollars, an average of 600 million dollars annually and, even as late as 1958–9, well after the conclusion of the Korean War, they were 'sufficient to pay for about 14 per cent of (Japanese) imports', an important boon for a country with a chronic balance of payments problem.[1] Expansion of the Vietnam War after 1965 was also a tremendous boon to Japan. Whereas the country's GNP rose 2.7 per cent in 1965–6, it rose by 7.5 per cent in 1966–7,[2] in which year military contracts with Japanese firms came to approximately $505 million, while other war-related contracts – for the delivery of goods to the U.S.A., Thailand, South Korea, Taiwan and the Philippines – were worth $1.2 billion.[3] To put it mildly, 'American war spending, in short, has been an important factor in revitalizing Japanese capitalism just as it has been in sustaining a prosperous American capitalism.'[4]

The Japanese economy was largely moulded by the demand for war materials. Seventy-two per cent of the plant designated for confiscation that was not confiscated was directly related to armament; 80–90 per cent of this production capacity was intact at the start of the Korean War. Organized Japanese business began in early 1953 to draw up plans for the rearmament of Japan, in 1954 to press for research into guided missiles; in 1955 it succeeded in getting orders for a start on the production of jet fighters.[5] In 1952 a joint Defence Production Committee (representative of business and military) had been set up to begin the institutionalization of military–industrial solidarity.[6]

The practice of 'descent from heaven', by which youthful admirals, generals and other military officials retire from their posts to join companies engaged in defence-related work is a

1. G. C. Allen, *A Short Economic History of Modern Japan 1867–1937*, with a supplementary chapter on 'Economic Recovery and Expansion 1945–1960', Allen & Unwin, 1962, ed., p. 173.

2. Peter Wiley, 'Vietnam and the Pacific Rim Strategy', *Leviathan*, June, 1969, p. 7.

3. D. Petrov, 'Anatomy of a Japanese Miracle', *New Times*, no. 36, 11 September 1968, p. 20.

4. Bix, op. cit., p. 34.

5. Takahashi Ryozo, op. cit., p. 78; Yanaga, op. cit., pp. 255 ff.

6. ibid., p. 256; Haruhiro Fukui, *Party in Power*, Berkeley and Los Angeles, 1970, p. 211.

long established one. During the 'Defence Secrets scandal' of 1967–8 it was learned that there were 265 Defence Agency officials, who had retired between 1962 and 1967, who were so engaged. According to Defence Agency figures, to the end of March 1969 there were 166 ex-generals or admirals, or candidate generals or admirals, employed in the 1,518 companies qualified to participate in bidding for their contracts at that time. In Mitsubishi Heavy Industries, the major contractor, there were fifteen.[1] Toshiba Electric, which appeared for the first time in the ranks of the top ten companies under contract to the Defence Agency in 1967, has since taken another four generals, for a total of five, onto its staff.[2] A general correlation of numbers of these 'descended from heaven' employees with Defence Agency contracts emerges from a comparative chart very clearly.[3]

The Mitsubishi group, and especially Mitsubishi Heavy Industries, has come to play an increasingly dominant role in Defence Agency contracting. In 1968 a total of 20 per cent of such contracts was awarded to Mitsubishi Heavy Industries, and a further 13 per cent to Mitsubishi Electric, for a total of 33 per cent. In 1969 the two Mitsubishi groups jointly undertook 45 per cent of all defence contracts, Mitsubishi Heavy Industries' total being no less than 70 billion yen, or 38 per cent.[4] In the United States even Lockheed only gets about 4.5

1. Murakami Kaoru, 'Mitsubishi Arms Factory – Actual Situation and Strategy', part one of a series on 'Japan's Military–Industrial Complex', *Asahi Journal*, 12 April 1970.

2. Shirota Noboru, Yamamura Yoshiharu and Shironishi Shinichiro, *Mitsubishi Gunshusho – Nihon no Sangun Fukugotai to Kaigai Shinshutsu* (*Mitsubishi Armament Factory – Japan's Military–Industrial Complex and Overseas Expansion*), Tokyo, Gendai Hyoronsha, 1971, p. 149.

3. Murakami, op. cit. For a comprehensive listing by name, rank and present position in the companies joined, see Akagi Shoichi, op. cit., pp. 164–8. In the U.S.A. the comparative figures are 261 of the rank of general and 1,400 of major and above in the top 100 defence contracting companies (cited by Akagi, op. cit., p. 168, from Jack Raymond's *Inside the Pentagon*).

4. Murakami, for 1968 details; for 1969 figures see Yagisawa

per cent of Pentagon arms orders. Makita Yoichiro, President of Mitsubishi Heavy Industries, protests too much when he claims, 'Defence Agency orders make up only less than 5 per cent of our sales. And we certainly don't make any money out of it. We wouldn't dream of making any money out of it.'[1] That defence contracts account for only about 5 per cent of gross company sales is no doubt true, but it is rather an indication of the enormous weight of the company in the economy. Mitsubishi group capital amounted in 1970 to 5.9 per cent of the total paid up capital of all Japanese companies, while gross sales (in 1969) amounted to 4.6 per cent of all Japanese company sales. The share enjoyed by the group in the Japanese economy as a whole is now greater than it was in 1937, and its strength as compared to other *zaibatsu* is also now greater.[2] The pious claim of disinterest in profit is a very traditional Mitsubishi one, 'service to the nation' being long the avowed *raison d'être*. The most recent Japanese study concludes that Mitsubishi, by heavy investment in its armaments section and contentment to date with minimal profits, has now secured for itself such a fund of experience and expertise, and established such a web of governmental contacts, that its dominance in the field will be increasingly unchallengeable in future, and thus big profits can now be taken.[3] The case of jet fighter construction is an example.

Since 1956 there have been three jet fighter models all produced by Mitsubishi under licence from three different American companies: from 1956 there were 300 F-86F produced under licence from North American at 120 million yen each for a total (including licences, etc.) of 42 billion yen, which left Mitsubishi in the red; from 1962 (after agreement in 1960) 200 F-104J were produced under licence from Lockheed at

---

Mitsuo, 'Mitsubishi Heavy Industries on the Attack', part one of a series, 'Big Business under Stagflation [stagnation–inflation]', *Asahi Journal*, 26 March 1971.

1. *Asahi Shimbun*, 15 August 1970, cited Yagisawa.
2. Shirota *et al.*, op. cit., pp. 88–9.
3. ibid., *passim*.

484 million yen each for a total of 96,800 million yen, on which Mitsubishi broke even; from 1968–71 104 F-4EJ Phantoms were to be produced under licence from McDonnell Douglas at a cost of between 1,800 and 2,000 million yen each, and on these Mitsubishi is expected to make a handsome profit.[1] The F-4E is reportedly already an 'old plane', being phased out in the U.S.A., as it is no match for the new MIG 23, and while the new F-15 is being developed the U.S. is said to be willing to sell F-4Es at 1,100 to 1,200 million yen each.[2]

One incident which drew public attention to the dangers of inordinately close ties, redrawn between government and Mitsubishi, was the award of the CX transport plane engine contract. In October 1966 MITI (Ministry of International Trade and Industry) awarded the large-scale CX contract to Ishikawajima-Harima, while the smaller T-63 and T-53 engines were ordered from Mitsubishi Heavy Industries and Kawasaki Heavy Industries. Powerful lobbying by Mitsubishi men behind the scenes, however, succeeded in having the large-scale engine contract transferred to them amid very strong rumours of scandal just before the elections of December 1969. After questions in the Diet on 26 February it emerged that Mitsubishi had no equipment and no technicians capable of work on the project, that its largest gas turbine engine experience to date was 317 HP while the CX was 25,000 HP, and that the new factory being built at Ajioka for the project was costing at least 2 billion yen.[3]

These figures suggest the importance of taking a close look at the Mitsubishi enterprise.[4] Since its foundation in 1870 in Osaka the company has maintained intimate governmental

1. Shirota *et al.*, op. cit., pp. 106–17.

2. Murakami, op. cit. The F-4E has a range of 3,700 kilometres, more than twice that of the F-104J, raising the question why Japan's 'Defence' Forces should need a plane with a strike capability stretching over much of Asia.

3. Sugioka Sekio, 'Big Economic Power and Toy Army', part two of 'Japan's Military–Industrial Complex', *Asahi Journal*, 26 March 1971; Shirota, *et al.* op. cit., p. 140.

4. The following account is based on Shirota *et al.*, op. cit., *passim.*

connections – growing symbiotically with the government through its various military and colonial enterprises, beginning with the Taiwan expedition of 1874 and continuing down to the Pacific war and now beyond. During the Pacific war Mitsubishi produced some 40 per cent of all aeroplane bodies and 50 per cent of engines for the air force, as well as all the tanks and a good many of the battleships used in that war. The 'Zero' fighter was a Mitsubishi product. At the end of the war there were thirty-one Mitsubishi factories employing a total of 400,000 workers. Mitsubishi Heavy Industries, the armaments division, was reluctant to undertake any voluntary disbandment in the occupation-sponsored reforms that followed the defeat, and indeed proved wise in delaying action since, with the shift in occupation policy, the beginning of the 'reverse course', a token separation into Eastern, Western and Central Mitsubishi Heavy Industries, was accepted. (Mitsubishi Trading Company, on the other hand, was divided into 140 separate parts.) From 1947 Mitsubishi Heavy Industries was engaged in weapons servicing and repair for the U.S. military, and in the Korean War boom, while largely ignoring the lucrative short-term business of munitions supply, largely of shells, bombs, etc., which went to new and smaller enterprises,[1] Mitsubishi continued to concentrate on servicing and repairing vehicles, battleships and jet planes, learning in the process much of American advanced weapons technology. In 1954 the Mitsubishi conglomerate was reorganized; Mitsubishi Trading Company, recently renamed Mitsubishi Corporation, was reformed from its briefly separated components; the 'Friday Directors' Meeting' of heads of all Mitsubishi enterprises was revived as the central planning and co-ordinating body of the group. The new Mitsubishi was formally different from the old in that the conglomerate was no longer structured around the centralized Iwasaki family holding company, but this may have actually served to enhance the efficiency and 'rationality' of the corporation.

1. Mitsubishi does not even figure in the top ten contractors for the supply of this kind of material during the Korean War (ibid., pp. 39–40).

Two important developments in Mitsubishi came in 1964, a crucial year in the development of Japanese capitalism. First was the reunification of the Western, Eastern and Central Heavy Industries, an important internal consolidation. The other was the appointment of Usami Makoto, Mitsubishi Bank President, to the Governorship of the Bank of Japan, a post which carried enormous political power in the sense of determining fiscal policy, and which had hitherto been filled only by bureaucrats from the Finance Ministry or from within the Bank itself.[1] These steps were preludes to the enormous expansion of overseas enterprise that followed 1965 (see elsewhere in this book), and to increasingly open advocacy of full-scale rearmament – two facets closely related in traditional Mitsubishi thinking since its expansion was concentrated heavily in Taiwan and South Korea especially, and since these are traditional first staging posts of armed Japanese expansion.

The next major developments within Mitsubishi came in 1969. An attempt was made from January onwards to merge the Mitsubishi and Dai-Ichi Banks, the one ranked third in volume of deposits in Japan and the other sixth. Such a tie-up would have had three main consequences: creation of a bank that would be the greatest in Japan and a powerful support in the competition expected under the forthcoming capital liberalization; a link with Fujitsu, a company of great strength in a field where Mitsubishi was comparatively weak and which was increasingly important in defence and missile contracting, i.e. computers; and also a link with Kawasaki Heavy Industries, a company second only to Mitsubishi Heavy Industries as a defence contractor, thus bringing about virtual elimination of all competition by the creation of one giant weapons monopoly company. (Both Fujitsu and Kawasaki Heavy Industries belonged to the Dai-Ichi group.) The move, as it happened, was defeated by opposition from within Dai-Ichi, but was

1. This appointment was reported to have been insisted on by Ikeda, when resigning the premiership at this time, in recognition for financial help rendered by Mitsubishi to the government during the July general elections (see Shirota *et al.*, op. cit., p. 56).

important, nevertheless, as showing the direction of Mitsubishi thinking. In 1969, also, Mitsubishi Heavy Industries was overtaken as the leading car exporter by Toyota, and in its traditional field of ship-building by Ishikawajima-Harima. With the domestic car market approaching saturation, and foreign competition in both cars and shipping intensifying, the unprofitable and heavily debt-burdened car section of Mitsubishi Heavy Industries was hived off altogether in May; a formal tie-up was agreed on with Chrysler of the U.S.A. which, it was anticipated, would give Mitsubishi access to the latest aerospace technology, and Makita Yoichiro, President from March 1969, indicated that defence would be given increasing priority by the company.[1]

At the 'Friday meeting' of the heads of the twenty-six Mitsubishi companies held on 12 September 1969, the line to be followed by the group in the seventies was defined as follows:

1. Mitsubishi as developer – promotion of a mass line by providing large-scale housing supply, the building of new towns, shopping centres, etc.

2. Mitsubishi as close support of the state – strengthening of Mitsubishi predominance in defence production, rocket development, marine development, the nuclear power industry, the

1. ibid., pp. 142–3; and article by Yagisawa Mitsuo cited above. Most of Japan's defence contractors are of course allied to their counter numbers in the U.S.A. by a series of licensing agreements and joint ventures. General Electric, for example, fourth largest in the U.S.A., has licensing agreements with about sixty-five Japanese companies and a 10 per cent interest in Tokyo Shibaura Electric. Bix (cited above) (p. 38) points to the tendency for U.S. pressure on Japan for liberalization of investment terms to be met in Japan partly by increased investment in defence production. *FEER* has also noted, 'The business magnates who have been pressing for easier entry of foreign investment into the motor industry have now almost unanimously begun to call for expansion of the defence programme.' (John Roberts, 'To Arms, Dear Friends', *FEER*, no. 31, 27 July–2 August 1969). The Dai-Ichi Bank, incidentally, recently merged with the Nippon Kangyo Bank to become the largest single bank in Japan (*The Financial Times*, 3 May 1971).

information industry. Especially in weapons production to take advantage of the present high technological level to go on to make faultless weapons and to expand the Mitsubishi share of the market.

3. Mitsubishi as world enterprise – to exercise the combined strength of Mitsubishi in international activities, such as development of resources and markets overseas, export of capital overseas.[1]

Finally, the organizational links between government and industry on a formal level, and Mitsubishi's part in them, should be considered. Since August 1952, when a Defence Production Council was first set up within the Keidanren (Federation of Economic Organizations), the post of chairman, beginning with the wartime president of Mitsubishi Heavy Industries, Goko Kiyoshi, has always been held by a Mitsubishi man.[2] The Defence Production Committee is the main body responsible for centralizing research, lobbying and marketing for the hundred or so large corporations involved in arms and munitions manufacture. Mitsubishi control over the key positions in weapons production on the industrial side reached a striking peak in 1970. Within the exclusively big business organization of Keidanren, the position was as follows:

Keidanren Vice-President – Kono Fumihiko, Chairman of Mitsubishi Heavy Industries.

Defence Production Committee Chairman – Okano Yasujiro, ex-President of, and consultant to, Mitsubishi Heavy Industries.

Finance and Monetary Committee Chairman – Tazane Wataru, President of Mitsubishi Bank.

Aviation Committee Chairman – Fujii Fukazo, Consultant to Mitsubishi Heavy Industries.

Electrical Committee Chairman – Seki Yoshihisa, Consultant to Mitsubishi Electric.

Japan Ordnance Association President – Okubo Ken, President of Mitsubishi Electric.

1. *Nikkan Kogyo Shimbun*, 13 September 1969, cited Shirota, p. 85.
2. ibid., p. 41.

Japan Aviation Industry Association Director-in-Chief – Makita Yoichiro, President of Mitsubishi Heavy Industries.[1]

In July and August of 1970 important and complementary documents relating to defence were issued by the Defence Agency ('Fundamental Measures Relating to the Production and Development of Equipment' – 15 July) and the Defence Production Committee of Keidanren ('Our Opinions on the Problem of Defence Equipment for the Next Period' – 12 August).[2] The former, from the government side, spelt out its two basic principles – promotion of the domestic production of arms and encouragement of the principle of competition among contractors. The latter, from industry's side, set out three institutional reforms which it desired, and which would create the formal channels, as distinct from the present quite informal and even secret ones, for the participation by industry in formulation of defence policy: (1) establishment of a National Security Council as principal advisory body to the Prime Minister on defence matters; (2) establishment of a Defence Commission, with representation by scholars, civilian specialists, etc., to plan and to advise the Director of the Defence Agency on the rational use of defence expenditures; (3) establishment of a round table conference on defence equipment, also with representation by civilians and government.

1. ibid., p. 134; Murakami Kaoru, article cited above. Yagisawa points out that on 22 September 1970, with the resignation through illness of Okano Yasujiro from the chairmanship of the Defence Production Committee, it was planned to replace him with Kono Fumihiko, Chairman of Mitsubishi Heavy Industries. However, total Mitsubishi control over the Keidanren five groups of Defence Production, Ordnance, Aviation, Shipping and Rocket Development was somewhat of an embarrassment and so the post was given for the time being to the Keidanren President. From May 1971 the new Japan Ordnance Association President was Toshiba Vice-President Tamaoki Keizo. Mitsubishi were anxious to be out of the job and to reduce their public exposure to attack as militarists, while Toshiba, faced with a continually declining market in colour television sets and the like, were anxious to increase defence orders, seeing this as the most secure growth sector (*Mainichi Shimbun*, 27 May 1971).

2. Yagisawa, op. cit.; Shirota *et al.*, op. cit., pp. 136–7.

If such recommendations are adopted, at least, leading industrialists have made quite clear the kinds of defence measures they believe necessary, and which until now they have been pressing informally on the government. Okubo Ken (Mitsubishi Electric President and President of the Japan Ordnance Association) favours nuclear weapons for Japan, an increase in defence spending to at least the level of France's 4 per cent of GNP (as against present 1 per cent), and a 300 per cent naval expansion.[1] At the 30th General Conference of Keidanren in May 1969, the then President (Uyemura) remarked in the course of his address of greeting: 'We have a duty to contribute to the preservation of peace in the Far East and to gradually increase self defence capacity, as well as to hold strongly to the Security Treaty system.'[2]

Sakurada, Director of the Japan Federation of Employers Associations (Nikkeiren), believes it necessary to take a careful look at the defence problem in view of the need to secure energy sources abroad, and thinks constitutional revision necessary to national defence.[3] Funada Naka, Chairman of the LDP's Security Treaty Investigation Association (Ampo Chosakai), proposed in the summer of 1969 that, because of the narrowness of the domestic armaments market, it was necessary, in order to develop a modernized industry, to allow exports to Taiwan, South Korea, Vietnam and South-East Asia.[4] And, to put the narrow defence consideration back into its proper perspective, there are the following words from Fujino Chujiro, President of Mitsubishi Trading Company, and who was head of Mitsubishi's Peking branch for six years through to the end of the war:

Go and take a look at Korea. If by chance in the early morning you happen to see a man pulling a cartload of kimche (pickled vegetable), his wife will be pushing from behind. The light in people's eyes is different there. Taiwan is like this too. These

1. Yagisawa, op. cit.; Shirota *et al.*, op. cit., p. 128.
2. Yagisawa, op. cit.
3. ibid.
4. *Atarashii Nihon Gunkokushugi*, op. cit., p. 22.

are countries we can co-operate with economically. Europe has its EEC. America is sufficient within itself. We coloured peoples who have become the world's problem people must even now unite our strength. I believe the old East Asian Co-prosperity Sphere was essentially right. The only trouble is that Japan looked only to its own advantage and resentment of this persists still. From now on we must meet a new age by changing our thinking both about giving aid and about being aided.[1]

1. Shirota *et al.*, op. cit., p. 245.

Chapter 4

JAPAN AND CHINA

THE TRADING AGREEMENTS

At the time of the victory of the Revolution in China, the U.S.A. forced Japan (then still not technically a sovereign nation) to adopt a uniquely severe embargo list as regards its trade with China. This was in 1951 – and the reason advanced was that, since Japan was benefiting more than any other country from the Korean War, it should suffer more from the trade embargo vis-à-vis China![1] At any rate, the result was a steep rise in American exports to Japan to replace those from China: 1951 U.S. sales of soya beans, coals and salt were up three, sixteen and eighteen times over the 1950 figures, while Chinese sales to Japan showed a catastrophic drop.

Apart from a brief interlude in the years 1955–6 (in 1956 Japan accounted for 21.8 per cent of China's total trade) Japan continued along the same path throughout the decade. However, after Kishi was brought down in 1960, his successor, Ikeda, a ruthless bureaucrat but less given to windy ideology

1. Haruhiro Fukui, *Party in Power*, Berkeley and Los Angeles, 1970, p. 228; Fukui has a long and useful section on Japanese–Chinese relations, particularly as they affect the ruling LDP. Information immediately below from the same source. This embargo was still in force in early 1972. MITI was reported pushing hard to get some sixty items de-embargoed and discriminatory tariffs lifted on a further thirty-one items at the February 1972 meeting of COCOM in Paris – as part of the overall drive to enlarge Japan–China trade (*JEJ*, vol. 10, no. 477, 15 February 1972).

than Kishi, accepted business pressure to revise trading relations with China. This pressure came from several sectors, particularly from Osaka, the big trading centre traditionally tied to the China trade; a sizeable section of the ruling LDP also pushed for better trade relations with China.

The aging LDP faction leader, Matsumura Kenzo, who knew both Chou En-lai and Chen Yi (then Foreign Minister) personally, went to China and talked with a member of the Central Committee of the Chinese Communist Party, Liao Cheng-chih (who was a graduate of Matsumura's university in Japan, Waseda). In November 1962 Liao signed an agreement with a Japanese businessman, Takasaki Tatsunosuke. Takasaki, like several of the big 'pro-Chinese' figures in and around the LDP, was a reactionary tycoon who had made his fortune in Manchukuo; in 1955 he headed the Japanese delegation to the Bandung Conference, where he conducted tentative talks with the Chinese delegation. The Liao–Takasaki agreement (usually referred to either as 'L–T trade' or 'Memorandum Trade') covered the five years 1963–7, and called for barter transactions of up to $100mill. Ikeda endorsed the agreement, which was warmly supported by the powerful Ministry of International Trade and Industry (MITI); the Keidanren, however, opposed better trade relations with China, although the Japan Economic Research Council, which was then headed by Uyemura Kogoro (now the head of Keidanren), came out in favour of increased trade with China at about this time.[1] In the year 1966, for example, L–T trade amounted to $200mill., and 'FF' trade to more than $300mill. In 1970, the first full year

1. Fukui, op. cit., p. 233. For a full study of the Liao–Takasaki arrangement see Norman Sun, 'Trade Between Mainland China and Japan under the "L–T" Agreements', *Hong Kong Economic Papers*, no. 4, November 1968, pp. 57–71 (on the 1963–7 period). L–T trade was confined to a few selected items. The term 'L–T trade' technically covers the years 1963–7, and 'Memorandum Trade' the years 1968 onwards. 'FF' (i.e. 'Friendly Firms') trade, referred to below, covers transactions between China and selected Japanese companies chosen for their political friendship. Many of these were small enterprises run by left-leaning businessmen.

after the Cultural Revolution, total Japan–China trade amounted to $820mill., of which L–T trade accounted for only $70mill.[1]

Japan's trade with China has been dominated by the question of Japan's relationship with Taiwan, rather than vice versa. In 1963 for the first time the Japanese government agreed to guarantee a $15mill. deferred payment loan on the export of a textile manufacturing plant to China. Taipei protested vigorously, and the Japanese decided to haul the semi-senile Yoshida out of retirement to go to Taipei and mollify Chiang Kai-shek. On his return to Japan, Yoshida wrote Chiang a letter promising that Japan would not allow any more deferred-payment plant exports to China – and the textile plant one fell through. The 'Yoshida letter' greatly irritated the Chinese government, and relations sank further with the advent of Sato, Kishi's brother, to the premiership in 1964. Sato announced that 'Japan–China relations will not change so long as I am in office.' Sato also gave his full backing to the efforts of his brother Kishi and of Yatsugi Kazuo in organizing the pro-Taipei and pro-Seoul lobbies.

After the Cultural Revolution China noticeably toughened its attitude to the Sato regime. In April 1970 Chou travelled to Pyongyang, where he signed a primarily anti-Japanese communiqué with the leaders of the Democratic People's Republic of Korea (D.P.R.K.). After that a succession of joint Chinese–Korean communiqués drew attention to the Japanese threat, particularly as regards Korea. U.S. imperialism, of course, remains the number one enemy, but the relationship is that of 'the United States pulling strings and Japan playing an on-stage role'. Also in April 1970 Chou enunciated the four Principles governing trade with Japan.

China concentrated its demands on Japan to the question of Taiwan. Chou stated that China was prepared to conclude a treaty with Japan upon renunciation of the current Japan–

1. Toshio Yoshimura and Koji Nakamura, 'Back Door to Peking', *FEER*, no. 5, 1971. L–T trade only accounted for about 10 per cent of 1971 Japan–China trade, which totalled some $900mill.

Taiwan peace treaty; the Security Treaty with the U.S.A. was *not* a stumbling block in itself.

Sato seemed to have felt the chill already before the announcement of the Nixon trip to Peking. On 5 April 1971, at a press conference in Fukuoka, he announced he was retracting his statement that relations would never change while he was in office, and that he would 'improve' Japan's relations with China. It is worth looking at the real pressures which obliged Sato to backtrack publicly before the Nixon move.

PRO-CHINA GROUPS INSIDE JAPAN

The groups working for a change in Japan's political relationship with China up to 1972 can conveniently be divided into two: those within the LDP and those outside it. Within the LDP there have traditionally been several potentates advocating close relations with Peking: the two best-known of these have been Matsumura Kenzo, who arranged the 1962 trade agreement (he died in August 1971), and Utsunomiya Tokuma. Both these worked for better relations with China, pointing out that the existing state of affairs was of great benefit only to the right-wing bureaucrats and militarists in Japan.[1]

More recently, the main agent of change has been Fujiyama Aiichiro, like the late Takasaki, a right-wing businessman who amassed a fortune plundering China during the Japanese occupation. He is close to big business, and was endorsed by part of business as its spokesman empowered to bring about the desired change. Prior to the events of summer 1971, the Keizai Doyukai (the second largest business federation), virtually the whole of the Osaka business community, and the *Nihon Keizai* (the *Financial Times* of Japan) had all come out openly for a change in policy.

Fujiyama organized a Dietmen's League with the support of more than half the MPs in both chambers for the *cause* of normal relations with China. Ninety-five LDP MPs, includ-

1. *FEER*, no. 4, 1971, p. 4; cf. interview with Fukui, op. cit., p. 257.

ing some from Sato's faction (possibly Trojan Horses?) had backed the League by summer 1971, and some estimates put the real support even higher – although this was belied by the Diet vote after the announcement of the Nixon trip.[1] The Chinese government responded to the formation of Fujiyama's League by inviting Fujiyama to visit Peking in early 1971 at the same time as the annual trade delegation which was coming to China to renew the Memorandum Trade Agreement. The Chinese, while politicizing their exchanges with the Tokyo regime as a whole, insisted on downgrading the political importance of the actual discussions on trade: the usual head of the delegation, LDP Dietman Furui Yoshimi, was demoted to the number two position by Japan (apparently at Peking's request), and replaced by the technocrat who heads the Memorandum Trade Office in Tokyo.[2]

In March 1971, the *Far Eastern Economic Review* wrote: 'The atmosphere in Japan has changed appreciably despite the rigid official government stand . . . It is evident that Sato has felt a "strong pinch" from the growing pro-Peking sentiment in Japan which recently crystallized into a supra-partisan parliamentary group consisting of 379 of the 743 members of the upper and lower houses.'[3] Already in January 1971 an *Asahi* poll showed that the number of those who gave priority to good relations with China had more than doubled in the previous eighteen months.

Fujiyama was only able to build his League thanks to two factors: sizeable financial support from business, especially from the Keizai Doyukai and from big Osaka concerns such as Sumitomo; and because of a big shift in public opinion and in the opposition parties. The Japanese Communist Party (JCP), in spite of its estrangement from Peking and its status as one

1. The LDP rode out the storm in the Diet. But this was too early for the ruling class to have been able to reorganize itself: not a single member raised the question of reappraising the pro-Taiwan, anti-Peking guidelines of Japanese foreign policy! (*FEER*, no. 32, 1971, p. 50.)

2. See *PR* nos. 10 and 11, 1971.

3. Koji Nakamura, 'Sato's Sinking Feeling', *FEER*, no. 11, 1971.

of the designated 'four enemies' of the Japanese people, is in favour of recognition and good relations; so is the Buddhist Komeito. After the Cultural Revolution the Japanese Socialist Party (JSP) also much improved its relations with China, and in late 1970 Narita, the head of the party, paid a warm visit to China.

The JSP has been active, along with the largest trade union federation, Sohyo, in organizing a new body, the National Congress for the Restoration of Japan–China Relations, which was inaugurated in early 1971. This Congress has organized a series of mass meetings and a vast campaign to galvanize public opinion on the China issue. It has pressured the government from the centre and the left, as a mass movement, while Fujiyama and his group apply pressure from within the ruling class. The two groups work together in the Diet and, even before the Nixon visit, it was taken as a foregone conclusion that Sato's successor would virtually be forced to undertake a full revision of China policy. Fukuda, Sato's designated heir, attempted to disengage Japan from the Washington-organized fiasco at the UN in autumn 1971.[1] He subsequently acknowledged that Japan should apologize to China. But even after the Nixon visit to China, he still seemed trapped in the contradictions of official LDP policy over Taiwan, and was still trailing along behind Sato in stating that Taiwan would only formally be acknowledged (by Japan) as part of China after the normalization of Japan's relations with China[2] – a preposterous position.

CHOU PRINCIPLES

Like the Lancashire cotton men in the nineteenth century who believed that an extra inch on every Chinese shirt-tail

1. The *Observer*, 12 September 1971; Fukuda told Rogers at the U.S.A.–Japan talks in Washington that Tokyo would not support the '2 Chinas' UN scheme. Fukuda was later overruled by Sato.

2. *The Times*, 4 March 1972. Note that the statement widely attributed to Sato that Taiwan is 'part of the People's Republic of China' was subsequently disowned.

would keep their mills in business more or less for ever, Japanese business has always eyed the China market as the potential solution to their eternal market quest and, like the Lancashire men, they have so far known only the promise and the disappointment. While the Taiwan/Korea/Japan axis was strengthened as described in a later section, not only did the China trade remain at low, though increasing, levels, but the strengthening of ties with the former became increasingly incompatible with developing ties with the latter.

A comparison of Japan/Taiwan with Japan/China trade shows the relatively undeveloped state of the China trade to 1971:

TABLE TWENTY-THREE Japan–Taiwan and Japan–China Trade 1967–71 (in $mill.)

	Taiwan			China		
	Japan's exports	Japan's imports	total	Japan's exports	Japan's imports	total
1967	328.1	137.0	465.1	288.2	269.4	557.6
1968	471.6	150.7	622.3	325.4	224.1	549.5
1969	606.3	180.5	786.8	390.8	234.5	635.3
1970	700.4	250.7	950.7	568.8	253.8	822.6
1971	767.0	267.0	1,034.0	577.6	322.1	899.7

Source: MITI, *Tsusho Hakusho, Kakuron*, 1970, pp. 277, 659; 1971, pp. 300, 700; *FEER*, 4 March 1972, pp. 44,67.

In other words Japan's trade with Taiwan is substantially greater than that with China as a whole, though Taiwan has only one fiftieth of the population of mainland China. In both cases the balance is in Japan's favour, grossly so in the Taiwan case. However, as reported recent interviews with Chou En-lai have underlined, the Chinese have become very conscious of the threat to them of the emerging politico-military bloc based on Japan, and are apparently shifting strategic priorities to some extent from South-East back towards North-East Asia. In doing so they are well aware that the weight of their trade with Japan, and the Japanese hopes for great increases in it, afford them considerable leverage which can be exercised to combat the threat of Japanese militarism. From 1968 three general principles were announced on which trade with Japan was to be based; these were expanded and codified only in the spring of 1970 by Chou En-lai, and since then used to great effect. The principles may be summarised briefly as these – that China will not trade with companies that aid or have large investments in Taiwan or South Korea, with companies that supply arms or weapons for the U.S.A. in South-East Asia, or that are joint enterprises or subsidiaries of American companies.[1]

In July and August, 1970, a considerable number of companies were excluded from the trade on one or other of these grounds. They included dummy companies set up specifically for the China trade by the four major trading companies – Mitsui, Mitsubishi, Marubeni and C. Itoh, forty companies which had participated in the 15th Meeting of the Japan–Republic of China Co-operation Committee, and which included Nippon Steel, Toshiba, Yanmar, Kawasaki Heavy Industries, Japan Air Lines, Mitsubishi Heavy Industries, Sumitomo Chemicals, Teijin. Others such as Asahi-Dow were excluded as joint U.S.A.–Japanese companies. The impact on Japanese industrialists was powerful. Some companies, like, for example, Sumitomo Metals, Kawasaki Iron, Japan Steel Tubing, Kobe Steel, were quick to announce acceptance of the principles.[2] Nagano Shigeo, President of Nippon Steel, which was deeply involved in the Korean Pohang project, announced in rather pained tones: 'We do business anywhere – Taiwan, China, or anywhere else. The discrimination is on the other side.'[3] This has been the general position adopted by those that have fallen under the Chinese ban. Yet it is hardly surprising that China should make some response to a situation in which large segments of Japanese industry declare them-

1. Yamamura Kenichiro, 'Japan's World Trade Hard Pressed', *Asahi Journal*, 6 December 1970, pp. 113–19.
2. ibid; also Shirota *et al.*, op. cit. p. 78–9.
3. Yamamura, op. cit.

selves, as many did at the 1969 Japan–Republic of China Co-operation Meeting, in support of Taiwan's efforts to 'liberate the mainland', or in which major Japanese figures are speaking of reviving the Asian Co-Prosperity Sphere. The popular liberal view that China has been 'childish' to impose these conditions, and to insist on denunciations of 'Japanese militarism' in the annual Peking trade negotiations, is a shallow and inadequate one.[1]

The shock effect in Japanese industrial circles produced by, first, the Pyongyang Chinese–Korean denunciation of Japanese imperialism and militarism in April 1970 (five months after the Sato–Nixon communiqué), and then by the many detailed elaborations of the same theme, of which the so-called 'Chou principles' is simply the most important, has been indisputable and probably salutary. Consider four important industries: chemicals, textiles, cars and steel. Over 60 per cent of domestic chemical fertilizer production is already being exported to China and this is an industry which more than any other depends for its survival on China. Even Mitsubishi Chemical has formally severed its ties with the Mitsubishi group to participate in this trade. Trade in 1971 was expected to hit a record total of 6 million tons. Negotiations dragged on in Peking from late April to the end of July without any settlement being announced, thus causing some fear in the trade.[2] Long-drawn-out negotiations with the U.S.A. have sent a very cold wind blowing through the textile industry and its leaders seem to be inclining very strongly towards China. The new President of the Japan Spinning Association (from April 1971) is reported to be thinking in terms of a long-term co-operative relationship with China, though the industry faces a long and difficult

1. As expressed, for example, by Derek Davies, Editor of the *Far Eastern Economic Review*, in an article in the *Guardian*, 14 April 1971.

2. Awata Fusao, 'Industry under Pressure from Moves towards China', (Big Business under Stagflation, no. 17), *Asahi Journal*, 6 August 1971, pp. 37–42. Agreement was finally reached in August on the purchase of $11 mill. worth of Japanese fertilizer, an important breakthrough (*FEER*, 2 October 1971, p. 36).

process of extrication from Taiwan and South Korea. In steel and iron 'voluntary' restrictions on exports to the major market, the U.S.A., are also forcing some reappraisal, though China now takes only 10 per cent of the industry's output. In the spring of 1971 the Managing Director of Sumitomo Metals and the Executive Director of Kobe Iron and Steel were sent

TABLE TWENTY-FOUR China's Mineral Resources – world standing (as at 1965)

Item	Rating in World Production	% of World Production	Self-Sufficiency	Reserves
Aluminium	9	2	adequate	considerable
Copper	10	2	insufficient	limited
Iron ore	4	6	adequate	no. 1
Lead	9	4	some surplus	limited
Manganese	6	6	some surplus	considerable
Nickel	low	—	considerable deficiency	slight
Zinc	11	3	some surplus	limited
Salt	2	13	some surplus	no. 1
Anthracite	2	12	adequate	no. 1
Coke	5	5	adequate	no. 1
Crude oil	17	0.6	self-sufficient	limited

Source: MITI, *Tsusho Hakusho*, 1971, p. 270.

to consultations in Peking, and even Nippon Steel's Chairman, Nagano Shigeo, who was a staunch backer of the R.O.K. (South Korea) and R.O.C. (Taiwan) Co-operation Committees, recently declined, on pretext of illness, to attend the meetings held in late July and August of these organizations.[1] These were held, incidentally, within weeks of the announcement of the Nixon China visit. The fact that China's reserves of iron ore, anthracite and coke are among the greatest in the world, must also be expected to play a large part in delibera-

1. Somewhat surprisingly, Nagano was recently included in a list of 'friends of the Chinese people', visited by Wang Kuo-chuan, Vice-President of the Chinese Japan–China Friendship Association, while he was in Tokyo in August for the funeral of Matsumura (*Ta Kung Pao*, 2 September 1971).

tions of the iron and steel industry. In the motor industry companies which have accepted the Chou principles, such as Nissan Diesel, Hino Motors, and even Toyota, which announced acceptance only in the autumn of 1970 and is currently engaged in withdrawal from Korea, were given good orders for trucks at the 1971 Spring Trade Fair in Canton, and, in view of anticipated requirements for the 4th Five Year Plan, expectations were high for further orders in the autumn.[1] The Chinese table tennis team even purchased some Toyotas after the 1971 world championships in Nagoya.[2] U.S. motor magnates are quite open in relating their Japanese tie-ups to the prospects of the China market.

Events moved with considerable speed in this field in the latter half of 1971, but they may be briefly recapitulated. The world's largest steel producer, Nippon Steel, was represented at the August meetings of the Japan–Republic of Korea Cooperation Committee, having abstained from the July equivalent meetings on Taiwan, but then, on 3 September, its President, Nagano Shigeo, accepted the four principles, and by November Nagano was in Peking wining and dining with Chou En-lai.[3] Japan's steel exports to China are now about two million tons a year, making it the industry's second largest market after the U.S.A., where voluntary restrictions keep sales to a limit of 5.75 million tons a year.[4] Also by late September the two biggest banks in Japan, Mitsubishi and Fuji, together with major companies in various sectors, including Hitachi and Sumitomo, had decided to follow suit,[5] and presently Hitachi's representative was reported to be in Peking to wrap up a major deal for the sale of a $21mill., 25,000 kilowatt gas turbine generator which Hitachi in turn is manufacturing under licence from General Electric.[6] Five of the six

1. Awata Fusao, op. cit.
2. *Asahi Journal*, 14 May 1971, pp. 16–17.
3. *Asahi Journal*, 13 August 1971, pp. 99–100; *FEER*, no. 40, 25 September 1971, p. 21; *Hsinhua*, 20 November 1971.
4. Christopher Reed, the *Sunday Times*, 12 September 1971.
5. *FEER*, no. 42, 16 October 1971, p. 52.
6. *Newsweek*, 29 November 1971.

shipping services which operate to Taiwan recently announced their withdrawal from the route, presumably hoping to open some China services in the future.[1] Japan Air Lines also refrained from attendance at the various 'Co-operation' committee meetings of 1971, and was reported to be hoping to extend its services to China some time, perhaps in competition with American carriers.[2] At the Autumn Trade Fair in Canton in 1971 a record 1,457 Japanese firms were represented. Yet, despite the painful volte-face involved for many Japanese companies in making the ritual kotow to Peking, and despite the intensive efforts being made especially by the Japanese steel and motor vehicle men to secure orders, the Chinese market was showing little sign of meeting expectations.

Yet there are a number of important considerations weighing heavily against any major redirection of Japan's present trading ties. One is simply the size of the China market. For all its 700 million people China's overseas trade amounted in 1966 only to $4,200mill., and then, after falling off for several years, to perhaps $4,190mill. in 1970. Compared to Japan's annual overseas trade of $40,000mill. it is tiny, and as China's foreign currency reserves are said to be only $500 or $600mill., prospects of dramatic growth in the seventies seem rather like the traditional fantasies about Chinese shirt tails.[3] For China is of course the last frontier, a glimmer of hope for further expansion to relieve the painful and increasing contradictions of monopoly capitalism, to avoid facing the bleak prospect of increasing production and contracting markets. In Japan, as no doubt in the United States, there is a considerable element of wishful thinking on the China question: there has to be a solution to so many problems and China must be it.

The second factor is the strength of vested interest in Taiwan and South Korea, to which one should possibly add the grow-

1. *FEER*, no. 42, op. cit.
2. *FEER*, no. 31, 31 July 1971, p. 57.
3. Figures taken from Awata Fusao, op. cit.; *FEER*, 4 March 1972, estimates China's reserves at $600–$1,000mill. Of course, the economic 'complementarity' of China and Japan gives plenty of scope to barter agreements.

ing competition between Japan and China in South-East Asia. The major trading companies and *zaibatsu*, Mitsubishi especially, have sunk virtually all their eggs into an anti-Chinese basket, and will exert their enormous political, and possibly their military weight too, to defend their interests, unless some extremely powerful counter advantage is to be gained by jettisoning them. At present industry is studying the options. Whatever happens the fabric of the past twenty-five years of political, and therefore to some extent trading, relationships, has been shattered by the events of 1971. The policy of faithful adherence to a conservative, pro-U.S. policy, of concentration on relationships with the anti-Communist, anti-China regimes of the Pacific rim in overall subordination to American imperial aims, has proved in the end utterly bankrupt. The fear now is that the U.S.A. has decided to apply a brake to the dramatic southern advances of Japanese capitalism, and that U.S. moves to a rapprochement with China arise partly from their common desire to restrain Japan. Increasing competition from Chinese goods in South-East Asia seems also to be a mounting Japanese concern. Already Chinese light industrial goods – bicycles, toys, fountain pens, etc. – are driving Japanese goods out of the markets, and Chinese sewing machines, cameras and other high quality goods are in increasing evidence.[1]

As Japanese capitalism studies what to do it is likely that the key decisions will be taken by the Sanken, or Council on Industrial Policy.[2] Since its formation in 1966 this group has rapidly developed into a formidable 'super-government'. Its

1. Awata, op. cit.

2. Principal source on the Sanken is Kimura Takeo, 'Sanken: The Brilliant Group in Industry's G.H.Q.', *Chuo Koron*, July 1971, pp. 166–96; an early article by Kato Hidetoshi, 'Sanken: a Power above Government', from the *Shukan Asahi* of November 1969 has been translated in *Japan Interpreter*, vol. 7, no. 1, winter 1971, pp. 36–42. This latter is rather superficial, and the members listed in it do not include the four most recent to join the group. It is, however, interesting on the Yawata–Fuji merger. *Pacific Imperialism Notebook*, December 1971–January 1972, pp. 11–16 is an excellent English language source on Sanken.

initial goals were the reorganization of the economy through promotion of mergers and elimination of competition, and the shifting of industrial policy decision-making power back from government (MITI) to private business hands. Its membership cuts across the lines of all pre-existing organizations and includes probably the twenty-four most powerful men in Japan – including figures like Uyemura of Keidanren, Sakurada of Nikkeiren, Hyuga of Keizai Doyukai, Nagano and Inayama of Nippon Steel, Kono of Mitsubishi Heavy Industries, Fujino of Mitsubishi Trading, Kikawada of Tokyo Electric Power, Iwasa of Fuji Bank, Mizukami of Mitsui Trading, Doko of Toshiba, Kawamata of Nissan, and other key figures in securities and banking, textiles and electronics. Membership is on an individual basis and it will be noted that the first three names are those of the central figures of the previously existing organizations in industry. It is clear that this group, more than any other, has power to make or break policy or government. A recent account of its activities concludes that it was this group which planned and executed the merger of Fuji and Yawata to form Nippon Steel, now the world's largest steel company, overcoming formidable difficulties from the Fair Trade Commission and from supporters of 'free competition' in the process, and that probably the most recent triumph for it was the emasculation of the 1970 Anti-Pollution Law.[1]

Relations with the United States (textile dispute, steel, and above all the dollar-yen question) and with China are the two questions concerning the Sanken above all else. Under its auspices an 'Asian Trade Structure Research Centre' was set up in May 1971, with Inayama Yoshihiro, President of Nippon Steel, as Director. Inayama is a representative figure of the industrialists who have given warm support to the coterie of war criminals and Co-Prosperity Spherists in the Co-operation Committees, and was consequently excluded from the China trade. As indicated above, he and his company have reconsidered their position. The strongest pro-China position on the Sanken is that of Sumitomo Metals President, Hyuga Hosai,

1. Kimura Takeo, op. cit.

who is also a leading Kansai[1] industrialist and member of the generally pro-China Keizai Doyukai. As might be expected, the strongest irredentist line on Taiwan and Korea was adopted by spokesmen for the Mitsubishi group, who seemed determined to continue to build up their stake there, and to think of these areas as, if not in the immediate future then eventually, key staging posts for moving into China, one way or another. Fujino Chujiro, President of Mitsubishi Corporation, put it this way:

> The Chinese value fidelity. It is more than likely that to recognize the 'four principles' now, and to cast aside Taiwan and Korea, would make the Chinese think of us as foolish and untrustworthy.[2]

The differences of opinion will not be easy to resolve. From the autumn of 1971 key political and government figures also have been making their run lest they too be left behind by what seemed to be a bandwagon rapidly gathering speed: Nakasone Yasuhiro, ex-Director of the Defence Agency and then Chairman of the LDP Executive Board, affirmed categorically that Peking was China's legitimate government, that Taiwan belonged to China and that it was time Japan came to terms with the fact. The then Foreign Minister, Fukuda Takeo, went one further by declaring that Japan was prepared to make a formal apology to the Chinese people for 'what they suffered during the Sino–Japanese war', as a condition for establishing diplomatic relations with Peking. The delegation of 'personages from Tokyo economic circles' as Peking blandly described the group visiting there in November 1971, was undoubtedly a mission of the highest importance, including as it did Nagano Shigeo of Nippon Steel, Kikawada Kazutaka of Tokyo Electric Power, Iwasa Yoshizane of Fuji Bank. Five of the nine in the group were Sanken members.

1. Kansai: the Osaka–Kobe–Kyoto area.

2. Awata Fusao, 'Mitsubishi Trading Company: Star Performer Comes from Behind', (Big Business under Stagflation, no. 13), *Asahi Journal*, 2 July 1971, pp. 41—6.

The visit by the delegation showed that big business was conscious of the dead end to which twenty-five years of rapid growth and obedient pursuit of a subordinate role in America's political/economic/military strategy had led. The patterns of twenty-five years (and more) are not easily broken. The mood was one of desperation rather than elation.

Chapter 5

THE TOKYO-TAIPEI-SEOUL NEXUS 1965-72

The announcement of Nixon's visit to China aroused considerable speculation about a change in Japan's policy towards the People's Republic. Such a change presented major difficulties, given the concentration of Japanese economic, political and military planning, especially during the years 1965–71, on solidarity with the regimes of South Korea and Taiwan. This was the kernel of Japanese strategic thinking at the highest level. It could not continue after the shift in American policy. But equally it could not be shattered without sending considerable shock waves through the entire Japanese establishment.

The changes in United States Far Eastern policy that have become apparent recently had their origin in 1964–5. With the drastic worsening of the U.S. position in South-East Asia, the decision greatly to expand the war there and the need to concentrate all available resources and attention on that area, imperial responsibilities in North-East Asia began to be foisted off onto Japan. The continuing rapid growth and generation of a substantial surplus within the Japanese economy, together with the assumption that Japan could now be regarded as safely assimilated into junior partnership in the imperial enterprises of the Pacific region, lay behind the first stage of the process – the commitment of Japan to hopefully inextricable economic involvement with the anti-communist regimes of the area. Secondary stages – Japanese military expansion and coordination with these same regimes – still continue, while the assumption of the identity of American and Japanese interests grows increasingly questionable.

U.S. aid to Taiwan ($1,420 million from 1953) ceased in 1965.[1] For its fourth 4-year plan which commenced in that year Taiwan succeeded in raising the following finance:

World Bank	$47.7mill.
Japan	$150mill. (in yen equivalent)

U.S. private investment did of course continue, as did the economic benefits of its military presence there. From 1965–9 private U.S. investment of $174mill. far outstripped the Japanese figure of $63mill. However, private Japanese investment, beginning slowly in the wake of the green light to industry which the government loan represented, then increased greatly in tempo, and 83 per cent of this $63mill. investment is accounted for by the years 1967–9.[2] Despite the Japanese claim that politics and trade are separate, it is clear in this, as in many other examples, that the lead came from the government, private industry following in the wake of what amounted to government assurance of the security of the investment. Following a Mitsubishi delegation of unprecedented size and weight in 1965, it and other Japanese trading companies moved first into the area, followed more recently by industrial and processing concerns.[3]

The attractions of investment in Taiwan are very obvious ones. First is the large pool of Chinese labour to be tapped

1. However, the 'Sino–American Fund for Economic and Social Development' continued to pour money into the country – $66mill. in fiscal 1967, $70mill. in 1968, $29mill. (estimated) in 1969. Grants of U.S. agricultural surplus also continued – $29mill. worth in 1968, for example (*FEER Yearbook*, 1970).

2. Asano Ryuzo, 'The Critical Structure of Japan–Taiwan Relations', *Gendai no Me*, August 1970, pp. 176–84; a recent estimate (March 1972) put Japanese investment at about $100mill. or one third that of the U.S.A. (*FEER*, 4 March 1972, p. 67).

3. Shirota Noboru, Yamamura Yoshiharu and Shironishi Shinichiro, *Mitsubishi Armament Factory – Japan's Military Industrial Complex and Overseas Expansion* (in Japanese), Tokyo , Gendai Hyoronsha, 1971, p. 196.

there – skilled, oppressed and cheap. Labour in Taiwan can be bought for about half the price of Hong Kong, one tenth that of West Germany, one fifteenth that of the U.S.A. Average annual income in Taiwan in 1970 was $258, one fifth the Japanese average, and about one fifteenth the U.S. average of $3,795. Furthermore the investment conditions leave nothing to be desired:

1. First five years are tax free for foreign investment, and only a cheap company tax payable from the sixth year.

2. Profits may be remitted without restriction to the country of capital origin.

3. Materials and equipment may be introduced tax free. Factories will be financed at low interest by the government up to 70 per cent.

4. Strikes are forbidden because of the 'War situation'.[1]

Japanese direct investment has till recently tended to be in a wide range of small items spread through the middle and small enterprises in the economy, while the U.S.A. has concentrated rather in a few key growth areas such as electronics.[2]

Of the total number of enterprises established with foreign capital between 1953 and 1969, 525 in all, no less than 307 were Japanese.[3] Japanese investment was concentrated in certain key manufacturing industries and in some cases dominated the Taiwan market. The Hualung Co., for example, set up by Teikoku Rayon, is the biggest chemical fibre company, its polyester fibre products supplying 70–80 per cent of the total needs. The New Taiwan Agricultural Machines Co. in Kaohsiung, which was founded by Mitsui and four other Japanese firms, has set up more than 100 agents in the Taiwan area and cornered 55 per cent of the island's farm machine market. The pharmaceutical market is dominated by enterprises set up by

1. Fujita Naoji, 'Crossing National Boundaries to Employ Cheap Labour', *Asahi Journal*, 25 October 1970, pp. 102–7.

2. Nozaki Yoji, 'Preliminary Moves towards the Second Taiwan Yen Loan', *Asahi Journal*, 2 April 1971, pp. 47–52; also William Glenn, *FEER*, 27 April 1971.

3. Ogiso Misao, 'Japan's Invisible Empire', *Chuo Koron*, June 1970, pp. 164–73.

even Japanese corporations.[1] Another important index of Japanese control is provided by looking at the instances of technical co-operation agreements entered into by Taiwanese business. Advanced technical knowhow has in almost every case to be imported and paid for, and of 327 recorded cases of such agreements between 1952 and 1966 251 were with Japanese interests, only fifty-two with the United States.[2] Another significant trend in Japanese investment is that more and more middle and small scale enterprises, increasingly squeezed out of the domestic market by rising labour and production costs and by the impossibility of competition with the monopoly cartels, are actually being forced to think in terms of overseas expansion as the only way to economic survival. Thus, according to a September 1969 report by the Japan Chamber of Commerce and Industry, only 50 per cent of Japanese enterprises going to Taiwan were in the black, 25 per cent were in the red and 25 per cent unclear. This would tend to support the idea that Taiwan served partly as a field for the resolution of increasing domestic contradictions.[3]

The following table gives details of U.S. and Japanese investment in Taiwan, however, from which it will be seen that in overall amount invested Japan has also been rapidly catching up with the United States:

TABLE TWENTY-FIVE Foreign Investment in Taiwan[4] (in $ 1,000)

	U.S.A.		Japan		Total (including others)	
	items	amount	items	amount	items	amount
1953–64	41	47,464	39	7,771	90	57,431
1965	17	31,104	14	2,081	36	35,140
1966	15	17,711	35	2,447	52	20,904
1967	19	15,726	77	15,957	109	38,688
1968	20	34,555	96	14,855	122	53,445
1969	31	27,882	79	17,642	116	82,221
total	143	174,442	340	60,753	525	287,826

1. *PR* no. 38, 17 September 1971, p. 11.
2. Ogiso Misao, op. cit.
3. Nozaki Yoji, op. cit.
4. Shirota *et al.*, op. cit., p. 202.

The figure for Japan in 1970 is reported to have been $28,530,000 invested in fifty-one items,[1] pointing to the likelihood that more Japanese than any other money, even U.S., was invested in Taiwan in that year. In terms of overall amount invested, however, Japan must still lag considerably behind the U.S.A.: the latest estimate by British sources puts the American total as of mid-1971 at $250mill. as against either $70 or $90mill. for Japan.[2] It is also important to note that overall foreign investment in Taiwan in the first six months of 1971 was only $39.5mill., or down 38 per cent from the figure for the first six months of 1970.[3] This was before the announcement of the Nixon visit to China, suggesting that investment in Taiwan may already have passed its peak.

As for trade, the comparative figures for U.S.A. and Japan, expressed here in percentages of the whole, are as follows to 1968:

TABLE TWENTY-SIX Relative Weight of Japan and U.S.A. in Taiwan's Trade.[4]

	Taiwan's imports from Japan	Taiwan's exports to Japan	Taiwan's imports from U.S.A.	Taiwan's exports to U.S.A.
1961	39%	28.5%	28%	24%
1968	43%	18%	29.8%	33%

1. Nozaki Yoji, op. cit.; Nozaki points out that from 1965–70 Japanese investment in Taiwan expanded by fourteen times.

2. *FEER*, 28 August 1971, p. 73 for U.S.A. figure; the same source variously reports Japanese investment total at $70mill. (p. 30) and $90mill. (p. 73). *The Times* supplement on Taiwan (8 October 1971) gives the figure of $90 to $100mill. for Japan, while Selig Harrison in the *Guardian* (4 August 1971) reports Japanese 'direct and indirect' investments in Taiwan amount to $200mill. *Fortune* (November 1971) gives $150mill. as the Japanese figure. *The Times* supplement also points out that Japan has now more than 400 very profitable licensing agreements with Taiwan, and that the profits from these agreements and from the marketing of the products, when re-invested in Taiwan, do not figure in the official investment statistics.

3. *FEER*, op. cit., p. 71.

4. *China Yearbook*, 1963–4 and 1969–70; for the volume of Japan–Taiwan trade 1967–70 see table 25. The most recent report

In 1970 Japan's Taiwan trade amounted to $950mill., with Japan selling nearly three times as much as it was buying.[1] Furthermore, at least half of Taiwan's total foreign trade, which amounts to a substantial $3,000mill., now passes through the hands of the big Japanese commercial interests – Mitsui, Mitsubishi, etc.

The volume of trade between Japan and Taiwan, together with ever increasing loan, investment and technical co-operation tie-ups, sustain in sum a powerful lobby reluctant to see its profitable relationship sacrificed in the interests of closer ties with China.

The principal exponent of this position is the Japan–Republic of China Co-operation Committee. This was set up originally in 1957, sponsored by the then Prime Minister, Kishi, as a committee of businessmen from both countries to promote economic ties between the two. It is only nominally a private business organisation, functioning rather as exponent of the foreign policy views of the ruling business-political clique, and is closely related to the two intra-party organs, the Soshinkai ('Pure-minded Association') and the Asian Problems Research Group of the Liberal Democratic Party far right.[2] The joint communiqué issued after the December 1964 meeting of this Co-operation Committee included the following sentiments:

> Japan and Republic of China being both important nations in Asia, the important problem which faces us at this moment is

---

states that 15 per cent of Taiwan's exports were directed to Japan, while 38 per cent of her imports were from Japan (*The Times*, 8 October 1971).

1. MITI, *Tsusho Hakusho, Kakuron*, 1971, p. 300; from the five years of Japan–Taiwan trade 1965–70 Japan has built up a cumulative trade surplus of $1,600mill. (*FEER*, no. 42, 16 October 1971).

2. Shirota *et al.*, op. cit., p. 187. As of 1966 members of this committee included apart from Kishi, men like Yoshida and Fukuda, and business leaders like Adachi and Ishizaka, the head of Keidanren. As Nathaniel B. Thayer (*How the Conservatives Rule Japan*, Princeton, N.J., 1969, p. 67) remarks, 'These men do not put pressure on the center of government; they are the center of government.'

how to promote the greater solidarity of the bloc of free nations, and how to stem the destructive force of Communist China and to overthrow it.[1]

The first yen loan and technical co-operation were promised Taiwan at this meeting. In 1969, while Prime Minister Sato was in Washington giving his signature to the joint communiqué with President Nixon which affirmed that the maintenance of peace and security in the Taiwan straits was a 'most important factor' in Japan's security, his brother, former Prime Minister Kishi, was in Taipei as adviser to the Co-operation Committee, where the communiqué on this occasion urged that

by the united efforts of the various countries of Asia a situation be brought about in which the mainland communist regime will collapse so that the Republic of China Government may succeed in its great task of recovery of the mainland.[2]

The Vice-Presidents of thirty-three large Japanese enterprises of the scale of Mitsui, Mitsubishi, Marubeni and C. Itoh Trading Companies, Mitsubishi Heavy Industries, Toshiba, Ishikawajima-Harima, etc., participated in the conference held on this occasion. A second 'yen loan', of $250 to $300mill., was one of the subjects of the meeting.[3] Its desirability was apparently agreed upon, and in July 1970, the Nationalist Chinese Vice-President, C. K. Yen, while visiting Osaka for Expo, was promised the loan by Prime Minister Sato. The loan was, however, held in abeyance due to protests of the Opposition and of the 'pro-Peking' moderates within the LDP. Instead, it seems loan items will be approved piecemeal and for individual projects for the time being.[4]

1. Shirota *et al.*, op. cit.
2. ibid.
3. Nonaka Kozo, 'The Real Face of the Japan–Republic of China Co-operation Committee', *Asahi Journal*, 12 July 1970, p. 103–7. Till April 1970, only two thirds of the first loan had been disbursed – suggesting the need for a newer and larger loan was as much political as economic (Nozaki).
4. A new loan of $22.5mill. for three projects including extensions to the Taipei telephone and telegraph system, for example, was agreed on 29 July 1971 (*Asahi Journal*, 13 August 1971, pp. 99–100).

At the 1970 meeting of this same Co-operation Committee a new trend emerged: the export not just of labour-intensive but also of pollution-intensive industries to places like Taiwan and Korea. Inaba Shuzo, President of the National Economic Research Society, adverted to this in his draft paper entitled 'Future of the Japanese Economy and Problems to be Faced in Japan–Republic of China Economic Co-operation':

> In order to deal with the problems arising in connection with harbours and with the increasingly large scale of industry, and in order to deal with pollution, Japan must seek new areas for its steel, electric power, oil-refining and petrochemical industries.[1]

The symbiotic relationship of Japanese government and business will be the better appreciated if it is understood that 65 per cent of the monies spent under the first yen loan was devoted to precisely those items of infrastructure – harbours, dams, bridges, electric power and transport facilities improvement – that would facilitate and encourage large scale Japanese industry to shift their large and dirty enterprises to Taiwan.[2] Maximum foreign capital involvement in Taiwan is of course an important political objective of Chiang Kai-shek, to serve hopefully as an insurance against 'sellout' of his interests. As late as November 1971, the U.S. Export-Import Bank was, rather surprisingly, reported to be putting up $93.4mill. as a loan for the construction of two nuclear power plants; the ADB was expected to put up $30mill. for an aluminium plant; an Austrian-based European consortium was taking over the arrangements for the construction of a major steelworks, the Japanese, after long consideration, having withdrawn from the deal; and Japanese investment in shipbuilding was reported to be on the rise – as Japanese domestic labour costs increased. With Japanese technical co-operation from IHI (Ishikawa-

1. Nozaki Yoji, op. cit.; Kishi also remarked at this meeting that 'the relationship of solidarity and co-operation between the economies of Japan, Taiwan and Korea can be expected hereafter to contribute greatly to the economic development of the Asian–Pacific region'.
2. Shirota *et al.*, op. cit., p. 201.

jima-Harima Heavy Industries) the Taiwan Government Shipbuilding Corporation is now building the biggest tankers in Asia outside Japan. The anticipated local production of steel will also help lower production costs in this industry. These various business deals, if they all go through, will obviously strengthen the hand of the administration on Taiwan.[1] Yet at the same time various big infrastructure projects, such as the $500mill. North-South freeway and the $150mill. fourth international airport on the west coast near Taichung, were delayed because of the tightening of Japanese purse strings.[2]

Reactions in Japan to the various Nixon administration moves on China and to the United Nations vote of the autumn of 1971 were initially ambivalent. The pro-Taiwan lobby remains of considerable strength in Japanese rightist circles, however, numbering no less than seventy-nine LDP Diet members led by former Premier Kishi for a start;[3] its influence should not be under-estimated. Traditionally, when frustrated in its aims by difficulties in the normal channels, the Japanese right has resorted to plots and under-cover activities. To save the day in Taiwan now a possible course would be for a switch from support of the hard-line irredentism of the KMT, evidently now a lost cause, to an apparently more flexible line of 'Taiwan Independence'. There are signs that moves in this direction are under way, and though they are not in themselves conclusive they are enough to sustain strong suspicion.[4]

In April 1971, *The Times* carried a report from its Hong Kong correspondent to the effect that the new Minister of Foreign Affairs in Taiwan was a 'realist' and in favour of an independent Taiwan republic.[5] In late July the Taiwan dele-

1. *Fortune*, November 1971, op. cit.; on the steelworks see *FEER*, 13 November 1971, p. 18.
2. *FEER*, 4 March 1972, p. 67.
3. *FEER*, no. 40, 27 October 1971.
4. Much of what follows is drawn from an article by Fujishima Udai, 'Taiwan: Whirlpool of Plots' in *Asahi Journal*, 12 November 1971, pp. 33–7.
5. *The Times*, 28 April 1971.

gate, Chang Ch'un, to the Japan–Republic of China Co-operation Committee meeting in Tokyo had two meetings with Premier Sato, ostensibly to ask for loan aid and for support in the forthcoming United Nations vote, but also with the reported aim of seeking Japanese support for a Republic of Taiwan in the event of expulsion from the United Nations. From mid-1971, when the crisis broke, intense activity was reported among 'Taiwan Independence' supporters.

On 23 September a group of twelve representatives of rightist Japanese organizations flew to Taiwan to gain '... an understanding of the situation', and on 6 October Kishi himself went to Taipei to participate in another Japan–Republic of China Co-operation Committee meeting, and then flew straight on from there to have talks with Nixon. In mid-October there were a number of meetings and demonstrations in Japan and the United States by Taiwan Independence Movement groups. Also in October three leading members of the Taiwan Independence League – Chien Wen-chieh, Liao Ming-shao and Shih Ch'ing-hsiang – returned to Taiwan declaring their solemn resolve to abstain from independence movement activity in the future. It seemed likely that rightist Japanese business men may have played some part in negotiating their return.[1]

At about the same time, October 1971, Chou En-lai remarked in an interview with several Japanese visitors that 'the Taiwan Independence movement has recently undergone some change as a result of secret moves by powerful members of the Kuomintang government' and that while 'Chiang (K'ai-shek) is a man of considerable pride, unlikely to do such a thing as to make an independent kingdom in a little island like Taiwan, yet Chang Ch'un, Ho Ying-ch'in and Ku Cheng-kang are plotting independence'.[2] The Japanese comment on this is that it was precisely these three, now important figures in

1. Fujishima, op. cit.
2. Interview with Nakajima Kenzo and Kuroda Hisao, cited in Fujishima.

Taiwan, who in 1937, just after full-scale invasion of China by Japan, were in favour of the 'Great South-Western-ism line', that is to say, offering Japan first the provinces of Hopei, Shantung, Shensi and Inner Mongolia, and then if that was not acceptable, the whole of China north of the Yangtze, while the Kuomintang should retreat to the South-West—to Szechuan, Kweichow and Yunnan – in order to reach a peaceful settlement. This defeatist line was strongly opposed by others in the KMT, including Chiang K'ai-shek, who finally overruled it saying: 'If we fight we lose, but the country will not necessarily be destroyed. However, if we don't fight, internal fighting will break out and the country will be destroyed. So let us fight Japan.'[1] It would not be surprising if the same KMT figures were now prepared to compromise with U.S.A. and Japanese imperialisms and to take again a narrowed 'Great South-Western-ism path', i.e. Taiwan independence, with the support especially of Kishi, Sato and their group.

Chiang K'ai-shek's strong emphasis on 'one China' at the KMT Central Committee meeting which opened on 28 October 1971, and his decision to stand a fifth term as President rather than resigning as planned in March 1972, may reflect his fear that even his son and heir designate – Chiang Ching-kuo – might be unable to resist the independence line gaining strength on Taiwan. Yet the U.S.A. support, without which invasion of the mainland could not even be considered, can hardly be hoped for by Chiang K'ai-shek now, and without it there can only be two possible paths for Taiwan – independence or some kind of agreement with Peking. The domestic situation in Taiwan is extremely volatile: unemployment is running at an estimated 25 per cent of the labour force[2] and reports of a liberation struggle, something quite apart from the Taiwan Independence Movement, are now appearing. It is significant that in the struggles of the past year or so – attacks on U.S. bases, banks, warships, press offices, peasant struggles against the expansion of U.S. bases or of

1. Fujishima, op. cit.
2. Alain Bouc, *Le Monde Diplomatique*, December 1971, p. 6.

petrochemical centres; student struggles against 'U.S.A.–Japan–Chiang K'ai-shek plots' – the slogans have been such as 'Taiwan is Chinese territory', 'Resolutely smash plots to build two Chinas', 'Down with U.S. imperialism' and 'Oppose Japanese militarism'.[1]

Clearly the Taiwan situation cannot continue very much longer in its present unresolved state. An independent Taiwan would be a much more tractable entity for Tokyo than a communist Taiwan, and it may be expected that in future there will be continuing undercover activity to try to achieve such an end.

Relations between Japan and South Korea have followed a somewhat similar pattern of development to those between Japan and Taiwan, and the two have been closely interconnected. Both territories have long experience of earlier forms of Japanese imperialism, and while Taiwan was described in the 1969 Sato–Nixon Communiqué as 'a most important factor for the security of Japan', Korea was described as 'essential' to it.

However, while postwar relations with Taiwan were normalized in 1952 with the signing of a treaty and reopening of relations between the two, those with Korea remained in abeyance until 1965. Hostility ran deep between Japan and Korea and Korean experience of Japanese oppression both in Korea and in Japan was qualitatively stronger and more bitter than Taiwan's. Since total incorporation in the Japanese empire in 1910 Korea suffered a repression as savage and an exploitation as total as any colony in modern times. Details of this are not well known and one or two should be mentioned here as necessary towards an understanding of feeling between the Korean and Japanese peoples today. The early phase of Japanese operations in Korea after annexation involved the harnessing of Korean agriculture and the squeezing of an ever greater surplus from it to feed a growing and industrializing Japan. Koreans were forced to produce more but eat less.[2]

1. Fujishima, op. cit.; *Hsinhua*, 4 October 1971.
2. Shiota Shobei, 'A "Ravaged" People: The Koreans in WW II',

Supply of cheap Korean rice also helped ease domestic Japanese contradictions by eliminating the shortages that had set off the rice riots of 1918, and keeping the rice price low also facilitated continuation of the low wage policy in Japan. The second phase came in the 1930s as the big Japanese *zaibatsu* moved in to extract more efficiently Korean underground resources (gold, iron ore, coal), and to industrialize, using cheap Korean labour to provide logistic support for Japan's further advances into the continent. Next came the forties in which Koreans were conscripted for military service and for slave labour battalions in Japan. Between 1939 and 1945 some 370,000 Koreans were conscripted into the armed forces and attached labour forces and another million into the labour forces for Japan itself – where many died under the intolerable conditions and the constant brutality they experienced in mines, harbours and construction projects they were employed on.[1]

The Japan Interpreter, 1971, vol. 7, no. 1, pp. 43–53. Shiota reproduces the following table at p. 45:

Production and Consumption of Korean Rice

Year	total output	export to Japan (in million koku)	total consumption within Korea	Annual per capita consumption (in koku) Korea	Japan
1912	11.6	0.5	11.1	0.78	1.07
1915	14.1	2.3	11.8	0.74	1.10
1918	13.7	2.2	11.6	0.68	1.14
1924	15.2	4.6	10.8	0.60	1.12
1930	13.7	5.4	8.6	0.45	1.08
1931	19.2	8.4	10.5	0.52	1.30
1932	15.9	7.6	8.4	0.41	1.01
1933	16.3	8.7	8.5	0.41	1.10

1. It was above all to the mines that the Koreans were drafted during the wars of the 1930s and 40s. One forty-seven year old Korean, Hyon Si-hon, recalled in a recent interview before returning to North Korea, being sent to the Tomakomai mines in Hokkaido at nineteen in 1943. The shift was 6 a.m. to 3 a.m.; only Koreans were driven

After the war Japan refused any reparations payments, refused also to invest or advance any aid to Korea, and, save for its very profitable collaboration with the U.S. war effort there from 1950 to 1953, relations with Korea were minimal. The state of vassalage to the U.S.A. was virtually total. However, the strains of the South-East Asian war in the mid-sixties forced America to shift some of the burdens of empire in the north-east to Japan. Where in Taiwan it was the $150mill. 'yen loan' of 1965 that signalled the beginning of the positive inroads of Japanese capital and influence, in Korea in the same year 'normalization' of Japan–South Korean relations was equally pivotal.

After his advent to power in the coup d'état of 1961 Pak Jung-Hi produced a comprehensive economic plan for the 1962–6 period under the slogan of an 'independent economy'. Oddly, the independence was to depend on the raising of $700mill. during the term of the plan. Main sources were to be foreign loans (62 per cent, or $426mill.) and foreign currency held in the country (i.e. U.S. military) 33 per cent. However, by 1965 only 30 per cent of the planned foreign loan of $426 mill. had been raised. The U.S.A. was sliding deep into war and dollar troubles, and Dean Rusk set about overcoming both problems relating to Korea by working to break the long deadlock in relations with Japan.[1]

With the re-opening of relations a considerable amount of Japanese money was pumped into the South Korean economy, some $300 mill. in goods and services 'gratis', and $200mill.

---

to the dangerous mine faces; those who died were often buried with cement in the mine wall (*Sekai*, July 1971, pp. 108–12). Maeda Hajime, currently the Executive Director of Nikkeiren (Japan Federation of Employers' Associations) was in 1943 Chief of the Personnel Section of the Hokkaido Collieries and Steamship Company (Shiota, p. 51). As late as 1958 over 80 per cent of Koreans in Japan were unemployed (*Sekai*, op. cit.), and severe discrimination against them is built into most areas of Japanese life.

1. Nihon Kokusai Boeki Shinko Kyokai (Japan Association for the Promotion of International Trade) *Atarashii Nihon Gunkokushugi* (*New Japanese Militarism*), Tokyo, 1971, pp. 57–8.

in yen credits, both payable in annual instalments over a ten-year period from 1965. A further $300mill. was set aside for private deferred payment loans on commercial conditions to Korean enterprises. Since this time ties with the south have grown enormously, while the question of responsibility for reparations towards the north is ignored, and the Korean population in Japan is much harried in attempts to conceal the fact that its majority is strongly in favour of Pyongyang.

Japanese 'aid' monies are used by South Korea to import commodities from Japan which are then sold. The funds realized in the process are then paid into a yen counterpart fund from which items such as miliary expenditure may then be met. The value of such aid to the ruling junta is thus clear. Furthermore Japan retains the right to decide what commodities are to be purchased with the funds provided. The significance of this is as follows:

> Thus, Japanese tax payers' money is paid 'gratis' to the South Korean government, which is then required to buy the products of, say, Mitsubishi. Big business rakes in the profit. Instead of directly subsidizing the zaibatsu, (which would hardly please the Japanese taxpayers), the Japanese government adopts the roundabout approach of giving 'gratis' aid to the South Korean regime, which then pays the money back into the coffers of monopoly capital.[1]

Many Japanese enterprises, engaged in continuous technical innovation and fierce competitive struggles, dispose of their domestic surplus production which is out of date or obsolete by exporting it as private 'aid' to Korea. Examples are Toyo Rayon's Shiga Synthetics Factory, Nihon Pulp's fertilizer factory, Nihon Chisso (Nitrogen)'s Chloride Vinyl factory. Kokan Synthetics, which imported an artificial silk plant that was about to be scrapped, soon came under banker's orders as a result. Daikan Plastics and Kyoei (Co-prosperity) Chemicals, who imported old-fashioned carbide acetylene equipment from

1. 'Ampo 70: South Korea in the Ampo System', *Ampo*, no. 3–4, March 1970.

Japan, paid a rate of $500 per ton, more than double the manufacturer's basic international price of $230.[1]

Clearly there has to be some rationale behind these apparently insane deals. It lies in the level of graft they support in Korea as well as the level of profit accruing to Japanese corporations. The *Mainichi Shimbun*'s Nishi Masao quotes Japanese Trading Company sources as authority for the figure of 3–4 per cent political donation necessary to win Korean government approval plus a further 4 per cent to certain powerful Korean business figures – 8 per cent of the loan total being thus expended in bribes.[2] Even after all such payments the Japanese returns can be very considerable indeed, as the case of Toyota for one illustrates. Having gained a monopoly on domestic car production from President Pak, Toyota proceeded to produce a Korean version of the Corona model, which is retailed in Japan at $1,650, and to sell it at $3,300, or double that price, in Korea.[3] In late autumn of 1971 Toyota decided to put its Korean holdings on ice and to recognize the Chou principles in the hope of thereby gaining access to the China market.[4] Whatever comes of its initiatives in that direction it can be assumed that bargaining with the Chinese will be a very different matter from bargaining with the Koreans.

The major single project so far settled within the terms of these 1965 agreements has been the Pohang integrated steel works, on which agreement was reached at the 3rd annual Japan–R.O.K. Ministerial Conference in 1969 for the provision of $73 mill. in Japanese government funds plus a further $50 mill. in deferred payment credits from the Import-Export

1. Hayashi Naomichi, 'The Economic Basis for the Revival of Japanese Militarism', *Gendai to Shiso* (*Ideas and the Present Age*) no. 1, p. 271; by October 1971 a staggering 85 per cent of loan enterprises in Korea had come under bankers' orders as unable to meet their commitments (Fujishima Udai, 'Policy toward Korea under Pressure to Change', *Asahi Journal*, 8 October 1971, pp. 17–20).

2. From his book *Keizai Kyoryoku* (*Economic Co-operation*), p. 105, cited *Atarashii* . . ., op. cit., p. 272.

3. Hayashi Naomichi, op. cit., p. 272.

4. *FEER*, 2 October 1971.

Bank. Estimated total cost of the works is $138.6 mill. The project had been dismissed as unfeasible by a European consortium (West Germany, U.K., France, Italy) shortly before the promise of Japanese help was made, and its announcement, shortly before the holding of the referendum on revision of the constitution to allow Pak a third term of office in South Korea, was a most welcome political boost. The role played by Mitsubishi Trading Company's President, Fujino, in liaising between Pak and Japanese business political circles seems to have been decisive, and on the request of the South Korean authorities Mitsubishi Trading Company thereafter became the official intermediary for all subsequent transactions relating to the project. Not surprisingly one of the first orders placed was for a $35 mill. hot strip mill from Mitsubishi Heavy Industries. Over 50 per cent of Japanese 'aid' money is reckoned to be going to Mitsubishi.[1] For General Pak the benefits of the deal are private as well as political, since he is a major landowner in the Pohang area.[2]

At the 4th Japan–R.O.K., Ministerial Conference in July 1970, agreement was reached on a further $59 mill. Japanese loan for the construction of four factories (heavy machines, pig-iron, etc.) which are to be related to the Pohang project, plus another $100 mill. loan for promotion of village industry and unspecified export industries. Nakagawa Nobuo, writing in the prestigious monthly *Sekai* in November 1970, reckoned that while the $59 mill. was for military-related industrial purposes, the $100 mill. was likely to provide key funds for

1. Awata Fusao, *Asahi Journal*, 2 July 1971, pp. 41–6.

2. Shirota *et al.*, op. cit., pp. 222–4. *Nihon Keizai Shimbun*, 25 July 1970. The story is actually told, attributed to the well known military affairs critic, Murakami Kaoru, that the Mitsubishi side had made a $5mill. contribution to the Pak Campaign funds for constitutional revision to enable Pak to serve a third Presidential term on the understanding that in return they were to be granted the Pusan–Seoul railway electrification contract, and that carriages, etc. were to be purchased from Mitsubishi. By some blunder on the Korean side this plum had already been promised to a West German syndicate, and it was to make amends for this that a very satisfactory Pohang deal was promised Mitsubishi (*Atarashii* . . . , op. cit., p. 70).

the 1971 Presidential and parliamentary election campaigns.[1] The final communiqué issued at this conference echoed the Sato–Nixon 'Japan–Taiwan–South Korea axis' line announced six months earlier: 'The peace and prosperity of the two countries are extremely intimately related and Asian peace and prosperity is the common goal of both.'[2] At the 5th Ministerial Conference in Tokyo a further $210mill. in credits was extended to the Korean side – $80mill. to finance the construction of a Seoul subway system, $85mill. for the purchase of freighters from Japan, and about $80mill. for four projected metal and machine plants, together with a promise of further assistance in other projects connected with Korea's third five-year development plan from 1972–6.[3] This was in accordance with the recommendation of the Japan–Republic of Korea Co-operation Committee meeting which immediately preceded it, that 'the proportion devoted to public loans and governmental aid should be increased as against that of commercial loans'.[4] In other words, despite the Chou principles and despite the news of Nixon's impending visit to China (announced a few weeks previously, on 17 July) the Japanese government was determined to increase the stake of Japanese involvement in Korea at an official level, and important sections of Japanese business were prepared to see this as sufficient guarantee of the 'security' of the operation. The Acting Foreign Minister, Kimura Toshio, described the purpose of the new loans as being 'to promote economic prosperity and civil stability in Korea', adding that: 'This should not become an obstacle to an improvement in diplomatic relations with China. Their way of thinking which holds that Japanese aid to Korea

1. Nakagawa Nobuo, 'Japanese–Korean Economic Co-operation in the 1970s', *Sekai*, November 1970, pp. 87–96.

2. ibid.

3. *New York Times*, 5 October 1971.

4. *Asahi Journal*, 13 August 1971, pp. 99–100; interest rates on these items are extraordinarily high, as much as 7 per cent on the freighter deal, indicating just how abjectly dependent the Koreans have become (Nakagawa Nobuo, 'The Political Consequences of the Formation of the Japan–ROK economic sphere', *Sekai*, November 1971, pp. 162–72).

will increase tensions in the peninsula or in Asia represents either dogmatism or misunderstanding.'[1]

However, despite the gradual increase of Japanese loans and investment in Korea since the 1965 settlement, Japan remains nevertheless very much secondary to the U.S.A. in general, though Japanese capital is dominant in Korean cement, textiles, fertilizers, synthetic fibres, chemicals and machine industries.[2] Of the total foreign loan and investment intake to September 1970 of approximately $2,800 mill., 40.4 per cent or $1,121mill. was from the U.S.A. and 20.2 per cent or $558mill. from Japan.[3] However, the weight is shifting more and more onto Japan. According to the most recent estimate Japanese investments almost equalled those of the U.S.A. in 1970, and outstripped them for the first time in the first five months of 1971 – $16mill. as compared to $13mill. for the U.S.A. – though as in the case of Taiwan in the overall or accumulated investment totals Japanese capital accounted for only 31 per cent of the total, U.S. capital for 58 per cent. (Japanese money is spread over 185 different projects, while the U.S.A. is involved in only ninety-nine.)[4] What is more, the troop withdrawals and reduced U.S. military spending in Korea announced in 1970 represented a severe blow to the Korean side. The dollar loss may be understood from the following:

	1969	1970	1971
Vietnam special procurements	$140mill.	$115mill.	$80mill. (estimated)
U.S.A. army in Korea	$155mill.	$137mill.	$108mill. (estimated)[5]

1. Sam Jameson, the *Guardian*, 14 August 1971.

2. Nakagawa, *Sekai*, November 1970; another estimate gives the following percentages of various sectors of Korean industry as being Japanese controlled: fertilizer: 90.2 per cent; chemical fibres: 64.2 per cent; foodstuffs: 62 per cent; cement and casting: 48.3 per cent; chemical engineering: 43.5 per cent (Hayashi, op. cit., p. 272).

3. According to the table from *Toa Nenkan* (1971), reproduced in Nakagawa Nobuo, 'Political-Economics of the Japan–Korea Unification', *Sekai*, May 1971, pp. 129–39.

4. *FEER*, 28 August 1971, p. 71.

5. Nakagawa, *Sekai*, May 1971; total U.S. expenditures in Korea

In the third Korean Five Year Plan (1972–6) formulated in 1970 the intake of another $2,500 mill. foreign capital was anticipated, of which two fifths, or $1,000 mill., was to come from Japan. Fulfilment of this plan will call for a tremendous increase of capital flow from Japan in the near future, and it seems almost certain that in the process Japan will replace the U.S.A. as the dominant financial backer of the Seoul regime.[1]

After the November 1970 visit of a powerful Korean business group to various centres in Japan to sell the idea of private investment there, further involvement of private capital may be expected.[2] Conditions of investment are more or less as in Taiwan. Companies may be 100 per cent foreign owned, and as of 1969 industries with foreign capital investment have been declared within the category of 'public interest enterprises' meaning that strikes are forbidden in them.[3] As for labour, it can probably be bought even more cheaply in Korea than in Taiwan.[4] A further characteristic that seems likely to distin-

---

until the year 1970 were set out in the following way for the House hearings on Foreign Aid in Washington on 6 March 1971:

1950–54 Korean war expenses	$18,000mill.
1954–70 Maintenance U.S. forces in Korea	$8,600mill.
1950–70 Non-refundable military aid	$3,000mill.
1946–70 Economic aid	$5,100mill.
Total	$34,700mill.

Source: Fujishima Udai, *Asahi Journal*, 8 October 1971.

1. *Nihon Keizai Shimbun*, 17 March 1971, Seoul correspondent report.

2. Nakagawa, *Sekai*, May 1971.

3. Nakagawa, 'The joint U.S.–Japan Communiqué and Public Opinion in South Korea', *Sekai*, June 1970, pp. 221–30.

4. The very low level of South Korean wages can be illustrated by testimony from U.S. Secretary of Commerce Stans, to the House Ways and Means Committee in June 1970: America, he claimed, was 'Uncle Sucker for the rest of the world'. According to Stans, U.S.A. textile workers were earning average pay of $2.38cents, compared with fifty-seven cents an hour in Japan, and thirteen cents an hour for men and seven cents an hour for women in South Korea. This would give a monthly wage for a woman textile worker working a sixty-hour week of $4.20. The exploitation value of Korean labour has

guish Japanese investment in Korea as well as in Taiwan is that of concentration, from now on, on export of 'dirty' industries. It is no accident that this point was made in 1970 at both the Japan–Republic of China Co-operation Committee meeting (by Inaba Shuzo, as quoted above) and at the Japan–R.O.K. Co-operation Committee meeting. Gradual awareness in Japan of the extent of the ecological disaster there, and the beginnings of a mass protest movement on the issue in 1969–70 also lay behind this step. At the meeting at Seoul in April, Japan's delegation was led by Kishi and the major policy blueprint from the Japanese side came from Yatsugi Kazuo, Permanent Director of the National Policy Research Society. Paragraph 2 of his memorandum, entitled 'Proposals for long-term Japan–Korean economic co-operation' is here quoted in full, and other sections summarized.

1. The need for the co-operation of Japanese capital and technology in Korean development.

2. 'As in the industries in which in particular Japan expects great development in the future – steel, aluminium, oil, petrochemicals, ship-building, electronics, plastics, etc., limitations are gradually being experienced in Japan because of coastal land use and anti-pollution measures, Japan is already doing its best to deal with this and must strive harder from now on, but I wonder if, with these considerations in mind, the Korean side would be able or would like to share the task, or whether it could be dealt with through Japanese–Korean co-operation.'

3. Expansion of free-port areas; expansion of the Joint Enterprise; more efforts to acquaint the labour force with high technology.

4. Agreement on division of labour within industries.

---

been enhanced by two devaluations of the South Korean won between November 1969 and June 1971. Japanese industrialists are remembering the good old days of the 'thirties, when, as Oji Paper Co. President, Fujiwara Ginjiro recalls: 'if we brought workers from Japan to Korea and provided them with housing, the daily wages were about two yen per worker. For Korean labourers, however, the daily wage was from about 20–30 to 40–50 sen at most' (100 sen = 1 yen), Shiota Shobei, op. cit., p. 45.

5. Promotion of imports to Japan of (cheaper) Korean fodder, livestock, agriculture, fishing and seaweed.[1]

To tie together the numerous links developing between Japan, Taiwan and South Korea, a 'Co-ordinating Committee of Japan/R.O.K./Republic of China Co-operation Committees' was formed in Seoul in November 1970.

Leading figures in its creation were Kishi, Yatsugi, Inaba, and many of the biggest of Japanese enterprises have given it their support. Joint development of the oil resources in the Yellow Sea and Tiaoyu Island areas was one of the first priorities of the new grouping. It was, until the upheavals and crisis of 1971 (¥ revaluation, etc.), the highest current articulated expression within Japanese business of the accelerating unification of Japan's new co-prosperity sphere, only five years after 'normalization' with Korea and the first 'yen loan' to Taiwan, one year after the line was endorsed in the Sato–Nixon communiqué, and concurrent with a new and greatly increased arms build-up.[2]

In terms of trade Japan became Korea's major partner, replacing the United States in that role, in 1969. Some 40 per cent of all Korean imports come from Japan, in a trade grossly imbalanced in Japan's favour.[3] At this point it is instructive

1. 'A Complete Picture of Yatsugi's Thinking', *Asahi Journal*, 14 October 1970, pp. 113–14. The National Policy Research Society is an organization which in prewar days was devoted to promotion of the line of unity of workers and employers. It was reconstructed in 1953 (Shirota, p. 187).

2. 'Machinations of the Japan/ROK/Republic of China Co-operation Committee', *Asahi Journal*, 29 November 1970, pp. 105–6.

3. Relative Weight of Japan and U.S.A. in South Korean Trade

	Korean Exports			Korean imports (U.S. $mill.)		
	1968	1969	1970	1968	1969	1970*
U.S.A.	235.4	312.2	395	489.0	530.2	390.7
Japan	99.7	133.3	234	623.9	753.8	530.3
Total	455.4	622.5	835.2	1,462.9	1,823.6	1,984

* The 1970 import figures from the U.S.A. and Japan are only to September; the total is for the whole year.

Source: Bank of Korea (Seoul), *Monthly Economic Statistics*, Decem-

to compare the trading relations of Japan/South Korea/Taiwan as they were in 1964 and as they had developed by 1969.[1]

Several points are striking: the tremendous growth in the volume of Japan's exports to both countries; the very slow

TABLE TWENTY-SEVEN Japan–Taiwan–South Korean Trade Relations: Imports/Exports (in $mill.)

	1964 Korea	Japan	Taiwan		1969 Korea	Japan	Taiwan
Korea	—	108.8	5.2	Korea	—	767.2	13
Japan	41.7	—	140.9	Japan	133.9	—	180.5
Taiwan	1.9	137.9	—	Taiwan	23	606.4	—

(read horizontal line for imports, vertical line for exports)

growth in the volume of their exports to Japan; the value of the overall trade, which amounts to 40 per cent of Japan's entire South-East Asian export trade. A further breakdown shows also that Japan's exports are overwhelmingly heavy industrial goods, while her imports are raw materials, foodstuffs and some textiles.

Yet it is generally assumed that the increasing interdependence of Japanese and Korean economies has brought many benefits to Korea. The economy grew at the impressive rate of 15.5 per cent in 1969; building goes on everywhere; there *is* a lot of money about. A few comments on the nature of the Korean 'boom' are in order. First of all, without the Vietnam war it would collapse, for the annual trade deficits of around $1,200mill. have to be made up by war procurements, payment for mercenaries, etc. Secondly the country is enormously in debt. To the end of 1970 $3,000mill. of foreign funds have been sunk into the economy and the investors and lenders overseas must now take their cut. Repayments on these moneys

ber 1970 and Bank of Korea, *Economic Progress in Korea*, Seoul, August 1971, pp. 11, 28–9. It should be stressed that these figures are not wholly reliable: the August 1971 document from the Bank of Korea states at p. 11 that 'exports reached $1 billion in 1970'; yet the actual figure given later is $835mill. – a gap of over $150mill.

1. Shirota *et al.*, op. cit., p. 193.

(excluding the $224.5mill. direct investment) are estimated as follows:

1971	$241mill.
1972	$335mill.
1974	$480mill.
1975	$583mill.
1976	$648mill.

As the loan intake in 1968 was $855mill. the projection indicates that if the present structure of financing growth were to be continued all this money would presently be going out in repayments![1] The U.S. dollar crisis is forcing drastic reduction in its various payments that have until now filled out the deficits on trading. Japanese involvement grows, and the Korean side, bereft of any alternative policy, must beg for more and more. But to keep Korea as an attractive field for Japanese investment, and for the establishment of Japan's large and dirty enterprises as outlined in the Yatsugi memorandum, domestic consumption must be held down to a minimum, labour costs kept to a minimum, and the population kept passive and compliant.

Perhaps hardest hit under the present regime are the farmers. The average annual income of the farming household actually dropped by 19.1 per cent between 1964 and 1968.[2] While rural conditions stagnate – and 73 per cent of the rural areas are still not electrified[3] – grain imports are up to a level of between $150 and $250mill. per year.[4] From Japan alone in 1969 $135mill. had to be spent in purchases of rice from the enormous surpluses stored there, and again $110 mill. in 1970.[5]

The situation in the urban industrial worker sector is comparable. While labour productivity rose by 2½ times between

1. Nakagawa, *Sekai*, May 1971.
2. Bank of Korea, 'Analysis of the Present Situation of the Korean Farming Household's Income', cited by Nakagawa, *Sekai*, November 1970.
3. *FEER*, 16 October 1971.
4. *Atarashii* . . ., op. cit., p. 63.
5. *Tsusho Hakusho* (*Kakuron*), 1971, p. 303.

1961 and 1969, wages in the same period rose by only 20 per cent and, according to the Korean labour problems specialist, Kim Yoon-han, wages of organized labour fell somewhat short of what is necessary for subsistence.[1] 1969 saw a 40 per cent increase in the number of workers involved in labour disputes and a 60 per cent increase in the number of work days lost.[2] The unemployment rate in Seoul stands at 23 per cent.[3] In November 1970, a twenty-year-old clothing manufacture employee in Seoul, named, Chun Tae-il, tried to organize a demonstration around these demands:

1. Reduction of average daily work hours from sixteen to nine.
2. Increase from two to four days off per month.
3. Improvement in working conditions.
4. Payment of a night work allowance.

Suppressed in his attempts by armed police, on 13 November, he burned himself to death as the only form of protest left.[4]

The plight of the urban middle-class consumer is only slightly better. While domestic fixed total capital formation increased from an average of 10.88 per cent between 1956 and 1960 to 27.4 per cent in 1967–9, in the same period private consumer spending fell by over 12 per cent.[5] A 19.5 per cent increase in prices of petroleum products granted in June 1971 had far-reaching effects on all kinds of commodities and services dependent on petroleum such as transport, power and various industrial products, while the 13 per cent devaluation of the won in June 1971 caused price rises of from 10 per cent to 20 per cent in cars, cotton yarns, sugar and so on. Rice, the

1. From an article in *Shin Toa* (*New East Asia*), January 1971, cited by Nakagawa, *Sekai*, May 1971.
2. From an article entitled, 'Industrialisation and the Deepening of Inequality', by Prof. Yim of Seoul Commercial University in *Shin Toa*, July 1970, cited Nakagawa, *Sekai*, November 1970.
3. *FEER*, 6 November 1971.
4. Nakagawa, *Sekai*, May 1971.
5. Nakagawa, *Sekai*, November 1970.

staple food, rose by 20 per cent in 1971.[1] While the rich are reported to be stowing their wealth overseas as crisis deepens in the country,[2] in late 1971 thousands of workers were reported to be laid off, undisclosed numbers of smaller urban and provincial businesses were folding overnight and almost unbelievably, the nation's largest banks are rumoured almost bankrupt'.[3]

It comes as hardly a surprise in this situation to find that protest movements are spreading through all levels of Korean society, save of course the top which is fighting a desperate rearguard action to keep the lid on it all. Many incidents occur, officially ascribed to the work of northern infiltrators and spies.

A few of these incidents are worth resuming in summary form. In July 1969 five people were executed – for belonging to the United Revolutionary Party,[4] the recently reorganized underground movement, grouping together the revolutionary left in the south. In the southern part of Kyongsang province, the area of greatest penetration of Japanese capital – where the Masan Free Export Zone is located – some 10,333 people were arrested and imprisoned in the space of one month in July 1970 in an attempt to put down unrest there.[5] In May 1970 a poem by the writer Kim Chi-ha appeared in the leading Korean monthly *Sa Sang-Kye* (*World of Ideas*), entitled 'The Five Bandits'.[6] It caused quite a stir, for the bandits were the plutocrats, bureaucrats, parliamentarians, generals and high officials who were represented in it to be waxing fat while behaving like the traitors who sold the country out to

1. *FEER*, 15 January 1972, 25 September 1971. The petroleum price rise was originally reported to have been 44.5 per cent (*FEER*, 25 September 1971) and the oil companies continued to press for this figure.

2. From the Korean paper *Toa Ilbo* (*East Asia Daily*) for 17 August, cited Fujishima Udai, *Asahi Journal*, 8 October 1971, pp. 17–20.

3. *FEER*, 11 December 1971.

4. *Atarashii* . . . , op. cit., p. 75. The URP is also sometimes referred to as the Revolutionary Party for Unification.

5. ibid., p. 76.

6. Translations of some of Kim's shorter poems and an interview with him in *Ronin*, vol. 1, nos. 1, 2, 4–5, and 7.

Japan at the beginning of the century. Kim was arrested under the anti-Communism law for conduct aiding the enemy and has served long periods in detention.[1]

In July 1971, there was a mysterious and ill-explained mutiny by an air force 'Special Education' detachment stationed on an island in Inchon harbour who were then annihilated as they began to move towards the capital.[2] In August massive protest demonstrations broke out among residents of a newly reclaimed town near Seoul calling for homes, work and better living conditions,[3] while in Seoul itself the owners of 200 retail shops in Pyongwa market closed their doors indefinitely in protest against tax assessments which they claimed were two or three times higher than they had been the previous year.[4] On 15 September some 500 manual labourers who had been employed under contract in Vietnam rioted at the offices of the company which had employed them demanding unpaid wages.[5]

The universities have always been a focus of opposition to the regime. Of late, however, unprecedentedly harsh repression has been seen to be necessary in order to try to contain that opposition.

On 5 October student leaders at Korea University were arrested and beaten by troops shortly after a campaign for reduction of military training hours had begun to take an overtly anti-regime, anti-establishment line and to speak out on wider social grievances.[6] As demonstrations spread and students became bolder in their attacks on corruption, and as slogans like 'Confiscate comprador capital' and 'Demand guaranteed right to livelihood' began to appear, President Pak sent in the troops again on 15 October, this time having them

1. Hayashi, op. cit., p. 272.
2. *Le Monde*, 10 September 1971; *Asahi Journal*, 22 October 1971.
3. *FEER*, 25 September 1971, where the numbers involved are put at 6,000 and *Asahi Journal*, 8 and 22 October, where numbers are put at 50,000.
4. *FEER*, ibid.
5. *Asahi Journal*, 22 October 1971.
6. *FEER*, 6 November 1971; *Asahi Journal*, 22 October 1971.

garrison all major universities. One hundred and seventy student leaders were arrested, and 6,332 more were reported to the conscription authorities for anti-military training – i.e. recommended for immediate conscription. All campus newspapers and magazines were suspended, and student organizations dissolved save academic ones which would have to be strictly guided by a responsible professor.[1] Student awareness of the crumbling social and political fabric has been much heightened of late as student fees have been massively increased. Increases of 20–30 per cent are imposed twice a term, coupled with immediate expulsion in the event of non-payment. The average private university student is now paying 70–80,000 won ($190–$220) per half term. To appreciate the significance of this it may be necessary to know that even with a 15 per cent rise in February, 1972 high school teachers will be getting 43,930 won ($122) monthly.[2]

The threat of a coalescing of the dissatisfaction rampant in all sectors of society was undoubtedly behind the crackdown on universities, as it has been behind the arrest of figures like the Dean of Seoul University's Law School, Ryu Ki-chon, on charges of sedition and complicity with the students[3], and of United Socialist party leader Kim Chul under the anti-communism law for calling for *de facto* recognition of Pyongyang,[4] and as it has been behind the declaration of a state of emergency and the recent suspension of most civil liberties.[5] In part, too, the desperation is prompted by the switches in U.S. policy, continuing troop withdrawals and pressures to come to an agreement with the north. It is in this context that urgent appeals for increased levels of Japanese aid and increasing military co-ordination between the two countries must be understood.

1. *Asahi Journal*, 29 October 1971, pp. 89–92; *FEER*, 6 November gives the figure of 9,307 students to be conscripted.
2. *Asahi Journal*, ibid.
3. *FEER*, 11 December, 1971.
4. Fujishima Udai, *Asahi Journal*, 8 October 1971.
5. Early December 1971, *FEER*, 11 December. The reason stated was the danger of attack from the north.

Pak, who came to power in a coup in 1961 to cut short moves towards reunification, has pursued a consistent policy of economic growth and Japanese dependency. Yet a government-sponsored survey of late 1969, released in February 1970, showed 90·61 per cent of the people desirous of unification. Another survey, reported in the *Koryo Ilbo* (*Korean Daily*) on 5 March 1970, showed that 97 per cent of the people interviewed were of the opinion that Korea should beware of Japan, while only 1 per cent was in favour of making friends with Japan.[1]

Five years after the 'normalization' of Japan–R.O.K. relations, an editorial in the *Koryo Ilbo* of 19 December 1970, noted that it was now quite clear to 'emerging critical public opinion' that 'apart from a section of politicians and merchants who have been able to profit by it, the establishment of the new relationship, the promotion of intercourse, which are expressed in the words "co-operation", and "friendliness" between the two countries has been not at all to the satisfaction of the citizens'.[2] The Opposition candidate in the 1970 presidential elections in a speech at the Seoul Foreign Correspondents Club on 30 October 1970 said:

> In the five year since normalization of relations the friendship between Japan and Korea has been no more than that between the governments of the two countries and the economic co-operation between Japan and Korea has aided corruption and built up the wealth of the Government party and a section of the *zaibatsu*.[3]

Japanese business shows no sign of feeling any need to modify the present relationship. President Nagano of Fuji Steel (in September 1969) expressed the following sentiments.[4]

> The future course of Japanese industry will be decided by three things: the 500 million people of India, the mineral

1. Nakagawa Nobuo, *Sekai*, June 1970, pp. 221–30.
2. Cited Nakagawa, *Sekai*, May 1971.
3. ibid. from *Asahi*, 18 December 1970.
4. Shirota *et al.*, op. cit., p. 223. (Nagano is now President of Nippon Steel.)

resources of Indonesia, and the prosperity of Korea, which is the defence perimeter of the Asian free world on the front lines with the communist sphere.

For all the 'Free World' aid and support of the South Korean regime its *per capita* GNP is still a mere $120 as compared to $210 in North Korea, as Senators Fulbright and Symington were much taken aback to hear during Senate hearings in 1970.[1] Once a rich agrarian country, South Korea has become a dumping ground for Japan's surplus rice.

With rising profits, an ever-increasing Japanese stake in the continuity of the present regime, and with frustration and discontent seething in all save the landlord/comprador class in Korea, the primary orientation of Japan's defence buildup towards the Korean peninsula was readily comprehensible.

1. Committee on Foreign Relations, U.S. Senate, *Hearing before the Sub-Committee on U.S. Security Agreements and Commitments Abroad*, January 1970.

Chapter 6

IMPERIALISM AT HOME

JAPAN PROPER

Since domestic developments are intimately bound up with Japan's activities abroad, a few trends which are significantly related to the main arguments of this book must here be briefly identified. Some aspects have already been touched on; here we shall consider or reconsider business and industry, agriculture, labour, education the environment, and, in a separate section, Okinawa.

Business and Industry

Japan's postwar recovery, its sustained rapid growth and the present strength of its economy – what is sometimes inclusively known as 'the Japanese economic miracle' – are well known, in a very vague way. There are important aspects of the 'miracle' which have received less attention than they deserve.

First, Japan's very high rate of capital accumulation has been achieved through an interlocking system of government supervision and private exploitation which has no equal in the other advanced capitalist countries. A recent estimate calculated that over 90 per cent of all government activity was devoted directly to looking after business.[1] Japan has by far the most inequitable overall tax system of the advanced capitalist countries, and extremely low expenditure on social services.

Second, this control over capital accumulation has been used to construct an economy whose structure is different from

1. Yanaga, op. cit., p. 3.

that of the other major capitalist powers. Japan, in spite of its popular image as a producer of consumer goods, has the heaviest based industrial economy in the entire world: as far back as 1965 the share of heavy industry in Japan's industrial output was higher than in any other industrial country. The disparity in growth between light and heavy industry in Japan in the years 1955–63, for example, was greater than it was in the Soviet Union throughout the period under Stalin when greatest attention was being given to heavy industry (1928–40).[1] This extraordinary strength in heavy industry is bound to determine the shape of Japan's import needs, the future development of the economy, and Japan's continuing export competitivity.

Third, along with this stress on heavy industry has gone an increasing trend towards monopoly and oligopoly. Concentration of capital is, of course, the number one feature of imperialism as defined by Lenin. One of the most important features of postwar Japanese capitalism has been the elimination of the old barriers which divided the *zaibatsu* from each other. After the war the American occupation regime essayed a feeble anti-monopoly programme, allegedly designed to break up the giant cartels and holding companies. The programme was little short of a farce; in particular, it failed to attack the core of the *zaibatsu* – the banks, and thus the key to all operations, credit. Since then, the *zaibatsu* have not only recovered their prewar position, but actually improved it. In particular, they streamlined their co-ordination so that now erstwhile rivals, such as Mitsubishi, Mitsui and Sumitomo can collaborate together in joint ventures.[2] Table 28 showing mergers between 1951 and 1969 demonstrates the trend.[3]

1. Angus Maddison, 'Japanese Economic Performance', *Banca Nazionale del Lavoro Quarterly Review*, no. 75, December 1965, p. 17.

2. These three, the three largest pre-1945 *zaibatsu*, and still the biggest groups in Japan, are the three largest shareholders in the Jyujo Paper Co. (Kozo Yamamura, 'Zaibatsu, Prewar and Zaibatsu, Postwar', *Journal of Asian Studies*, vol. 23, no. 4, August 1964, p. 554; Yamamura, *Economic Policy in Postwar Japan*, Berkeley and Los Angeles, 1967. On the whole Yamamura is most useful on the whole

The government, in spite of the vain gesticulations of the Fair Trade Commission (FTC), has pressed ahead with assisting concentration: MITI has been particularly active in this. On the whole, the tactic has been to ensure a high degree

TABLE TWENTY-EIGHT Company Mergers in Japan 1951–69

	1951–5	1956–60	1961–4	1965–7	1968	1969
Total (annual average)	345	402	812	933	1,020	1,163
Companies with capitalization value of more than 1 billion yen	4	8	27	35	28	36

of concentration well before a specific sector is opened up to foreign capital penetration. Thus, the Ikeda government (1960–64) which marked the key period of capital reorganization after the relatively sloppy Kishi administration (1957–60), was the real powerhouse behind the merger drive. There has been a high degree of concentration in such key sectors as steel, automobiles, banking and now the computer industry. The Fuji–Yawata merger (or, strictly speaking, re-merger) produced the world's number one steel company (Nippon Steel).[1] Toyota is now the number three car producer in the world (and is in active collaboration with the number two Japanese producer, Nissan – for example, in a joint venture in

economy, but, of course, mergers have speeded up greatly since. *PR*, no. 4, 1971 ('Zaibatsu Stage Comeback') points out that the ten pre-war big groups have, through concentration, now become a mere six. For an invaluable up-to-date survey of the *zaibatsu* see 'Who's Who in the Zaibatsu', *Pacific Imperialism Notebook*, vol. 3, no. 1, December 1971–January 1972.

3. *OECD Economic Surveys, Japan*, June 1971, p. 29.

1. The two had been part of the Yawata *zaibatsu* prior to 1945 (Yawata was the smallest of the 'big four' *zaibatsu*); when the merger took place it was widely predicted that the new conglomerate would overtake U.S. Steel by 1975; in fact Nippon Steel became the world's number one in 1971! Note that Japan's per capita output of steel was already equal to the U.S.A.'s per capita output in 1967.

Thailand). The vast Mitsubishi empire has been streamlining its internal co-ordination even further (as detailed above). The formation of the two huge banking consortia is an important step towards further centralization of credit (already centrally controlled by the Bank of Japan). In the vital area of computers it would seem that a desperate push is on to consolidate the Japanese-owned part of the industry, as the remaining barriers against foreign capital are slowly withdrawn.[1]

It goes without saying that one of the inevitable results of this further concentration is the elimination of a number of small and medium enterprises: many of these either have to accept being taken over, go broke, or export themselves to other parts of the region – Taiwan, Korea, etc. The narrow profit margins on which these small businesses (often family-operated) were being run were in many cases sliced to nothing by the effects, first of the U.S. 10 per cent import surcharge slapped on in mid-1971, and then of the December 1971 yen revaluation[2] (which, of course, made it relatively cheaper to buy

1. Two of the largest Japanese companies, Fujitsu and Hitachi, recently merged their computer interests; and two others, Nippon Electric Co. and Toshiba were reported about to sign a computer arrangement. This would give the industry the following structure: two purely Japanese groups: NEC–Toshiba, and Fujitsu–Hitachi; one joint venture group: Mitsubishi Electric Corporation + Oki Electric Industry Co. + Nippon Univac Kaisha + Oki Univac Kaisha (Univac being a division of Sperry Rand): see *JEJ*, no. 463, 9 November 1971, p. 9. For details of the Fujitsu–Hitachi tie-up, *JEJ*, no. 461, 26 October 1971, p. 1.

2. Japanese textile unions expected to see 215,000 people out of work as a result of the U.S.A.–Japan agreement restricting the export of woollen goods and synthetics; in Fukui Prefecture alone it was reported that 353 small firms had gone out of business by the beginning of December 1971 as a result of the various 'shocks'. The leading Japanese textile tycoon, Ohya Shinzo, stated that he expected 300,000 layoffs in Japan because of the textiles agreement with the U.S.A. (*Wall Street Journal*, 18 October 1971). In general, 'Ruin faces makers of wigs, dolls, fishing rods, ping pong bats, parasols, pen nibs, guitars, plastic buttons and Xmas tree lights, all heavily oriented to North America' (Peter Wilsher, the *Sunday Times*, 5 December 1971).

into South-East Asia); the general slowdown in trade, particularly in textiles, has also had a serious effect on these smaller companies which, like much of Japanese business, run on very tight credit. The big businesses, in liaison with the banks, have traditionally used recessions as a good occasion for consolidation. The government has usually given a hand in this by 'tolerating' what are called 'recession cartels'.

There are two other domestic phenomena which are certain to have a big effect on the location of future Japanese investment: rising wages and pollution (the latter dealt with more fully in a section below). Japanese industrial wages have been rising at a rate of 15–18 per cent per annum in recent years: not an intolerable rate when compared with increases in productivity, but in combination with the revaluation of the yen (particularly vis-à-vis the U.S. dollar), all the same a sizeable amount. Cheaper wages abroad are obviously becoming more and more attractive: Taiwan, for example, has an estimated 25 per cent unemployment rate, and Indonesia perhaps 35 per cent (unemployed and semi-unemployed), compared with a Japanese figure of just over 1 per cent. Given such items as martial law (in Taiwan) and this huge pool of unemployed, the local proletariat is unlikely to be able to exercise the kind of pressure on wages which the Japanese working class can. Protests against industrial pollution in Japan are also making business emigration more popular. In addition, American and other tariffs against Japanese goods produced in the homeland, make it more attractive to move production to, say, Macao[1] – or perhaps even the United States itself. And these pressures are increased by the lavish incentives offered by many of the South-East Asian countries to foreign investors (see above).

1. There is no U.S. textile quota on imports from Macao. It has preferential access to Portugal and the Portuguese colonies, as well as to South Africa; and special favourable treatment from France. Wages are up to 30 per cent lower than in Hong Kong, land 20–30 per cent cheaper, and accommodation one third the Hong Kong figure.

Agriculture

The increasing dominance of monopoly capital and multinational business has had drastic repercussions on agriculture no less than on other sectors of the economy. In Japanese agriculture the basic patterns were set with the occupation-sponsored land reforms, by which the powers and prerogatives of the prewar landowning class were restricted, though only to the point where agrarian peasant discontent was defused while at the same time '. . . preserving enough of the substance of dependency and inequality to enable the upper class to deliver the rural vote regularly for the anti-communist conservative parties'.[1]

Placation of rural power has remained a key political principle through the postwar period, while the 'rationalization' of agriculture has assumed greater and greater significance but is actually a contradictory goal, since 'rationalization' of agriculture, as of industry, means redundancies, restriction of autonomy and co-option to the purposes of big business and empire. The Fundamental Law on Agriculture of May 1961 envisaged the need to cut the number of farming households to 2–3 million since there were only 15 million acres of arable land in the country, and a lot of five acres was reckoned the minimum necessary to bring the farmer's income into line with that of other sectors of the population.[2] But a positive policy to force such a 'rationalization' has been so far ruled out for political reasons – after all, boundaries for Diet seats were fixed according to 1950 population distribution figures, so that some 50 per cent of Diet members represent rural constituencies, in general staunchly conservative, while only

1. Al McCoy, 'Land Reform as Counter-Revolution', *BCAS*, vol. 3, no. 1, winter/spring 1971, pp. 14–49, at p. 21. McCoy's article is a brilliant reconsideration of the whole 'land-reform' question in relation to Japan, Taiwan, the Philippines and South Vietnam.

2. Ouchi Tsutomu, Namiki Masakichi and Nakamura Takahide, 'A Look at the Changing Face of Japanese Agriculture', *Sekai*, November 1971, pp. 227–46.

18 per cent of the population is now actually engaged in agriculture.[1]

The anomalies of the electoral representation system are such that, for example, the maximum differential in the weight of urban/rural votes is 5:1 (*The Times*, 29 April 1971) – i.e. that a Dietman can be elected from a rural constituency with as few as one fifth the votes it might take from an urban one. Incidentally, the general assumption that the ruling Liberal Democratic Party (roughly two-thirds of the seats in the Diet – 300 from the election of 1969) must enjoy the support of something like a majority of the people is quite false. In 1969 it won 47.6 per cent of votes cast, which was 32.6 per cent of the electorate, and in the highly urbanized areas of Tokyo and Osaka it won a mere 34.2 per cent and 26.16 per cent of the votes cast.

Even in the absence of a positive policy, however, the rural population has come under increasing pressure in recent years. According to the government's 1970 White Paper on Agriculture there were at that time 6.76 million people employed in agriculture and fisheries (in 5.43 million households), but of these no less than 4 million had to have regular employment elsewhere as well.[2] Many husbands commute to nearby small or medium-size factories and tend their land only during the busy seasons of sowing and harvest, sometimes even hiring labour for that. In the case of bleak northern districts like Tohoku and Hokuriku, snowbound for much of the year, they must be away for much of the time, working in seasonal jobs in Tokyo and other urban centres. As the Nissan example discussed below indicates, they are nothing but an 'industrial reserve army of Japan, obliged to work under less than satisfactory conditions, laid off first when business becomes dull'.[3] Thus it is often only the women and the old over sixty who remain at home – making up in fact 70 per cent of the agricul-

1. ibid.
2. ibid.
3. 'Economic Analysis (1): Junk-Yard Development', *Ampo*, no. 11, p. 25; on Nissan see the 'Labour' section in this chapter.

tural labour force.[1] Although they bear the brunt of the agricultural work, however, no less than 2.28 million farming wives have to work outside the home as well in order to make ends meet – in small rural enterprises or small-scale manufacture often under contract from large enterprises. Even in relatively 'prosperous' districts favourably located near the big Pacific coast urban centres farmers' wives are often obliged to do spells as, for example, builders' labourers, road construction workers, packaging tea or canning fish. Average wages for this female labour are between 500 and 1,000 yen ($1.60 to $3.20) daily.[2] Their lives are thus an experience of multiple drudgery and exploitation – regular domestic duties, land tilling, part-time jobs, and child-nursing. Furthermore, village educational and medical services are deteriorating because of the decreasing enrolment in schools and the poverty facing rural medical practices. The Japanese peasantry is, in effect, being turned into 'a hoard of wage-earners with tiny plots of land', which, as a last resort, they see as possible sources of money when desperate, as the demand for industrial sites will greatly boost land prices.[3]

Over the decade to 1971 8 million workers were extracted from agriculture to other sectors, and, as there are still 2 million households working holdings of one and a quarter acres or less, as against the minimum economic holding of five acres that the government had decided was necessary in 1961, the outlook for the farmers left is far from bright.[4] In 1970 54 per cent of the farming family's income came from working not on the land but in various 'side jobs' in the towns and cities.[5]

The political mobilization of Japanese farmers around their many grievances has been made more difficult by government manipulation of the Food Control Programme, a subsidized rice price support system which is the focal point in the

1. 'Economic Analysis (1).'

2. Oshima Kiyoshi, 'Japanese Agriculture: Is the Present State of Affairs Good Enough?', *Sekai*, November 1971, pp. 247–55.

3. 'Economic Analysis (1): Junk-Yard Development', *Ampo*, no. 11.

4. Ouchi *et al.*, op. cit.

5. Oshima, op. cit., p. 249.

LDP's vote-oriented propaganda to the farmers. The system works like this: the government buys rice from the farmers at a price of 140 yen per kilo, which, by the time storage and collection costs are included, means about 170 yen from the public purse. This is nearly double the international price for rice and, as production greatly exceeds demand under the present system, much of the surplus has to be sold at a considerable loss – for fodder at 21.2 yen per kilo, for foreign export at 50 yen, or for industrial use at 60 yen, or stored, which is also very expensive. The net result is a cost to the taxpayer of what amounted by early 1971 to $3.2 billion (1,000 billion yen), much of which is eaten up, however, in the enormous government bureaucracy of 280,000 odd employed in the programme.[1] As a percentage of GNP the deficit in the special account for foodstuff control has risen steadily from 0.1 per cent in 1958 to 1.2 per cent in 1967, and, if it continues at this rate, might reach 2.2 per cent or $8.8 billion in 1975.[2]

There are few possible solutions to the problem. On the one hand, a Chinese-style, socialist 'rationalization' of agriculture – based on commune farming, a degree of central planning and great crop diversification to reduce imports – is out for obvious reasons. Indeed, on the contrary, present policies demand an increase in imports from South-East Asia in order to help level out the massive trade imbalances in Japan's favour, and at least a maintenance of U.S. agricultural imports (currently over $1 billion per year)[3] in order to ease the difficulties of that trade too. It is towards the other, U.S.-style 'rationalization' that Japanese monopoly capital is moving – elimination of the domestic, 'low-productive' agriculture, and its replacement with 'profit-oriented, mechanized and systematized farming by capitalist corporations and large, rich farmers', despite the considerable political risks this entails for the rural-based

1. Ouchi *et al.*, op. cit. (The figure 280,000 is *Ampo*'s.) Rice for domestic consumption in Japan is sold at 152 yen per kilo.

2. *The Times*, 29 April 1971.

3. MITI, *Tsusho Hakusho*, op. cit. (1971), (wheat: $173.6mill.; soyabeans: $329.6mill.; corn: $217.7mill.; fodder: $399.1mill. for a total of $1.1 billion).

ruling Conservatives.[1] For one thing, domestic rice production is now being positively discouraged, to the extent that in 1970 the government was paying out sixty-eight yen to the farmers for each kilo of rice they did *not* produce, with the result that 10 per cent of the country's rice fields were left uncultivated.[2] Furthermore, revision of the Agricultural Land Regulation is under way to enable the land to be easily bought up and converted to other purposes. According to *Shinzenso* (a comprehensive, long-term, national development plan drawn up in 1969), at least one sixth of land currently used in agriculture will be converted to industrial use by 1985.[3]

All in all, the agricultural problem may be expected to worsen greatly in the future; levels of discontent are rising among the farmers, who have so long been urged to produce as much rice as possible and are now being urged to stop producing it at all, and who on the whole have never made a decent living out of their back-breaking work anyway; and also on the part of the general consumer, who sees enormous sums of money being eaten up in a highly irrational rice programme and enormous sums going out, on the other hand, to buy wheat and corn from the United States. Meanwhile, also, rising pollution levels are making any agriculture at all difficult and are crippling the small-scale fishing industry.

There are a number of concrete examples which illustrate the farming situation more powerfully than any generalizations. One case in which many salient features of the emerging Japanese state are brought out is that of the farming community of Sanrizuka, a village about forty miles east of Tokyo. Sanrizuka is situated in rather poor agricultural land, much of it only brought under cultivation by dint of intensive effort after the Second World War, and until recently, was producing crops of wheat, peanuts, taro, ginger and watermelons. In June 1966, however, the Japanese government announced that Sanrizuka was to be the site of the new Tokyo International Airport. Apart from the immediate problem this raised for the

1. 'Economic Analysis (1): Junk-Yard Development', *Ampo*, no. 11.
2. ibid. 3. ibid.

local people of the area, the plan had important ramifications in terms of Japan's military alliance with the United States and in terms of comprehensive planning for Japanese agriculture.[1]

In military terms one of the main reasons for the overcrowding of Haneda Airport, which in turn made a new one necessary, was its much increased use by military charter flights following the escalation of the Vietnam war. Free use of Haneda is guaranteed the U.S. military under the Security Treaty and of course the same would apply to the new airport. Another relevant factor is the existence of what is known as the 'Blue 14' air route which, as stipulated in the Security Treaty, is reserved for the exclusive use of U.S. military aircraft, and which makes it impossible to put the airport to the west of Tokyo, for example.

The second, and more general, point argued by the opponents of the plan, especially the farmers, is that it is aimed in effect at the destruction of agriculture in Japan. The rationale behind this thinking is set out as follows by Kitazawa Yoko:

> The Sanrizuka International Airport is one of the main pillars of a redevelopment plan for the entire Hokuso plateau on which Sanrizuka stands, which in turn is to be a test for a vast plan for the reorganization of the entire economic structure of the nation. This plan involves the transformation of present agricultural areas into industrial areas, the destruction of farmland and the uprooting of peasants from their life and culture to be transformed into an industrial labour force. It is not quite correct to call this a 'decentralization' plan, since it involves the expansion, not the dissolution, of the metropolis. Thus the airport is part of a general plan to urbanize the entire Hokuso area, to bring in metals and machine industry to be tied in with the Kashima and Keiyo industrial areas along the coast. Narita New City is to be built on 487 hectares of Sanrizuka land, to accommodate the labour force associated with the airport. A new transportation network is to be built both within the area and between the area and the capital. Most important is a plan to alter the rivers in the area so as to divert the waters from agriculture to industry, which will mean the final death of the farmlands.[2]

1. The Sanrizuka struggle has been extensively dealt with in Japanese sources. The best account in English is Kitazawa Yoko, 'Vietnam in Japan: Sanrizuka', *Ampo*, no. 9–10, 1971, pp. 3–7.
2. ibid., p. 3.

This point has also to be related to that emphasized above – that Japan has to promote the import of agricultural commodities from South-East Asia and from the United States – so that, extreme and irrational as it may sound, the destruction of agriculture in Japan is actually 'necessary'. The struggle which has developed in Sanrizuka has thus tied together opposition to Japanese complicity in, and support for, the Vietnam war, opposition to the entire Hokuso Development Plan, and general opposition by the people against the tendency of monopoly capital to expand, modernize and rationalize for its own benefit.

Since 1967 the resistance movement at Sanrizuka has developed into a struggle of epic proportions. Though the airport was supposed to be open to traffic early in 1971, by the end of that year the issue had still not been finally resolved. For the state, massive contingents of para-military riot police – up to 5,000 in the September 1971 clashes – have been employed in full-scale assaults, but, despite massive arrests, had not been able to break the resistance. On the side of the farmers, there was initially a tendency to rely on established opposition forces of Japan Socialist and Communist Parties, but as these stood aside, counselling non-resistance when forced surveys and takeover of the land commenced, an alliance gradually developed between local people and radical worker and student groups prepared to fight with them. In the resistance much has been learnt from the experiences of peasants in Indochina: permanent guards have been set up; living quarters have been moved underground into an elaborate complex of caves and tunnels and, gradually, the method of resisting has changed from the early days when farmers simply hurled excrement at the riot police or lay in front of the tractors, to the position now where booby traps are dug, and bamboo spears and Molotov cocktails are freely used. Three policemen died in the September 1971 assaults and the struggle continued.

The seeds of a potential second Sanrizuka have been sown recently in a remote region of northern Japan. Till around 1969, Aomori prefecture had been famous for little but the taste of its apples, the enormous U.S. air force base at Misawa, and the depth of its winter snow. Then it was decided that it was one of the best possible sites left for development of a large-scale industrial complex. The scale of the plan that was drawn up is indicated by the geographical scope – the whole eastern side of the province – and by the output that was planned for the development: 20 million tons of pig iron, one million tons of non-ferrous metals (smelting is now forbidden in most Japanese towns because of the pollution hazards), 2.6 million tons of petrochemicals, 15 million tons of refined petroleum, and 8 million kilowatts of electricity. Yokkaichi, renowned as the petrochemical centre of Japan and as one of the most polluted cities, operates on barely one fifth of these levels.[1]

When the people of Rokkasho, some 12,000 farmers and fishermen, heard that they were to be at the heart of the new plan, and that most of them would be expected to leave, they were understandably shaken. Many of them went, under village sponsorship, to see what had happened to the people of Kashima, a similar if smaller development scheme that has been growing over the past four years or so about fifty miles north of Tokyo. They were shocked at what they found, reporting back to the village that pollution levels were already severe, even though the Kashima development was nowhere near completion. Strong village opposition was partly responsible, along with the 'Nixon shock', for a rethinking of the Rokkasho plan, to the extent that the area affected has been halved, and parts of the project – notably the steel, non-ferrous metals and electricity generation plants – put on ice for the time being, though this is likely to be only a temporary step. Above all it is important to note that this plan, known as the Mutsu-Ogawara project, is only the first of eleven gigantic

1. For a detailed account of the Rokkasho situation (in Japanese) see 'The Development of Mutsu-Ogawara in a State of Confusion', *Asahi Journal*, 12 November 1971, pp. 105–20; the English account by Peter Wilsher in the *Sunday Times*, 19 December 1971, sums up the main points of the *Asahi Journal* articles.

industrial complexes planned under *Shinzenso*.[1] In fact the Mutsu-Ogawara project may well be the world's largest development plan – a thought which holds little cheer for those who live there.[2]

It would be absurd to suggest that Sanrizuka and Rokkasho are typical Japanese villages. Yet they are concentrated expressions of some of the most advanced tendencies working themselves out in relation to Japanese agriculture. The attacks on, and the attempts to eliminate, Japanese farming communities at points and in areas where they are thought likely to be weakest – communities working newly-reclaimed land or in remote districts – and the attempts to put in their stead giant pollution-intensive, high-profit industrial complexes or mammoth, semi-military air-fields are not haphazard steps. The logic of the policies being pursued by the present government is such that these attacks must be expected to continue and multiply, and in this sense the bitter scenes from Sanrizuka may be expected to be re-enacted many times over.

Labour

Virtually the whole of this exposition has been concerned with Japanese business, government and military. To what extent has the Japanese working class been co-opted into the various

1. For more on the *Shinzenso* plan see 'Junk-Yard Development', op. cit; *FEER*, 4 March 1972, p. 47, estimates that the country's total requirement of industrial space is expected to reach 300,000 hectares in 1985, compared with 1965's 100,000 hectares.

2. 'Giant Development on the Way', *Chuo Koron*, February 1972. One may note the callousness and stupidity of Herman Kahn's comments on the *Shinzenso* only three years ago: 'It is a blueprint for the rational and efficient decentralization of the entire country, tying all areas together into a rather closely knit but decentralized unit . . . [the Japanese] solution to all these current problems of civilization are (*sic*) likely to be an aesthetic and cultural delight as well as an economic, technological and engineering miracle.' (Herman Kahn, *The Emerging Japanese Superstate*, London, 1971, [U.S.A., 1970], p. 132.) The *Shinzenso* in its 1969 form has been shelved, but Tanaka, immediately on taking office as premier, set up a special 80-man group to work out a 'super-*Shinzenso*'.

processes and plans of these ruling groups? The common stereotype of the Japanese work-force is of one which puts a high premium on loyalty, thrift, and hard work, and which sees the enterprise, and the boss as some kind of extended benevolent family and father figure. It is true that the high growth rate in the sixties, featuring regular wage increases and close to full employment, was not a time of great labour activism. Industrial action centred either on the spring struggles, through which the 'base-up' or basic wage increases for the year were negotiated, either with or without recourse to a brief strike, or occasional political gestures – demonstrations, token strikes – in opposition to the Security Treaty with the United States, to the terms of the Okinawa reversion and so on.

Now things are obviously changing. For one, the expansion cannot be expected to continue. The irreparable harm it has wrought to the environment has recently become all too clear, and the markets to absorb the flow of goods being produced have also begun to shrink. Late in 1971, in the wake of the various Nixon shocks and the textile deal with the United States, large scale sackings were reported in the electric, steel, automobile, shipping, textile and chemical industries, with the figure for unemployment expected to continue to rise until it levels out at about the one million mark.[1] For another thing, the possibility of securing labour, on close enough to slave terms, elsewhere in the Asian region encourages the attempt by Japanese management to reduce the home labour force to, as near as possible, the same condition. The strains of the latter part of 1971 served to expose the degree to which the position of workers has been undermined over recent years and the inadequacy of the established trade union response to the policies of 'rationalization' of the work force in the interests of capital.

During the sixties a whole series of new management measures, some new, some not, was elaborated into a comprehensive code of worker control: time control, personnel

1. Yamada Koji, *Asahi Journal*, 29 October 1971, pp. 93–6.

control, efficiency wages, a pay scale tied to 'ability', rigidly hierarchical status rankings for workers, and the shop supervisory system known as 'shokusei' (literally 'work control'). This was part of the process of rationalization of the home labour force which coincided with, and was necessary to, the period of dramatic overseas expansion of the economy.

While the process of alienation and dehumanization of the workers proceeded apace during these years the established labour movement contrived to urge workers to stick to conventional pay rise demands. Furthermore the unions themselves became increasingly integrated into the supervisory structure of the company, partners of capital, united with private enterprise in helping Japan compete for international markets.

Before looking at one or two examples which illustrate these trends it is important to note several things: first, many Japanese workers, especially white-collar workers, are not unionized at all; second, that unions are organized on an enterprise rather than a craft basis and every effort is made within a system weighted heavily against free labour mobility to reinforce loyalty to the enterprise and thus weaken class solidarity among workers; third, that the labour movement is organized within several main federations, and that even within these federations there is also considerable difference of political line. The two main federations are Sohyo, the General Council of Trade Unions, and Domei, also a nation-wide labour federation. Sohyo is by far the largest federation, grouping under its umbrella some 4,200,000 workers, being particularly strong in public enterprises like National Railways, Postal and Telegraph Workers; it is a kind of People's Front force, its political weight divided between the Communist and Socialist parties, and, as its consciousness of class is constantly eroded, its position becomes a more and more innocuous one, being vaguely for peace and democracy and defence of the constitution.[1] Domei was founded in 1964, very likely with American trade unions from the AFL–CIO playing some part

1. Kamizuma Yoshiaki, 'The Present State of the Confused Labour Movement', *Ekonomisuto*, 20 April 1971, pp. 16–23.

in its origin, and has functioned largely as a minority ginger group on the right of the labour movement, in broad agreement with the existing business and political establishment.[1] The differences between these two groups should not be emphasized too much, however, and since 1970 there has been a wide area of agreement between them, allowing co-operation in joint political rallies, for example.

The most important development of recent years, however, has been the emergence, within these established unions, of a radical anti-imperialist caucus known as the Hansen, or Anti-War Youth Committee. Hansen began in 1965 as the expression of two powerful sentiments within the labour movement: rejection of the labour bosses because of the timidity and bureaucratism evident in their failure to carry through the projected 1964 general strike; and absolute opposition to the ready complicity of the same union leadership with imperialism. Significantly, Hansen was born out of actual struggle – a militant effort by direct action to disrupt the transport over Japanese railway networks of munitions and fuel destined for U.S.A. operations in the stepped-up Vietnam war, and to block the 1965 Treaty 'normalizing' relations between Japan and South Korea, a major watershed in the development of Japanese imperialism generally. Hansen has from its inception specialized in direct action, whether through wildcat strikes in industry or through street actions on wider political issues, as, for example, apart from those mentioned above, attempts to prevent the visit to Japanese ports of U.S.A. nuclear submarines, or to oppose the terms of the Okinawa Reversion Agreement. Because of the loose and decentralized nature of Hansen there is no way of knowing how many 'members' there are. It can mobilize very considerable numbers for demonstrations, however, and there is no doubt that its ideological influence within the labour movement is considerable.[2]

1. See the section on 'The Labor and Cultural Front' in Herbert P. Bix, 'The Security Treaty System and the Japanese Military–Industrial Complex', *BCAS*, vol. 2, no. 2, January 1970.

2. For one brief account in English, see 'Street-fighting Workers: Hansen Seinen Iinkai' in *Ampo*, no. 6, 1970.

Several important recent tendencies within the world of labour are brought out by considering the case of Nissan Automobile Company. With a capital of 40 billion yen ($112mill.) it produces some 1.2 million vehicles annually, thus ranking seventh in the world. (Toyota, with an output of 1.5 million, is third.) Employing 45,000 workers, Nissan is the sixth largest enterprise in Japan.[1]

Within the Nissan factories there is an elaborate hierarchical structure linking management and supervisory staff and labour. The three grades of upper-level supervisory staff must be either university graduates or workers of at least fifteen years experience in the company, while the three lower-level grades must be at least thirty-five years old, or have passed through high school and served at least four years in the company. Workers fall into four categories – from 'regular' workers through probationary and provisional staff to seasonal workers at bottom. In the Japanese context the latter mean generally farmers from poor districts which in winter and spring are deep under snow and where some supplementary income is necessary to make ends meet. Nissan keep these workers heavily segregated, engage regular staff to keep them under surveillance, and house them in barracks-style huts with an allocation of approximately two square metres of space per man. Throughout the year there is a substratum of labour of status clearly beneath the regular workers: after the seasonal workers depart in the spring they are replaced by those just emerging onto the labour market from schools, of whom there is often a rapid turnover; in the summer it is vacation-working students who fill the role.

To remain more than three years at Nissan it is necessary to become either a member of the supervisory staff, at no

1. The following details on the Nissan situation are drawn from the article by Matsuo Kei, 'Nissan Capital: the Domination of Workers by Unions and the Formation of Fascism in the Work Place', *Kozo*, June 1971, and based on a French translation of that article kindly made available to us by Bernard Béraud of Tokyo. Some information has also been taken from *Asahi Journal* of 12 February 1971.

matter how low a level, or a union official (the significance of which is explained below). The criteria for promotion are those of fidelity and obedience to the company and support for its policies. Correct attitudes of mind are heavily emphasized as in the 'Three Elements' movement, for example:

> Responsibility is the worker's backbone, and responsibility rests on (1) doing one's work in depth, (2) doing one's work actively, and (3) doing one's work conscientiously.

The manuals aimed at ideological formation of the workers are sprinkled with expressions like the following:

> After leaving school and finding a place in an enterprise, there comes a time after two or three years when one tires of this work ... But whether pleasant or not one must do the work that one has to do. Perseverance is necessary ... those not worthy of confidence cannot but be dropped by the enterprise.

The factory assembly lines operate virtually non-stop throughout the day, which necessitates frequent overtime work. Even in the case of accidents the Nissan lines only very rarely stop, as the following table indicates.

TABLE TWENTY-NINE Industrial Accidents January–November 1969 (the Seven Automobile Manufacturing Companies)

	Deaths	Permanent Injury	Work Stoppage	Without Stoppage	Total
Nissan	3	19	135	1,559	1,756
Toyota	0	65	66	817	948
Isuzu	0	6	37	380	423
Fuji Juko	0	2	6	404	412
Mitsubishi	1	1	10	318	330
Hino	0	6	12	166	184
Nissan Diesel	0	6	32	128	166
TOTAL	4	105	298	3,812	4,219

While one might think that this general situation presented some scope for activity on the part of the union in Nissan such is certainly not the case. Actually the Nissan union, headed by a major figure in the labour bureaucracy who is also an administrator in the ILO and a Vice-President of Domei, exactly parallels and reinforces the company's supervisory hierarchy, demanding qualifications for union office identical with those required for company posts, preserving the same distinctions, and collaborating enthusiastically with management in rationalization and productivity programmes. The following are passages taken from the handbook distributed to new employees by the union:

> While being a good employee doing your job the most important thing is to be proud of belonging to the Nissan union.
>
> Our goal is stability and prosperity for the enterprise. It is to bring happiness and a better life to those who work here, to offer more advantages to the consumer, and to provide society with always more and better vehicles.
>
> In 19xx turnover increased but profits went down. From the point of view of international competition there are still many ways in which it is necessary to strengthen the system.
>
> To catch up with and to overtake other enterprises in the automobile industry the strengthening of the constitution of our enterprise ought to be the principal theme.

Even on the annual wage increase 'base-up' campaign the union position is 'not to demand unreasonable amounts, to ask for acceptable amounts'. Sohyo is criticized because 'Sohyo demands the unacceptable. Sohyo struggles just for struggle's sake.'

The important role played by this union *on behalf* of management, as watchdog of capital and accomplice in the efficient exploitation of workers, provides both a flashback to the Japanese labour scene of the 1930s and a preview of what a labour force fully co-opted in the interests of the new Japanese imperialism would be like.

As it happens the transformation is not proceeding completely smoothly. In late 1970 and early 1971 the production line was actually stopped in the course of a movement arising from the lowest, unco-opted sectors of the work force. In November 1970, an eighteen-year-old 'probationary' worker was dismissed after taking two weeks off, despite having presented a medical certificate explaining the reasons in advance. A 'Defence Committee' was formed among ex-school friends, young workers and activists (not union men) to begin agitating and leafleting for his reinstatement. Then in January 1971 the management of the Kyoto factory suddenly, and without notice, announced changes in the terms and conditions of work of the seasonal workers employed there. The changes amounted to an effective loss in wages of 4,000 to 6,000 yen ($11 to $14) per month, thus sparking off a revolt among them which soon fused with that over the dismissed worker and began to develop into a comprehensive attack on the enslaving nature of the work process and on the enterprise itself. While unrest at the factory was at its peak, a 'goon squad' of company and union men was got together to beat up the dissidents and intimidate them from further action. This group of thugs became known as the Nissan SS. Uniformed and some 300 in number they represent a refinement in repressive technique over earlier labour troubles in which goon squads or the regular police force have been called in *from outside* to act as strike breakers or to crush radical student movements.

What the eventual outcome will be of these struggles cannot be known. In the case of the seasonal workers Nissan decided that they were 'unstable' and 'lacking in feeling of belonging to the enterprise' and announced in March that they would be employed no longer. They are mentioned here, however, simply as indications of the serious resistance which does exist to the 'rationalization' policies currently being pursued by the management of many Japanese enterprises.

In the JNR (Japan National Railways), to cite one other example which is of a public enterprise, productivity theory, which has been pushed hard in a productivity drive since November 1969, is referred to as a 'philosophy of love'.[1] The campaign stresses the outdatedness of class confrontation and the need for co-operation by all, and even boasts a productivity song, beginning with the line, 'Arise, ye shock troop of reconstruction . . .' It is based on three principles: 'expanded

1. 'Productivity Movement Runs Wild off the Rails', *Asahi Journal*, 15 October 1971, pp. 41–5.

security of employment, co-operation and consultation between workers and management, and fair distribution of the results'. Since the campaign has been under way management has been applying strong pressure on workers to abandon the established reformist unions, National Railway Workers (Kokuro) and Locomotive Men's (Doro), and to join the Railway Workers' Union (Tetsuro). Tetsuro is a supporter of the productivity line, and no doubt the exhortation to join it is powerfully reinforced by the suspicion that the anticipated 110,000 workers to be made redundant in the course of the productivity drive are not likely to be chosen from the ranks of the collaborationist union.

The impression of the extremely widespread nature of this new unionism, fully integrated with management, is strengthened by the findings of a recent survey carried out by the Kansai (Osaka/Kyoto/Kobe area) Productivity HQ, of 258 companies and 260 unions in that area.[1] The findings, announced in July 1971, were that all union offices were held by middle and upper rank employees, that 40 per cent of the supervisory staff (shokusei) had formerly been office bearers in the union, and that union men who became shokusei would then automatically become members of the union committee. Nissan, in which all 118 permanent officials of the union are members of the supervisory staff, is simply one of the most advanced examples of a very widely-based trend in Japanese industry.

Education

The process of reorganization of the Japanese state so that it can more efficiently carry out an imperialist and counter-revolutionary role, and so that opposition forces within Japanese society itself can be either co-opted or suppressed, has considerable ramifications throughout the field of culture. Some of the most vivid illustrations of the growing strength of repressive and reactionary ideology and of the gradual

1. Yamada Koji, op. cit.

abandonment of the façade of 'peace and democracy' on which the postwar Japanese state has supposedly been based, come in the field of education and educational policy.

A determined effort is at present afoot to turn back from the freedoms spelt out in the Fundamental Law of Education (1947), and to impose strict control over the content of teaching materials in schools, especially in subjects like history. The prewar pattern was one of strict state control through a system of licensing of textbooks to ensure the elimination of any 'dangerous thoughts' and to foster the virtues of emperor worship, militarism, imperialism and racism. This is now being revived. Certification of textbooks by the Ministry of Education was continued after the war, supposedly as a temporary expedient till the task could be transferred to elective boards of education. Likewise the 'course of study' prepared by the Ministry was to serve only as a guide to teachers. Yet certification has remained a government prerogative, though till recently very loosely exercised, and the 'course of study', which became binding in 1958, has undergone continuous, retrogressive revision, democratic, pacifistic and scientific elements being gradually whittled away from it.[1] From 1963, when the system of free state supply of textbooks to primary and secondary schools was instituted, further regulation became possible, and since the passage of the Textbook State Control Law of 1966 only those textbooks which are approved by an official Textbook Certification Commission may be published.[2]

Some examples of the kind of revisions, deletions, and amendments to textbooks demanded by the Ministry are indicative of the trend of official thinking. The following relate to texts for use in Middle Schools:

From the treatment of the development of Hokkaido, delete completely 'From the latter Meiji period the Government

1. Ienaga Saburo, 'The Historical Significance of the Japanese Textbook Lawsuit', *BCAS*, vol. 2, no. 4, Fall 1970, pp. 2–12.
2. *Atarashii Nihon Gunkokushugi*, op. cit., pp. 116–17.

strove to expand into Taiwan and Korea, and soon afterwards into the continent.'

On the independence of various Asian countries after World War II, 'the democratic movement was of such strength that it could not be held down' is inappropriate. Change to 'the democratic movement again flourished and presently the mother countries too found it necessary to grant independence.'

In 'civil war broke out between the Republic of China and the Chinese People's Republic' make it clear that two Chinas emerged as a result.

For the 'American occupation of Okinawa' substitute 'administration'.

In the case of the Kuriles write of Soviet 'occupation' not 'administration'.

In treatment of the causes of the Sino–Japanese war it reads as if Japan did something wrong. Mention the wrongs on the other side.

From the Japanese point of view the expression 'invasion of Korea and China' is infelicitous. Change the expression 'invasion'.

The expression 'Japan advanced into Korea' is one-sided. There were wrongs on the other side too. Amend.

The illustrations of 'anti-Japanese slogans' in China are humiliating to the nation. This is a Japanese textbook.

'Sovereignty rests in the people' may cause misunderstanding. Change it.

Avoid any mention of the Emperor's declaration that he is a mere human (and not divine).

The argument about rights to self-defence (forces) is over. Write that war potential for self-defence is not unconstitutional.

Reconsider the point about 'our country, especially in the Pacific war, caused countless suffering and damage to the peoples of Asia'. Since there is also the opinion that the 'Greater East Asian war afforded the opportunity of independence to the peoples of Asia' delete it.

Do not write that there were differences of opinion over foreign policy within the country.

To write about reconsideration of the war is unnecessary since present-day pupils had nothing to do with it. (These) pupils were born long afterwards. The expression 'Japan, together with the Asian and African countries . . .' is too facile, and does not conform to the present situation. The countries of Asia and Africa are underdeveloped.[1]

The current trend of thinking in the Education Ministry emerges clearly enough from directives such as these to make comment on them unnecessary.

In the Japanese courts at present a long and closely contested suit is under appeal in which the constitutional rights and wrongs of such interference by the government are at issue. In July 1970 a District Court in Tokyo held that the Ministry's right to certify textbooks was limited to indicating 'typographical errors, misprints and clear errors of historical fact'. In upholding the complaint of Ienaga Saburo, a Professor of Japanese History at Tokyo University of Education, the court warned against scrutinizing an author's selection of illustrative material or his interpretations and conclusions. The court also held that the state may not require teachers to use any particular textbook in the classroom.[2]

However, after Ienaga's apparent victory in this case, the Director of the Bureau for Primary and Middle School Education in the Ministry of Education issued a directive to all prefectural governors and Directors of Education forcefully reiterating the Ministry's objections to the judgement and stating that no changes of any kind were to be made in the textbook system pending the appeal.[3] This may take years and, given the record of subservience of Japanese higher courts to government policy in the past, it is difficult to see this judgement being sustained at any higher level. Among the specific amendments to his Japanese history textbook that Ienaga is protesting against are the deletion of pictures of war damage, crippled veterans and so on, as giving 'too dark a picture'; of the word 'reckless' as a description of the Pacific war; of the caption 'People as the mainstay of history' from several pictures of peasants and labourers; of statements to the effect

1. From *Hogaku Jiho* (*Law Review*), August 1970, cited in ibid.
2. Ienaga Saburo, op. cit.
3. R. P. Dore, 'Textbook Censorship in Japan: the Ienaga Case', *Pacific Affairs*, vol. 33, no. 4, winter 1970–71, p. 556.

that the legends of the origins of the Imperial House are not historical fact.[1]

The senior official responsible for textbook certification in the Ministry of Education, Murao Jiro, is on record as holding the following opinions on present-day textbooks: 'If I were to give 100 marks to a textbook I had written myself I would give maybe 20 to present-day texts. They are all biassed and ignorant.' In the same interview, to remove any possible doubt about where he stood, Murao added: 'I prefer to be called a rightist. I am an ultra-nationalist (kokusui-shugisha).'[2]

The new school curriculum, announced by the Ministry of Education in March 1971, to be implemented from 1973, contained *inter alia*, the following points:

> General housekeeping becomes compulsory for every girl. The theory and practice of 'everyday manners' will be taught to make girls more genteel and to break the 'trend of argumentativeness'. The making of kimono . . . will be a compulsory subject so that wives 'can at least make their husbands' yukata'. Gymnastics for boys are also to be increased by 22 per cent and kendo and judo are both to be made compulsory.[3]

This is not just a minor reform: it is a viciously reactionary attempt to block social, sexual and political emancipation; and, looked at together with the censorship and political indoctrination referred to above, represents part of a comprehensive attempt to turn back the clock by re-establishing the Japanese education system firmly upon the authoritarian and militaristic principles which were basic to it during that hey-day of ultranationalism, the 1930s.

Environment

Many of the details of the destruction of the Japanese environment through the heedless pursuit by monopoly capital of the

1. Ienaga Saburo, op. cit.
2. *Shukan Asahi*, 1 August 1970, p. 32.
3. *FEER*, 13 March 1971, p. 13. *Yukata* are a kind of loose-fitting robe. Kendo is a form of Japanese sword-fighting, closely associated with militarism.

goals of economic growth, increased GNP and higher rates of profit, are well enough known in the West, if often in a fragmentary way, through the mass media. It should be sufficient here simply to resume some of the main points in this process and to point out their relationship to our overall argument.

So far there have been outbreaks in four different parts of the country of a disease known now as Minamata, after the fishing hamlet where first it appeared. In Minamata itself forty-six villagers were killed and more than seventy paralysed and blinded by mercury poisoning. They had eaten fish and shellfish from local waters into which the Shin Nihon Chisso Fertilizer Co. had been discharging industrial waste which included a heavy concentration of mercury. The first deaths were in 1956; a 1959 report by a special committee within the Welfare Ministry directly linking the disease to mercury discharge was suppressed and the committee dissolved; only in 1968 did the government publicly recognize the connection. By that time the disease had struck in other places too, and since then compensation cases have been under way in various courts. Meanwhile fishermen have to go into deeper and deeper water to get a 'safe' catch; the effluent continues to be discharged into the sea; and sufferers from the disease were beaten up by right-wing toughs hired by the company when they attempted to address their appeal directly to stockholders at the Annual General Meeting of the company. (For the November 1970 meeting 1,000 thugs and gang members were hired by the company for this purpose; likewise in May 1971; and their activities have been widely publicized on television and in the press.)[1]

Cadmium poisoning, which affects the liver and kidneys and agonizingly softens the bones, has claimed more than 100 lives since the early 1950s. The Mitsui Mining and Smelting Company was accused of contaminating large stretches of rice

1. Jonathan Unger, 'Measuring Japan's Misery', *FEER*, 14 August 1971, pp. 32–3; Ui Jun, 'Basic Theory of Kogai', *Ampo*, no. 9–10, 1971, pp. 15–26.

fields and water in Toyama prefecture and of poisoning more than 500 people. After three years of legal action a district court awarded damages amounting to $160,000 to thirty-one victims and their families, and the company lodged notice of appeal. A recent government survey indicated that rice fields were increasingly being contaminated by cadmium.[1]

In Tokyo itself half the residents of the city fear that they will personally fall victim to pollution-related diseases and a startling 65 per cent believe that they will have to wear 'gas masks' in ten or fifteen years' time. In the heavily industrial district of Kawasaki near Tokyo a recent survey found that 10,000 residents suffered from chronic respiratory diseases caused by air pollution, and in May 1971 some 100 cases of a pollution-induced disease affecting the brain – unrecorded elsewhere – were announced from the city hospital. Since the summer of 1970 Tokyo has suffered from recurrent bouts of 'photochemical' smog, during which citizens are advised to stay indoors and to refrain from any unnecessary activity. Legislation supposedly to deal with this problem came into effect in June 1971. By it the Governor can order emergency actions such as factory closures when the smog reaches .5 ppm (parts per million); the smog which hospitalized 4,000 in July 1970 was somewhat less than .3 ppm.[2]

While aerial pollution is intensifying over the great Pacific conurbation into which most of Japan's population is being concentrated, in the country it is the fish and the rice – the two staple foods – which are being poisoned. The belief that waste can be disposed by simply pouring it into the sea persists, and yet the Maritime Safety Agency in June 1970 announced that Japan's coastal waters were on the verge of turning into dead seas. Half of the country's commercial fishing grounds are now unfit for fishing.[3] Yet fish is an absolutely essential part of the Japanese diet: while the average daily consumption of fish in Europe and America is something less than ten grams

1. Ui Jun, op. cit.
2. ibid.
3. ibid.

per person it is over fifty grams in Japan, from which the seriousness of this problem may be understood.[1]

Since mid-1970 citizens' organizations concerned with mounting evidence of the multiform dangers to the environment have mushroomed throughout the country and pollution has become a central political issue. The fact is, however, that pollution is an essential part of the structure of the capitalist economy of Japan. Two examples, adduced by the engineer and leading anti-pollution campaigner Ui Jun, illustrate this. He considers first the pulp and then the steel industries:

> The principal pulp producing countries in the world are six or seven: first, the U.S.A.; second, Canada; and after that Sweden, Finland, the U.S.S.R., and Japan. If we compare these six countries, it is obvious that all these countries except Japan have rich supplies of wood and water. Japan is a country with little wood and water, and with a population density for its habitable land of twenty to a hundred times that of the other countries. Nevertheless, in Japan there are few pulp factories that make any reasonable effort to treat their waste. The most blatant example is Fuji City, where the big factories have been located right in the middle of the crowded city, and not one of them is making any attempt to treat its waste. There has been no objection, and so it has been possible to locate the factories there and develop the 'rapidly expanding economy'. In other countries it has been a matter of common sense that 10–20% of the productive facilities are necessarily directed to treatment of waste so that it does not do severe harm to the fish. In Japan they can use that 10–20% for production . . . So Japan is ranked among the world's first six pulp-producers, where it has no business being.
>
> Someone might object that the pulp industry is not a principal industry. So let me talk about an industry which anyone would agree is central: the steel industry.
>
> Steel engineers say that the most important factor in the rapid recovery and modernization of Japan's post-war steel industry has been the Oxygen LD furnace. We are familiar with the multicolored smoke that comes from the chimneys of steel mills,

1. Ui Jun, 'Ui Jun Report', *Asahi Journal*, 1 October 1971, pp. 14–17.

which is a necessary product of this LD furnace. In Europe or the U.S.A. this kind of furnace cannot be used unless its smoke is cleaned in a dust collector. But if this dust collector is taken into account, the LD furnace is not particularly cheap. This dust collector and the necessary connecting ducts are several times larger than the furnace itself. Of course we cannot judge their cost just from their size, but they cost at least 30% of the whole setup . . . and the small furnace itself is already very expensive. In Japan it has been possible to operate this furnace without the cooling duct and dust collector. Thus the steel companies in Japan have profited some 30% on each furnace, a profit which can be turned to more profit, and so on.[1]

Ui concludes that Kogai – pollution – is not just a side effect or a distortion of rapid economic growth, but that, along with low wages and protection, it is a vital factor in it. This makes it easier to understand why Japanese government and industry are unable to conceive of any solution to the problem. An Environment Agency was recently set up but no action against *big* business can be expected from that quarter. Rather the kind of thing that is likely to recur is action against public bath houses for the smoke they produce, or, as in a recent case in Kyoto, against traditional pottery works because of smoke from the kiln.[2] The difficulties big business faces will come largely from increased awareness and organized opposition on the part of the long-suffering people. This is undoubtedly intensifying, as indicated for one thing by the reaction to the Aomori development plan.[3]

Throughout the country there are some 1,000 cases of local citizens' groups recently formed to fight the destruction of their environment, and, as the *Asahi Shimbun* has noted, they 'have a strong revolutionary tendency similar to peasants' risings'.[4] Yet the response by industry is not to rethink the concepts of growth and GNP, and, more importantly, profit, but rather to set about shifting their difficult and dirty enter-

1. 'Basic Theory of Kogai', *Ampo*, no. 9–10, p. 18.
2. ibid.
3. See 'Agriculture' section above.
4. *FEER*, 22 January 1972, p. 23.

prises to areas where opposition to them will certainly be quickly put down – as spelt out in the Yatsugi memorandum discussed above.[1] As part of foreign 'aid' programmes they will be exported to places like Korea, Taiwan, Thailand and so on.

Apart from this move to shift the location of offensive industries, there is also a notable tendency for companies, in difficulties because of complaints over environmental pollution, to contribute heavily to LDP funds, in the belief that this is the best insurance against any effective restraint of their activities. Only a small proportion of political party contributions in Japan is ever made public, but of that, in the case of the Sato faction in the LDP, the three main sources in 1969–70 were: first, three colour television companies under attack for price rises; second, a number of companies engaged in pollution controversies; third, private railway companies that had just implemented substantial fare increases.[2] Thus, although various anti-pollution measures are passed through the Diet, 'Premier Sato has yet to demonstrate any enthusiasm for enforcement, presumably for fear of alienating big business contributors to his party'.[3]

OKINAWA

Okinawa has to be considered here both because it is a special case of U.S.–Japan relationships and because it raises questions very relevant to other sections of this work – Japan and South-East Asia, the military, and the Japanese domestic situation.

Japan and the U.S.A. first 'joined hands' in Okinawa in the fighting of March to June 1945, some of the fiercest of the whole Pacific war. A lot of people died in the process – far more of them non-combatant Okinawan civilians than soldiers

1. *Mainichi Shimbun*, 26 December 1970.
2. ibid.
3. *Time*, 12 April 1971.

of either side.[1] The Okinawan people were caught then in the crossfire between the defeated Imperial Japanese armies, returning broken from their attempts to impose imperial rule on South-East Asia, and those of the United States, embarking, though few may then have thought of it that way, on their greatest imperial expansionist phase in Asia since 1898, when they had seized and laid waste to the Philippines. Now the Okinawan people are caught again, this time in a different crossfire, as the retreating U.S. and the advancing Japanese armies prepare to join forces in a determined effort to suppress popular and revolutionary movements throughout the region.

Okinawa's experience of Japan began with the dispatch of an expedition to punish the islands, then an independent kingdom, for their tardy response to a Japanese request for troops to join in the Hideyoshi-led expedition against Korea at the end of the sixteenth century. Thereafter a continuous, and on the Okinawan side continuously unhappy, relationship persisted, alongside the ongoing relationship of tribute and trade with China, until 1879, when Japanese troops were again dispatched, this time to see to the severance of the long tie with China and to effect the firm incorporation of Okinawa within the burgeoning Meiji state system. The consolidated state moved on quickly from this step to swallow up Korea and Taiwan, and to make its fatal moves against China and South-East Asia. Okinawans were always amongst the lowest of the Emperor's subjects – their culture, language and tradition thoroughly suppressed – the poorest of all Japanese Prefectures. In the last days of the Pacific war whole villages were put to the sword since food supplies would not support both the Imperial forces and a local population as well.[2]

Okinawa's experience of the United States began in 1945, from which date it was ruled as, in effect, a U.S. colony,

1. Okinawan civilian deaths were 160,000, as against 12,520 U.S.A. soldiers, and 110,000 Japanese soldiers (which figure also included many Okinawan conscripts) *Ampo*, no. 7–8, p. 14.

2. ibid. (historical essay on Okinawa). Also Mark Selden, 'Okinawa and American Colonialism', *BCAS*, vol. 3, no. 1, 1971, pp. 51–63.

governed by an American general, based on the dollar, occupied by legions of troops. The best land was confiscated and turned into bases, and the traditional livelihood of the people destroyed, so that the economy has become a typically colonial one-crop one – and the crop is war.

Forty-four per cent of the arable land (14.8 per cent of the land surface) has been converted into bases; one sixth of the entire work force is employed by the military.[1] The base complex, occupied by some 45,000 U.S. troops, has been to the U.S.A.' the Keystone of the Pacific': source of bombing raids against Indochina; location of major depots for nuclear, gas and chemical and bacteriological weapons supply, and of guerrilla warfare schools in realistic Asian conditions; convenient surveillance and spying post against China and North Korea, and important staging post for dry-run exercises in counter-revolutionary warfare in Korea or elsewhere in Asia.[2] Precisely because it has been a colony, not subject to 'interference', Okinawa has been the prize possession of the American military.

The million 'indigenous personnel' have provided a useful supply of cheap labour, both directly on the bases and indirectly as servants, prostitutes and the like, to be engaged as such in the grand design, but that usefulness has weighed progressively less heavily in the balance against the difficulties of keeping them sufficiently repressed and downtrodden as to be amenable. A Ryukyuan Diet, with Chief Executive etc., has existed, but with no jurisdiction over Americans and little power otherwise. Till 1968 the Chief Executive was a direct U.S. nominee. Thereafter the left candidate, Yara Chobyo, who has filled the post by election since, has foundered in efforts to win concessions from either the U.S.A. or Japan

1. ibid., p. 57. There are 40,000 base workers. But, as Selden points out, 'this is but a fraction of those forced to live off the American presence. There are an estimated 15,000 to 25,000 prostitutes and bar girls, more than 10,000 maids employed by servicemen alone . . . Tens of thousands of others work in the wide range of subsidiary industries and services which cater to American pleasures.'

2. See, for example, *Newsweek*, 30 August 1965.

(removal of poison gas, nuclear weapons or B-52s from the one; aid, non-militaristic reversion from the other), while he has had to try to quench the popular movement from which he sprang.

After considerable Japanese pressure, and in the context of the Nixon doctrine, the U.S.A. agreed, in November 1969, to the 'return' of Okinawa to Japan. The document announcing agreement in principle on the return, which is discussed elsewhere in this book, stressed the Japanese side's recognition of the invaluable role the U.S. forces in the Far East had played hitherto in promoting the peace of the region, and committed the Japanese to see the defence of Korea, Taiwan and South-East Asia as 'essential' or 'very important' to their own security, and to effect the return of Okinawa in such a way as not to prejudice '. . . the United States' efforts to assure the South Vietnamese people the opportunity to determine their own political future without outside interference'.[1] Premier Sato elaborated on this in his address to the National Press Club in Washington after signing these agreements with Nixon, when he emphasized that '. . . in the real international world it is impossible to adequately maintain the security of Japan without international peace and security in the Far East'.

The meaning of this apparently innocuous statement had to be spelt out for the Senate Foreign Relations Committee in January 1970, by U. Alexis Johnson, Under Secretary for Political Affairs and former Ambassador to Japan:

> Hitherto the Japanese Government, the Japanese people in general, have tended to take the attitude that their security arrangements with the United States had significance only in so far as the security of Japan itself was concerned. That Japan was not interested in nor concerned with the security of other areas nor should it in any way get involved with security of other areas. . . . What they are saying here for the first time is that they recognize that the security of Japan cannot be separated from that of Korea, Taiwan, and our obligations elsewhere in the

1. For the text of this important document, see Appendix III.

area and, thus, in looking at the question of our bases and our facilities in Japan, they will look at it in terms of the security of the whole area rather than in the security just of Japan itself . . . it represented a quite new stage of thinking in Japan.[1]

In other words, with U.S.–Japan unanimity on basic policy towards Asia, 'return' of Okinawa could be contemplated in Washington without any qualms. While negotiations on 'return' went ahead so did plans to extend U.S. port facilities at Oura, which is the main base for Polaris and Poseidon submarines;[2] plans were announced for $60mill. extensions to Kadena Airport to continue to 1976;[3] and, on 16 March 1970, it was actually revealed to Congress that the logistical centre for all U.S. troops in the entire Pacific, South-Eastern and North-Eastern Asian areas was to be moved to Okinawa.[4]

Recently, with the signing of the Reversion Agreement in June 1971, and its ratification in November 1971, further details of the deal became clear. Of greatest interest is the fact that, of the total of 145 bases at present in Okinawa, no less than eighty-eight are not being returned at all, and no major U.S. units will be withdrawn; twelve of the remaining bases will be taken over by Japanese troops and thirty-four will be 'de-activated'. Japanese studies have established that the area actually returned will be less than 5,000 square metres, of which 75 per cent is not even base land but land held on one-year leases by the United States, some of which has already been abandoned, the rest apartment buildings, a gas tank and so on. U.S. bases, in short, will be reduced from their

1. Hearings before the Sub-committee on U.S. Security Agreements and Commitments abroad of the Committee on Foreign Relations, U.S. Senate, 91st Congress, 2nd Session, 26–29 January 1970, *U.S. Security Agreements and Commitments Abroad – Japan and Okinawa*, p. 1,162.

2. Koji Nakamura, 'Ryukyus: Anguish of Doubt', *FEER*, no . 1, 1971.

3. *New York Times*, 5 July 1970; *Asahi Evening News*, 20 August 1970.

4. *Ampo*, no. 7–8, p. 36.

present 14.8 per cent of total land surface to 12.3 per cent.[1] And as U.S. Commander General Chapman put it: 'Even after the return of Okinawan administrative rights I am of the opinion that we can freely take operational actions in order to protect the common interests of Japan and the United States.'[2]

Secondly, it is notable that for return of these 'administrative rights' and facilities Japan is to pay the United States the sum of $320mill.[3]

Thirdly, the significance of the entry into Okinawa of Japanese troops ('Self-Defence Forces') needs to be understood. It is necessary to look at their numbers, composition and role. In June 1970 the Defence Agency first announced that '3,000 to 4,000' troops would be sent; in October the figure of 3,300 was decided upon; in March 1971 it was amended to 3,100 within six months of 'return' and a total of 6,100 within one and a half years; by the time the text of the Reversion Agreement was settled in May 1971, the figure was 6,800.[4] It seems reasonable to assume that the anti-

1. The documents pertaining to the return are notably (and understandably) obscure on what is and what is not to be returned. They actually list only 109 bases in all, but include all of the twelve to be turned over to the Japanese forces, and some of the thirty-four to be de-activated, among the eighty-eight to be retained by the U.S.A.! A number of Japanese correspondents have examined the figures and generally agreed on the figures given here, see *Asahi Journal*, 22 October 1971, p. 95; Miyagi Zensho, 'Okinawa Crushed by Bases', *Sekai*, August 1971, pp. 89–95; 'Problem Points in the Okinawa "Return" Agreement', by the editorial staff, *Sekai*, November 1971, pp. 105–23 at p. 113.

2. At Okinawan Press Conference, 21 January 1971 quoted *Asahi Journal*, 22 October 1971, p. 54 (translated back from the Japanese).

3. Clause 7 of the Reversion Agreement. See Nakano Yoshio, 'The Okinawa Reversion Agreement and its Surrounding Circumstances', *Sekai*, August 1971, pp. 10–15.

4. Sasaki Ryuji, Shinzato Keiji and Toyama Shigeki, 'The Present Condition of Japanese Nationalism: Criticisms on the "Reversion" of Okinawa', *Rekishigaku Kenkyu* (*Historical Research*), no. 377, October 1971, pp. 40–60. The Tokyo government has stated that Okinawa will be treated exactly the same as the mainland; but it should be noted that the proportion of troops to population on Okinawa will be nearly three times the national average.

American riots of December 1970 in Koza city and the obvious deterioration in relations between the U.S. military and the local population has had something to do with this expansion. At any rate, the Japanese military are obviously delighted and their taste for expansion has been whetted by moves into Tiaoyu. Their equipment in Okinawa will include anti-submarine reconnaissance planes, F-104s, mine-sweepers, Nike and Hawk missiles, and many facilities – training grounds etc. – will be shared with the United States. With some 45,000 American troops presumably well able to take care of any possible invasion of the islands from outside, the role expected of Japanese troops might seem puzzling. A spokesman from the Defence Agency, however, in the *Mainichi Shimbun* of 1 May 1970, is quoted as follows: 'The Self-Defence Forces will perform mainly counter-insurgency functions.'[1] It is preferable, in other words, for the Okinawan people's struggle against the bases to be put down by Japanese rather than American troops.

At the same time, as described above in the section on the military, they will fill in the gaps in the U.S. naval and aerial reconnaissance and patrol network in the eastern Pacific region in overall subordination to U.S. strategic planning.

Fourthly, the agreement conspicuously fails to state that Okinawa will be returned to Japan 'nuclear-free', i.e. under the same terms as are supposed to have applied to Japan itself. For obvious reasons the nuclear issue is one that excites powerful emotions in Japan and for years the conservative government has sought ways to break down what Sato has apologized for as a 'peculiar' attitude: thus the enormous

1. It appears that the American side in the negotiations brought pressure to bear to have the Japanese commitment to the defence of U.S.A. bases spelt out specifically in the Reversion Agreement. The Japanese pleaded the embarrassing domestic consequences of this and the agreement – 'Arrangement concerning the assumption by Japan of the responsibility for the immediate defence of Okinawa' was announced instead at the meeting of the Japan–United States Security Treaty Consultative Council meeting on 29 June (Miyagi Zensho, *Sekai*, August 1971, pp. 89–95).

expansion within Japan of all conventional armaments, and the promotion, against strong opposition, of visits by nuclear submarines and aircraft carriers. The return of Okinawa, a nuclear base with both B-52s and Polaris bases, is seen as useful in helping to undermine further this 'pathological' Japanese hatred of nuclear weapons. The treatment of the nuclear issue in the public diplomatic record has been extraordinarily obscure and ambiguous. In the joint Sato–Nixon Communiqué of 1969 it was stated (paragraph 8):

> The Prime Minister [Sato] described in detail the particular sentiment of the Japanese people against nuclear weapons and the policy of the Japanese government reflecting such sentiment. The President [Nixon] expressed his deep understanding and assured the Prime Minister that, without prejudice to the position of the U.S.A. government with respect to the prior consultation system under the Treaty of Mutual Co-operation and Security, the reversion of Okinawa would be carried out in a manner consistent with the policy of the Japanese government as described by the Prime Minister.

Then in paragraph 7 of the Reversion Treaty (which oddly enough deals with financial provisions) it is stated that the reversion will be carried out 'not in contradiction' with this understanding. However, even if the weapons were once withdrawn, and Premier Sato has admitted that there is no way the Japanese side could verify whether they had been or not – 'All we can do is to trust the U.S.' – requests to reintroduce them could be made any time under the 'prior consultations' clause; Sato promised, at the National Press Club in Washington in November 1969, that he would deal with such requests in a 'positive manner'. Furthermore, there were clear intimations during the visit of Secretary of Defense Laird to Japan in June 1971 that the Nixon doctrine called for the nuclearization not only of Okinawa but of Japan proper as well.[1]

1. Nakano Yoshio, op. cit.; *Ampo*, no. 7–8, p. 30; *Ampo*, no. 11, p. 17.

Later assurances that Okinawa would be returned nuclear-free – by Secretary Rogers to the Senate Foreign Relations Committee in October 1971, and in the joint communiqué issued after the San Clemente meeting of Nixon and Sato in January 1972 – have consequently to be taken at rather less than their face value. They are regarded in Okinawa with outright disbelief and in Japan with profound scepticism.

Finally, there is the broader sense in which the conservative administration clearly hopes to use the Okinawan 'return' to change public opinion. In his 1969 National Press Club speech Sato referred to the Okinawa issue as a 'mental block' for the Japanese people, and as a 'symbol of defeat'.[1] The choice of words is revealing. By calling Okinawa a symbol of defeat rather than of imperialism and war he was actually saying that war is not so bad in itself; what is bad is losing. By getting Okinawa back he hoped to give the Japanese people a small taste of what it would be like to win. The first seizure of Okinawa in 1879 can be seen as the first step in Japanese imperial expansion, which led into Korea, China and South-East Asia. Clearly Sato wanted to interpret the present return of Okinawa in a similar way, as a symbol of national strength, as something to whet the nationalist appetite. While Sato rhapsodized about the 'new Pacific age' that the occasion symbolized, his then Defence Minister, Nakasone Yasuhiro, spoke as follows:

> The return of our Okinawan brothers and the unification of the nation must be cause for a spiritual maelstrom among the people. We may expect a newer nationalism to well up strongly, and a ground swell to emerge such as has not been known in the spiritual history of our people since the war . . .[2]
>
> It is not necessarily so that the postwar period is over. There is still the problem of improving again on General MacArthur. The constitution is a large part of that, and it is only to be

1. *Ampo*, no. 7–8, p. 33.
2. Miyagi Zensho, op. cit. Address to graduating students of the Self-Defence Forces Officer Cadet School in Fukuoka Prefecture, 21 June 1971.

expected that it will be re-examined after the return of a million of our brothers to the motherland.[1]

The question of constitutional revision is treated elsewhere in this work. The subject of the 'million brothers', however, calls for more comment at this point. What has been the nature of their experience under U.S. occupation in the past and what is it likely to be like under joint U.S.–Japan occupation in future? To General James B. Lampert, U.S. Administrator of Okinawa: 'The typical Ryukyuan is an extremely likeable, friendly, unsophisticated person. We (Americans) travel around freely in Okinawa, to the cities and markets and so on, and we do live and work in a friendly environment.'[2] One would hardly realize, reading Lampert's impressions, that Okinawa has been shaken by a series of massive popular protest movements, anti-American riots and general strikes over the past few years, and that the experience of those years has bred a considerable political sophistication into the 'typical Ryukyuan'.

To take a few examples. In Koza city, which lies just outside the highly strategic Kadena Airbase, some 10,000 citizens took to the streets to fight with the U.S. military, storming the gates of the base and burning eighty American cars in the process, after an incident on 20 December 1970, in which a car driven by an American serviceman ran over and injured an Okinawan outside the base and the military police immediately released the culprit.[3] Police statistics show that of the average 1,000 crimes committed annually by GIs in Okinawa, (and therefore outside Okinawan jurisdiction), only in 1 or 2 per

1. Ise Hidekazu, 'Harbinger of the 4th Defence Plan System: the Dispatch of the SDF to Okinawa and the Opposition to the Military', *Asahi Journal*, 23 July 1971, pp. 4–9.

2. *U.S. Security Agreements and Commitments Abroad – Japan and Okinawa*, op. cit., p. 1,307.

3. *Ampo*, no. 7–8, pp. 1–5; the Koza incident followed hard on the heels of a not-guilty verdict in the case of a GI who ran over and killed an Okinawan housewife; tempers frayed as the U.S.A. continued to stall on the removal of poison gas from the islands (Selden, op. cit., p. 58).

cent is the culprit punished.[1] Ten days after the Koza incident, at Kunigami in northern Okinawa, farmers invaded a Marine artillery range, drove away the troops guarding it, and succeeded in preventing the scheduled firing practice.[2] In March 1965, 100 Middle School students were injured in the course of poison gas war exercises conducted by the 173rd Brigade.[3] In July 1968, 237 Primary School students from a Naha school suddenly turned bright red and swelled up agonizingly when they went swimming; they were presumably affected by materials which had leaked from the nearby U.S. army fuel dump.[4] At about the same time farmers from near the town of Gushikawa reported finding frogs of strange colours and with anywhere between three and eleven legs. No definitive cause was ever established, but nearby was a section of the 267th Chemical Squad, specialists in chemical and bacteriological warfare,[5] and the Okinawans drew their own conclusions. In November 1968, Professors Hattori of Rikkyo University and Michiie of Tokyo University announced findings of cobalt 60 in the waters of Naha harbour in the vicinity of the nuclear submarine base; the same material was later found also in the fish, and following the Japanese reports the Americans admitted the fact, but announced that the cobalt was in such small quantities as to present no danger.[6] In 1971 a bar hostess was murdered by a serviceman in February and another in March with no arrests made. *Sekai* reported in August that incidents of rape, murder and injury were occurring this year at a rate of three per day, generally with impunity.[7]

As all of these incidents involved, or are believed to have

1. Yü Yi-ch'ien, *Jih-pen chen-hsiang*, Hong Kong, 1971, translated into Japanese as *Nihon no Razo* (*Japan Unmasked*), Tokyo, 1971, pp. 210–11.
2. *Ampo*, no. 7–8, p. 6.
3. Yü Yi-ch'ien, op. cit., p. 204.
4. ibid., pp. 197–200.
5. ibid., pp. 201–4; *Ampo*, no. 7–8, p. 40.
6. Yü Yi-ch'ien, op. cit., pp. 192–6.
7. Fukugi Akira, 'The Day of the Signing of the Okinawa Reversion Agreement', *Sekai*, August 1971, pp. 75–85.

involved, the American military, it might be thought that Okinawans would have no particular reason to oppose the dispatch of Japanese military to their islands in future. This would be a very mistaken view. Public opinion polls taken by the *Ryukyo Shimpo* newspaper show that while 31 per cent of Okinawans opposed the stationing of Japanese troops in Okinawa in October 1970, that percentage had grown to 47.4 per cent in June 1971 (after the signing of the agreement), and to 56 per cent by late August 1971 (as against 35, 16 and 22 per cent respectively in favour). Only 15 per cent of Okinawans believed in August 1971 what the Japanese government was saying about the return being effected nuclear-free and with mainland level restrictions on the bases, and only 13 per cent thought the opinions of Okinawans had been adequately taken into account in working out the terms of reversion.[1] The meaninglessness of 'reversion' has evidently been well understood on Okinawa itself, and the massive struggles of 1971 – the base workers strike of February and the general strikes of May and November – reflect a mature opposition to militarism in all its forms. Where the main demands of 1969 and 1970 were for removal of nuclear and poisonous weapons and for protection of the livelihood of base workers, in 1971 they were 'take away the bases' and 'keep out the Self-Defence Forces'.[2]

The immediate future prospects for Okinawa are far from bright. Militarily the signs are clear enough. On the day of the signing of the reversion agreement in May 1971, Nationalist Chinese navy men were in port about to proceed to Korea to take part in manoeuvres to complete their course graduation, while in northern Okinawa Japanese and Korean officers were taking part in U.S. exercises, practising assaults initiated from landing craft dropped from jets.[3] Economically, too, the pattern is clear enough. Both American and Japanese money

1. Polls of October 1970, and June 1971, cited in Sasaki Ryuji *et al.*, op. cit. Poll of late August cited in Uema Seiyu, 'Bearer of History', *Asahi Journal*, 22 October 1971, pp. 10–13.

2. See especially Fukugi Akira, 'The Okinawan General Strike of May 19th', *Sekai*, July 1971, pp. 128–36; *Ampo* for earlier strikes.

3. Fukugi Akira, 'The Day of the Signing . . .', op. cit.

are pouring into Okinawa, but that is no reason for the people to rejoice.

Caught between two economic giants, the plight of the Okinawans was highlighted in the late summer of 1971 by the then *de facto* devaluation of the dollar against the yen. *The Times* of 30 August 1971 estimated that this would inflict a loss of about 30,000 million yen (some $97mill.) on the Okinawan people. In the forty days between 15 August and 8 October when the Japanese government finally reacted to the fierce agitation of the Okinawans by agreeing to indemnify some of the losses on the new conversion rate, commodity price rises, in percentages, were as follows: instant coffee, 15.3; tomato ketchup, 18.3; sugar, 12.5; chicken, 33; tuna fish, 20; cheese, 16.7; tangerines, 16.7; apples, 33.3; butter, 50.[1] In Tokyo, or indeed in many places, such staggering increases might well have caused a riot.

Even the belated measures announced by the government in October were far from answering the Okinawans' need. Private savings accounts were converted at the 'old' rate and $ notes were likewise accepted for exchange at the 'old' rate for one day in October; but for all other losses, against which the Okinawan government claimed the figure mentioned above – $97mill. – Tokyo responded by offering $3.2mill. (¥1,000mill.). Applications for compensation from this fund – which is supposed to cover the case of food importers and the like – are hedged with infinite bureaucratic complexity and the amount paid out, to December 1971, was a paltry $14,791 against twelve claims, out of a total demand for $2.7mill. in 2,173 claims. For most Okinawans a steep fall in income and in living standards is inevitable. The $50mill. price received for their crops by pineapple and sugar cane farmers in February 1972, for example, fell outside the scope of the relief measures, so that the 90,000 farmers concerned suffered a loss of some $8mill. (¥2,500mill.), or more than double the total

1. Survey by the Women's Section of Okinawan Base Workers' Union, reported in Ichiizumi Chieii, 'The Return which is not a Return', *Asahi Journal*, 22 October 1971, pp. 100–106.

compensation offered by the government.[1] Workers' losses were no more part of Tokyo's concern than were those of the farmers and, on 6 March 1972, some 50,000 Okinawan workers went on strike to demand that their wages in dollars be converted into yen at the old rate of 360 yen to the dollar.[2]

As for the inflow of U.S. capital into Okinawa, the rationale behind this is to be found in the notion that Japan had always exercised 'residual sovereignty' over the islands. Thus the investment was not only a safe and attractive one in itself but also a backway around the various barriers on capital investment which had applied to Japan proper, a *fait accompli* which would mean the opening of the whole Japanese market to such investments upon reversion.

As of 30 June 1969, total American investment in Okinawa, *excluding* banking, insurance and airlines, came to $229,254,000 – out of a total of $240,055,000 'foreign' (i.e., including Japanese) investment. Japanese investment came to a mere $8mill. as of that date, concentrated in sugar refining, hotels and canning. U.S. interests dominate in the colony's banking: both the Bank of America and American Express are powerful institutions, and the U.S. Administration holds more than 50 per cent of the capital in the official Ryukyu Bank. But the main American interest is in oil: some 95 per cent of all American investment was in this one sector in June 1969: $217mill. out of the $229,254,000 total. Four firms are involved: Gulf, Caltex, Esso and Kaiser Cement. This investment, writes *Ampo*, 'overshadows the remainder of the American economic stake and suggests important dimensions of the struggle not only for Okinawa but for entry into lucrative Japanese markets. In establishing refineries in Okinawa shortly before its reversion to Japan, these companies seek a springboard to Japan and a means to evade tight Japanese restrictions on foreign-controlled enterprise.'[3]

1. Fukugi Akira, 'Okinawa: Changeover to Yen Economy', *Sekai*, February 1972, pp. 197–205.

2. *Le Monde*, 8 March 1972.

3. *Ampo*, no. 5, p. 9. As of June 1971, 54 per cent of foreign (then including Japanese) enterprises in Okinawa were American, and

The pattern of linking of major sectors of Japanese and American capital that has since emerged in this sector is also suggestive of overall trends. Esso, which now has a refinery capable of producing 80,000 barrels a day, was to tie up with General Sekiyu and Sumitomo Chemical, while Gulf Oil, which is building a refinery with a capacity of 100,000 barrels a day, was to link with Toho Oil and Mitsubishi Chemicals. They will export 30,000 to 40,000 barrels to Korea, 20,000 to 30,000 to Japan proper, leaving 120,000 to satisfy Okinawan demand, and, incidentally, Japanese producers will be excluded from refining any oil at all in Okinawa.[1] Gulf has even been granted a yen loan to the tune of 5,000 million yen to aid in construction of its refinery.[2]

The pattern of planned 'development' is thus of oil, petrochemicals and aluminium[3] in giant, industrial complexes along the Okinawan coastline which, with their effluvia, will poison the fish, the sugar cane and other crops, and force the population into even more restricted enclaves wedged between them and the bases, and which, while earning considerable profits for investors far away, will deprive the islanders of any livelihood but that of wage labour in a sterile, sooty, polluted and militarized slum.

---

certainly the largest sums invested – $60mill. by Gulf, $100mill. each by Esso, Kaiser and Alcoa, meant absolute American control of key sectors. The largest Japanese sums were a total of $250mill. by Japan Light Metals and four other companies (Ichiizumi Chieii, op. cit.).

1. *Tokyo Stock Journal*, 8 November 1971.
2. ibid., 13 November 1971.
3. An aluminium smelter is to be installed in Okinawa by five Japanese companies at a cost of $292mill. (*JEJ*, no. 476, p. 4).

Chapter 7

CONCLUSION

JAPAN'S RELATIONSHIP WITH THE UNITED STATES

Although the United States is in the grip of a severe economic crisis, it is still the biggest economy in the world and U.S. imperialism cannot be taken lightly. Moreover, the U.S.A., through the so-called Security Treaty, has a politico–military relationship with Japan which is not comparable to that which it has with, say, Western Europe through Nato. The Security Treaty gives America powers approximating to those of an occupation, as top Washington leaks have recently been emphasizing.[1] Furthermore, up until May 1972, the U.S.A. was in fact occupying a part of Japan as a colony and was able to use its hold on Okinawa as a bargaining counter in economic, political and military negotiations (and, by hanging on to so many installations in the Ryukyus probably can go on doing so for some time).

Certain aspects of the U.S.A.–Japan relationship have already been outlined. Here we shall try to resume briefly the overall relationship.

1. An unnamed White House source, who is unofficially acknowledged to be either Nixon or Kissinger, has at least twice recently stated that one of the purposes of the Security Treaty is to prevent the resurgence of Japanese militarism. A correct emphasis on the dangers of reviving Japanese militarism risks obscuring the fact that it is the U.S.A. which has largely structured the re-militarization of Japan, and which remains *dominant* in Japanese military actions. The Japanese army is considerably more subordinate to the U.S.A. than is, say, the West German army.

Investment. American investment in Japan, as noted above, was, until recently, nearly ten times the size of Japanese investment in the U.S.A.; it was still six and a half times as big in 1970.

Trade. At present Japan depends on the U.S.A. for about 30 per cent of its trade: in 1970 Japan sent 33.7 per cent of its exports to the U.S.A., and took 34.4 per cent of its imports from there (as against only figures of 28.2 and 28 per cent, respectively, for the whole of Asia and the Middle East). The U.S.A., on the other hand, sent only 14.7 per cent of its exports to, and took 10.8 per cent of its imports from, Japan in 1970.[1] Moreover, quite apart from the fact that Japan is much more dependent on international trade than the U.S.A., there is a significant difference in the structure of each country's exports to the other. In 1970, 72 per cent of Japan's sales to America were heavy and chemical industry products; 24 per cent were light industrial products, and a mere 4 per cent were raw materials. Of the U.S.A.'s exports to Japan in the same year, 58 per cent were made up of foodstuffs and raw materials, 7 per cent of chemicals, and 25 per cent of machines, instruments, etc. In other words, the relationship was not unlike that of an industrialized (Japan) to an underdeveloped (U.S.A.) country.

In 1971 Japan ran a fairly large trading surplus with the United States – more than $2 billion, which accounted for about 30 per cent of Japan's total trading surplus for the year.[2] The United States government, as is well known, counteracted sharply in a number of ways. These can, roughly, be broken down into two groups: measures to restrict Japanese imports into the United States, and measures to increase American penetration of Japan.

The most publicized protectionist measures by the Nixon Administration have been connected with textiles. In order to

1. *JEJ*, no. 476, 8 February 1972. Information below from same.

2. The 1972 trading surplus was forecast at about $3 billion by Treasury Secretary Connally in January (*The Times*, 10 January 1972). See below (p. 247) for later estimates.

repay his political debt to Strom Thurmond, Nixon went down the line to impose a particularly harsh and stupid programme restricting textile imports from the major South-East Asian producers: five-year agreements were imposed on Hong Kong, Taiwan and South Korea, and a three-year agreement on Japan, pegging increases in detail, by type of product, to tiny amounts per annum. By this deal, Nixon paid off Thurmond and his southern textile backers and, at the same time, undercut Wallace and Wilbur Mills. The textile fight, which was of little economic importance to the United States, was a striking indication of the fact that the United States still calls the shots for Japan when the chips are down. The textile industry is economically and politically extremely powerful inside Japan (even though it is a declining industry): but it failed to get the terms of the agreement modified in the slightest way. In the end the Sato regime was simply obliged to let some 300,000 people be thrown out of work – although the government did mobilize a sizeable sum of money for emergency relief for the industry.[1]

Other commodities are in fact of much greater economic importance to the Americans: steel, cars, TV sets, for example. The Americans wheeled out a veritable arsenal of countermeasures, ranging from special credit schemes for domestic producers, to tax rebates, tariffs, quotas and even the threat of employing the Trading With the Enemy Act to repel Japanese goods.[2] As a result, the Japanese agreed first to

1. After the voluntary restrictions programme came into effect on 1 July 1971, the Tokyo government allotted ¥75,100mill. relief for the textile industry; after revaluation a further ¥127,800mill. (£158mill.) was set aside for the industry. On the textile dispute cf. Jon Halliday, 'Washington *v.* Tokyo', *NLR*, no. 67, 1971, and references there.

2. This is a law dating from the First World War, and originally resuscitated to prevent private American interests investing abroad against the U.S. government's wishes. The textile dispute with Japan was the first time it had been evoked in such a context – with predictable results (*The Times*, 28 September 1971; cf. *International Herald Tribune*, 6 October 1971 for a sober American assessment of the damage done by such a move). At a U.S.–Japanese business

'voluntary restrictions' in, for example, steel exports. Then, of course, the Americans hit them with the 10 per cent surcharge, and finally with the forced revaluation of the yen.

America would like not only to cut down Japanese exports to the States; it would also like to increase U.S. exports to Japan, and American investment in Japan. The recent economic dispute between the two countries was usually referred to exclusively as a trade war, whereas it was also an investment war. American capital desperately needs to invest in areas where it can restore its badly depleted profit margins: during the recent American recession, it has only been investment in the EEC (which kept growing faster than the U.S.A.) which kept many American companies going. Japan is still the fastest growing capitalist economy in the world, and it is only natural that American capital is very much attracted to it. The various car projects referred to above are only the most reported of many such attempts at penetration. In the crucial field of video-cassettes, for example, the giant 3-M Corporation has already done a deal with Sony. Until very recently Japan kept very tight controls over foreign capital coming into Japan. In the car sector, for example, maximum foreign participation was restricted to 35 per cent for a number of years ahead. In other existing industries the ceiling was 50 per cent[1] – although in new industries it was set at 100 per cent. Other restrictions on the repatriation of capital contributed to keeping foreign interests out of Japan in most sectors,

gathering in Hawaii in September 1971, the American side handed round the lyrics from a southern ballad, *The Import Blues*; a laid-off racist mill-hand laments: 'Now the people of Jay-pan have it made./ They make cheap-john goods in a sleazy style.' Even his wife, he complains, wears minis produced by 'slant-eyed people of the country of the Rising Sun flag' (*Time*, 4 October 1971).

1. In October 1971 the Americans scored a major breakthrough when Superscope Inc. was allowed to acquire 50 per cent of Standard Radio Corporation: this was the first time the Japanese government had sanctioned acquisition of 50 per cent of the stock of a domestic electronic firm; and MITI announced formally that such deals would continue to be approved 'if foreign firms are willing to comply with government conditions' (*The Times*, 30 October 1971).

except oil and the few others mentioned earlier. Throughout the negotiations over Okinawa and the textile fight the Americans kept hammering away at these restrictions on foreign investment, which have been Japan's number one line of defence in safeguarding its own autonomy in the worldwide capitalist dogfight.

On the whole, Japan, although its own capitalist class exploits its proletariat and foreign workers ruthlessly, has been greatly maligned by its capitalist rivals. For, among the world's seventy-six biggest exporting nations, Japan stood only sixty-second in the ratio of its exports to GNP in 1971.[1] Furthermore, it had a much higher percentage of its trade (some 45 per cent in 1970) with the underdeveloped countries than did any other advanced capitalist country. Even by 1975, if generally accepted projections turn out to be true and Japan is then accounting for about 10.5 per cent of total world exports, it will still be below a figure commensurate with its share of total world output: it is now *relatively* a much lesser exporter than France, or Britain, or Holland. Having said that, and repeated that some of Japan's exports, such as textiles, were a threat to no one and nothing, except Nixon's diseased 'Southern strategy', it is necessary to examine what Japan's objectives are at the present stage.

Japan would like to retain maximum control over its own domestic industry, meaning primarily over production; it would also like to keep control of its own large – and still, comparatively, very fast-growing – domestic market. It has long understood that there is no such thing as free trade, but within the distorted terminology used among capitalists, Japan supports free trade.[2] As outlined in the October 1971 White

1. *Time*, 4 October 1971.

2. The Nixon administration trundled out some very dangerous arguments during the textiles dispute (see reference to Secretary Stans' testimony quoted above, p. 154). Textiles, of course, is one of the few industries in which an underdeveloped country can hope to compete with an advanced industrial economy. In October 1971 the House labour committee added an amendment to the minimum wage bill which would seek to limit (and often bar) any exports from 'low

Paper on Resources, Japan would also like to take rapid steps to try to control more sources of raw materials, now largely in the hands of its main rivals. In theory, Japan has three ways out of the present situation: direct deals with the third world producing countries (such as the deal with Saudi Arabia mentioned above); a big deal with the U.S.S.R.; or a continuing, essentially subordinate relationship to the United States, as exemplified in the post-1965 carve-up of Indonesia.[1] The evidence is that, in most of the South-East Asia area, Japan will continue to be essentially subordinate to the United States. One of the reasons for this is that Japan is still not in a position to exercise the required military surveillance of the area, which is a highly explosive one – and here Japan's continued reliance on American military technology is bound to continue to be of vital importance (even if Japan actually manufactures the hardware itself).

The 1971 White Paper on Resources pointed out that no less than 44.3 per cent of Japan's total imports (up from 38.7

---

wage countries' – defined as those paying 'substantially' less than the U.S.A. minimum wage! (*The Times*, 14 October 1971). A further 'protectionist' move in the air is an AFL–CIO suggestion to pass a bill (originally suggested as a rider to the dollar devaluation bill) to make it less financially attractive for U.S.A. companies to invest abroad (*The Times*, 2 March 1972). The outlines of a vast, all-embracing protectionism are more than clear.

1. On an earlier occasion when Japanese interests were pondering participation in the development of Siberia, Western oil and gas firms are reported to have exercised colossal, and successful, pressure against this: as the Teikoku Oil Co. was about to commit itself to developing the gas fields at Okha in Sakhalin, Shell offered it a deal to extract gas from Brunei (n.a., 'Japan's Role in the Economic Development of Siberia', *JQ*, vol. 15, no. 2, 1968, pp. 153–4). More recently in Indonesia, in spite of intensive Japanese lobbying, big copper resources in West Irian were granted to the U.S. Freeport Sulphur Company rather than to Mitsubishi. Nickel mines in south-central Sulawesi went to International Nickel (Canadian-based, but-U.S.A.-controlled) rather than to the Japanese consortium bidding for them – though Japan did gain some other reportedly rich nickel rights in the Halmahera area (Hayashi Naomichi, 'The Economic Basis for the Revival of Japanese Militarism', *Gendai to Shiso*, 1 October 1970,

per cent in 1960) was accounted for by raw materials; and dependency is particularly striking towards the great U.S., Canadian and European corporations that have a stranglehold over present world supplies of oil, copper, nickel, etc. Japan is making a big effort to alter the situation but even if present government plans are fulfilled Japan will still control only 30 per cent of its estimated domestic requirements by 1985.[1] Long-term co-operation and integration with the centres of international capital remain, therefore, a necessity for Japan.

In addition, as Japanese business moves into more modern advanced sectors – atomic energy, pollution, ocean (*sic*), housing, etc. – for which they need the most advanced technology, their bargaining position weakens and they have to accept direct investment and partnership rather than rely on licensing and copying. Japanese policy can be expected to move more and more from undercutting to interlocking. As the president of the Japan Iron and Steel Federation put it, 'Now is the time for us to drop the mean idea of trying to beat foreign competitors and face the reality of Japanese interdependence with them.' (Quoted in the *Montreal Star*, 24 January 1970.)[2]

---

pp. 283–4). Alcoa (U.S.) has secured bauxite rights on every island except Bintan (where the deposits are worked by the government) and U.S. capital dominates in tin and other mining sectors ('Indonesia: The Making of a Neo-Colony', *PR & WET*, vol. I, no. 1, August 1969). After several vain attempts at competing with their U.S. rivals, Marubeni Corporation announced in June 1970 that they were linking up with Kaiser Steel to jointly develop coal resources on Sumatra (Hayashi, op. cit.). By mid-1971 U.S. investments accounted for no less than 78.6 per cent of the total foreign investments in mining in Indonesia (*FEER*, 28 August 1971, p. 48). The same situation prevails in Oil (*v.* Caldwell, 'Oil and Imperialism in East Asia', *JCA*, vol. 1, no. 3, 1971) – yet the bulk of both oil and mineral exports from Indonesia are going and will continue to go to Japan. Independent Japanese investment seems to be powerful only in fisheries, especially shrimps (Yü, op. cit., pp. 172–5), lumber and certain forms of manufacture.

1. *The Times*, 8 October 1971. Cf. *JEJ*, no. 459, 12 October 1971 pp. 10–11.

2. Stephen Hymer, 'The United States Multinational Corporations and Japanese Competition in the Pacific', p. 7 (paper prepared for the

A revealing index of both Japan's governmental backing for the drive to develop overseas sources of raw materials and of the extent of America's desire to draw Japan into its plans, is given by the various investment guarantee projects recently operationalized or mooted. On 15 May 1970 the Japanese government set up an insurance system for Japanese investment overseas. This guaranteed to make up up to 90 per cent of losses 'from foreign political or credit troubles'.[1] In fiscal 1972 ¥350 billion were set aside for the fund ($1,136mill.). In other words, the Japanese government has given a cast-iron guarantee to any private interests who will invest in approved sectors abroad. But Japan has realized it cannot possibly go it alone. In November 1971 Tokyo hosted a UN-sponsored conference on advanced capitalist countries' investment in the developing countries, at which Japan's role in the *relatively* integrated exploitation of the third world was a major topic.[2] Immediately after this it was announced from Washington that the U.S.A. and Japan were about to launch a mammoth worldwide investment insurance body, via the World Bank. Japanese investment abroad, lamented William Rogers, had been enjoying a 'honeymoon period' in that it had not faced expropriation to the same extent as American investors had. He called for a 'multilateral approach' to insure capitalist investments throughout the world. The Japanese agreed 'that it would be desirable to establish an international investment programme supported by industrial nations and developing countries'.[3] The upshot of Rogers's outrageous suggestion is clearly that the U.S.A. wants to establish closer control over the forthcoming burst of overseas investment which is bound to come out of Japan.

Conferencia del Pacifico, Viña del Mar, Chile, 27 September–3 October 1970, and kindly made available by John Gittings).

1. *JEJ*, no. 476, 8 February 1972, p. 10.
2. *JER*, vol. 4, no. 1, January 1972, p. 8.
3. *The Times*, 29 September 1971. The following day World Bank president McNamara made a major speech threatening tighter international capitalist intervention, through the World Bank, to protect exploitation and profits (*The Times*, 30 September 1971).

For one of the new phenomena connected with Japan is the recent multiplication of the country's reserves: these rose from \$7,927mill. at the end of July 1971 to \$12,514mill. at the end of August 1971, putting Japan ahead of the U.S.A., and then to \$15,235mill. at the end of the year, and \$16½ billion by the end of February 1972, when many estimates calculated they would top the \$20 billion mark by the end of 1972.[1] The vast majority of the reserves is composed of dollars, at present not convertible. Japan has always had very low gold reserves.

The December 1971 currency realignment meant an effective devaluation of the dollar against the yen of 16.88 per cent; obviously, in the first place this makes Japanese exports to the U.S.A. more expensive (although minus the 10 per cent surcharge) and U.S. exports into Japan relatively cheaper. But it also makes it more expensive for American firms to buy into the Japanese economy, and cheaper for Japanese firms to invest in America (and other places).

The U.S. government has leant mercilessly on Japan in the recent economic dispute. Treasury Secretary Connally called on Japan to make up some 40 per cent (i.e. \$5 billion) of the \$13 billion turnaround which, he alleged, was needed in the American balance of trade. One of the simplest ways a contribution could be made, it was repeatedly pointed out, would be if Japan would increase its purchases of American military equipment. It is reported that under great pressure Japan agreed to double its purchases in 1972. It has also agreed to pay all the foreign-exchange costs of keeping U.S. bases in Japan.[2]

Ironically, too, the U.S.A. has now reached a situation where it would like Japan to bring investment to America. The self-interested actions of the Detroit motor manufacturers are

1. *The Times*, 1 and 14 March for the end of February reserves.

2. *Newsweek*, 27 December 1971, p. 13. To our knowledge, this has not been officially made explicit. The precise figure for arms purchases is not clear. At the time of Connally's visit the Japanese were suggesting they might spend about \$540mill. in 1972 for American arms – about 80 per cent of the figure America wanted (*JEJ*, no. 462, 2 November 1971, p. 8).

already in danger of boomeranging: in early 1972 the United Auto Workers union announced a boycott of some of the products of the Detroit–Japan automobile tie-ups unless the American firms brought their investment back to the States. Japanese textile manufacturers have even set up in North Carolina! It is easily forgotten that one of the objectives of American trade policy (tariffs, quotas, etc.) is to force Japanese capital into the United States – investment means not only profits, but also jobs. The Japanese are not entirely unhappy about this situation. The government, in this case MITI, has given its attention and backing to a general plan to boost investment in the States on a long-term basis. The government is extending the overseas investment insurance cover to Japanese ventures in the industrialized countries – 'to include losses resulting from strikes or other troubles peculiar to advanced countries'.[1]

Japan is also being pressured to put several billion dollars back into the U.S.A. economy by buying either U.S. Treasury bills, or medium and long-term bonds – perhaps to about the same level as Canada ($2,290mill. as of July 1971).[2] Of course, this is only another way of Washington forcing its allies to prop up the American economy. But Japan does not have much alternative, particularly while the dollar is not convertible.[3]

In addition to these moves in quasi-antagonistic co-operation with the U.S.A., Japan is looking for other ways to utilize its

1. *JEJ*, no. 476, 8 February 1972, p. 10, p. 1.

2. This was the figure being suggested at the time of the Connally visit in late 1971 – before revaluation (*JEJ*, no. 462, p. 8). It may well have risen since then, and the kind of bonds also may differ (see *The Times*, 9 March 1972).

3. It may well be that almost the totality of Japan's reserves have never left the shores of the United States, and are not really 'reserves' for Japan at all – but for the U.S.A. Professor Inoue Kiyoshi, from whose stimulating ideas the authors greatly benefited just as this book was going to press, emphasized that Japan's failure to buy gold and other non-dollar currencies can only be interpreted as a sign of weakness and subordination to the U.S.A. Japan does not have complete control over its reserves, whose main function is still to prop up the dollar.

vast reserves. The natural move is to step up investment overseas, and there is every sign that this is in the process of increasing by leaps and bounds. The sheer size of the Siberia deal offered by Moscow would have been unthinkable only a couple of years ago. At the end of February 1972 the well-informed Kyodo news service reported that the Japanese government was planning to solve some of its surplus foreign exchange problem by lending some of the reserves to private businesses and banks for investment overseas.[1] This would complement the existing government guarantees and accelerate overseas investment.

Besides this, the experience of being dependent on the dollar has been a very nasty one. The overwhelming percentage of Japan's business contracts were in dollars, and many sectors of business would have lost gigantic sums of money through the December 1971 revaluation arrangement had the government not come to their assistance with lavish support funds. One obvious way out of the predicament would be to establish the yen as an international currency, sign contracts in it and deal in it in most or all foreign transactions. There is a still unresolved debate going on about this in Japan. On 4 January 1972 a plan for a 'yen settlement union' was cautiously unveiled in Tokyo: this would require the participating South-East Asian countries to deal in yen rather than dollars with Tokyo. In return Japan would offer its most lenient credit to those in the 'settlement union'. This yen economic bloc, wrote the *Guardian* correspondent, is 'reminiscent of the pre-war "co-prosperity sphere"'.[2] A few weeks later Finance Minister

1. *International Herald Tribune*, 29 February 1972; *The Times*, 9 March 1972. A move to try to convert some of its dollar holdings into SDRs (*Le Monde*, 30 September 1971) would appear to have been frustrated.

2. The *Guardian*, 6 January 1972; a subsequent report (the *Guardian*, 6 March 1972) gives official Japanese estimates that yen-based trade had risen to 13 per cent from 6 per cent only three months earlier. At the time of the penultimate Deutschmark revaluation, Germany was estimated to have had about 80 per cent of its contracts in Deutschmarks; the Japanese figure for shipping in mid-1971 was about 1 per

Mizuta let it be known that he did not favour an international role for the yen. Britain, he pointed out, had suffered 'extreme hardships' while the pound was the world's major means of trade settlement, and Japan should avoid getting into a similar position.[1] The upshot of his remarks was that Japan might not block the gradual advance of the yen as an international currency, which, he implied, would in any case strengthen it. Short of this, Japan can use its reserves not only to boost investment, but also to advance credit to South-East Asian countries, and increase its 'aid' programmes. This may become not only attractive (to Japan) but necessary. The well-honed transformation capacities of the Japanese economy are such that the natural response to the slowdown in world trade and the domestic recession is for Japan to boost its exports – which is in fact what happened.[2] But with the trade imbalance already acute, Japan can only conciliate the antagonisms aroused by this by advancing more and more money to the regimes on the receiving end of the export drive. As these countries become increasingly hostile to the flood of Japanese exports (a process already well under way), the pressures to oblige Japan to move more and more production to the South-East Asian states will build up – pressures which Japan can easily respond to by exporting more capital.

It is very easy to fall into one extreme position on the question of the relationship between Japan and the U.S.A. Their military and political relationship is *closer* than that between the U.S.A. and any of its European allies. Until the winter of 1971–2 Japan had no independent foreign policy at

---

cent. Of course, there are already strong rumours of a further forced revaluation of the yen, which must put a brake on the development of a 'yen bloc'.

1. *The Times*, 27 January 1972.

2. A February 1972 Mitsubishi study showed that the recession had boosted exports. The key sectors of cars, motorcycles and steel products had continued to expand their exports; TV sets and toys had 'slowed down'; chemical products and fertilizers had 'slackened' (*JEJ*, no. 478, 22 February 1972, p. 3).

all. The Security Treaty gives the U.S.A. veto rights over Japanese moves. Japan is terribly closely tied to the dollar. In terms of the respective investment in each other's economies, there is no comparison.[1] On the other hand, in trading terms, Japan is certainly the toughest capitalist competitor America has had since 1945 – but this competition is only so acute on the domestic U.S.A. market. Indeed, elsewhere in the world, there is no reason why the two should not promote their interests in common: Connally offered to help Japan promote its exports to Europe, just as Foster Dulles once arranged to help Japan increase its exports to South-East Asia.

Yet it is also obvious that the relationship between the U.S.A. and Japan *is* different from that between other major capitalist powers. In spite of America's influence in Tokyo, it is still not sure of its alleged ally. In a speech in Kansas City in October 1971, Barry Goldwater predicted – without a precise timetable – that Japan would become 'the world's most modern military system, far, far better than ours and far better than the Russians . . . The biggest problems that we face in the Pacific in the coming years rest neither with China nor with the Soviets. They rest with Japan.'[2]

In the wake of the 'Nixon shocks' Japan has definitely found itself obliged to start playing poker. It has moved on the question of a Peace Treaty with the Soviet Union, which had been stalled since the war. It broke with its American ally for the first time to recognize Bangladesh. It sent an official mission to Hanoi, headed by a senior Foreign Ministry official.

1. Direct U.S. investment in Japan at the end of 1970 (preliminary estimate) was $1,491mill. The net U.S. international investment position at the end of 1970 in Japan was $1,183mill., and assets amounted to $7,237mill. Japanese direct investment in the U.S.A. at the end of 1970 came to $233mill. – up from $181mill. in 1968 and $176mill. in 1969 (*Survey of Current Business*, October 1971, pp. 28, 38).

2. *International Herald Tribune*, 6 October 1971. Goldwater should not be dismissed as an observer of no reliability, since he is known to keep in excellent contact with the U.S. air force, which should be in a position to assess the Japanese challenge.

It recognized Mongolia. It allowed a Diet delegation, headed by an LDP Dietman, to visit North Korea and initiate a trade settlement of the kind negotiated originally with China in 1962.[1] It has certainly allowed the issue of massive participation in Siberia to be floated. And it let the Americans know that it would revise its trade policy towards China and compete with the U.S.A. there wherever possible.[2] Nearly a decade ago Mao Tse-tung is reported to have told a delegation of visiting Japanese Socialists that Japan then belonged to one of the world's two intermediate zones. But Japanese monopoly capital, he noted, 'is discontented with the United States, and some of its representatives are openly rising against the United States. Though Japanese monopoly capital now is dependent on the United States, the time will come when it too will shake off the American yoke.'[3]

Certainly a sector of Japanese capitalism wants to shake off the American yoke. But the indications are that Japanese capitalism is still essentially subordinate to U.S. imperialism, and that the signs and signals of 'independence' are more

1. On Japan's relations with the D.R.V., see *Le Monde*, 8 February 1972 and *JEJ*, no. 478, 22 February 1972, p. 2 (where Pham Van Dong is reported having suggested the setting up of 'representative offices' in Hanoi and Tokyo); on relations with the D.P.R.K., see *FEER*, no. 5, 1972 and *JEJ*, no. 478, p. 12 (for the setting up of a North Korean trade corporation in Tokyo; Japan is also scheduled to lift its ban on Export–Import Bank guarantees for loans to Japan–D.P.R.K. trade – cf. below re China).

2. Selig Harrison noted that it was after Sato heard that American businessmen would be allowed to the 1972 Spring Canton Fair that the Tokyo regime lifted its ban on Export–Import Bank low-interest loans to China, which had been at the origin of the démarche by Chiang which had led to the famous 'Yoshida letter' in the mid-sixties (the *Guardian*, 6 March 1971). Harrison also notes that 'Tokyo is moving rapidly to line up Mongolian copper, North Korean iron ore, and North Vietnamese anthracite as part of new trade patterns.'

3. As given in Franz Schurmann and Orville Schell, eds., *Communist China* (*China Readings 3*), New York, 1967 (Penguin 1968), p. 369; this is an abridged translation from the conservative Japanese journal *Sekai Shuho*, 11 August 1964. To our knowledge this very interesting statement by Mao on Japan has neither been acknowledged nor denied officially.

shadow than substance. Moreover, it must be repeated that, while Japanese imperialism is a real danger to the peoples of Asia, including the people of Japan, U.S. imperialism is the main enemy, and is itself largely responsible for the restoration of Japanese imperialism and Japanese militarism.

THE NATURE AND FUTURE OF JAPANESE IMPERIALISM

Among the world's imperialist powers, Japan has always been something of a maverick. Courted and feared by its capitalist competitors, admired by much of the Russian anti-Tsarist movement in the years after the Russo–Japanese war of 1904–05, at a time when it was equally loathed by the masses of Korea and Taiwan, Japan has presented no less intractable a problem to those trying to analyse the nature of its state and its imperialist activities.

As noted in the preface, Japan is largely absent from the current debate on imperialism. But it is also largely absent from the classical texts on imperialism, too. In his preface to *Imperialism, The Highest Stage of Capitalism*, Lenin almost apologizes for using Japan as an example on the question of annexation.[1]

Much of the discussion on the subject of the nature of contemporary Japanese capitalism (and therefore imperialism) in Japan itself, and in Chinese political texts, hinges on the question of the relationship between Japanese capitalism and U.S. capitalism. Emphasis on Japanese *militarism* is designed to indicate that Japanese capitalism is essentially subordinate to the United States.[2] This is certainly the case. Nonetheless,

1. V. I. Lenin, *Imperialism, the Highest Stage of Capitalism*, Preface, 26 April 1917, p. 6 (Moscow paperback ed.).

2. Chinese statements in particular have tended to concentrate on Japanese militarism, rather than on Japanese imperialism. Our understanding of postwar Japanese imperialism is that it differs structurally from pre-war Japanese imperialism. In the postwar period and parti-

Japan is an imperialist power, with its own relative autonomy within the world imperialist system. One of the most important features of postwar Japan has been the unusual speed with which the economy, and Japan's position in Asia, have changed. After the initial postwar lull, Japan first structured its relationships with South-East Asia largely through trade; in the present phase investment is becoming increasingly important; and it may well be that military presence will become an integral feature of the next phase. In the text we have indicated as precisely as possible the exact role of militarism within contemporary Japanese imperialism. While stressing that the military establishment has maintained its own identity (*v.* the struggle over the 1972 Defence Budget), it must be reiterated that it is structurally only a component of Japanese imperialism.

The basis of Japan's very fast economic growth in the postwar period, the highest in the capitalist world, has been its high rate of capital accumulation and investment. The share of GNP devoted to capital investment was about 31 per cent in 1965, 35 per cent in 1970 and is scheduled to hit 39 per cent in 1975. As noted above, an extraordinarily high proportion of investment went into heavy industry, thus laying the foundations for sustained future expansion. Until very recently, too, Japan exported only tiny amounts of its capital compared with other industrialized countries. At the same time it restricted foreign capital penetration to an extent which no other advanced capitalist state has done.

---

cularly in recent years, it has been big business which has been the main proponent of greatly expanded arms budgets. The military, of course, has its own *relative* autonomy, but it does not occupy the same position in the state as it did prior to the 1945 surrender. Postwar Japanese militarism, which certainly exists, is only a component of Japanese imperialism, which ultimately must be explained structurally by reference to the economic base. On this problem see the extremely valuable and stimulating text by Herbert P. Bix, 'Report on Japan 1972' *BCAS* vol 4, nos. 2 and 3, especially part 2 ('The Economic Dimension'). Bix's conclusions differ somewhat from ours.

As far as inter-imperialist competition is concerned, there are two absolutely central issues: the degree of capital concentration (Lenin's first principle), and the level of technology. Wages, of course, are important: but, as Emmanuel has vividly argued,[1] Japan has historically been able to advance technologically without a 'comparable' rise in wages, until very recently.

The relationship between high technology, economies of scale and wage levels lies at the centre of the discussion between Ernest Mandel and Martin Nicolaus about U.S. imperialism.[2] More detailed study is needed before a definitive position can be adopted. In the meantime, the situation can be outlined as follows. On the whole, the United States still has the advantage as far as the size of enterprises is concerned, but it is in the process of being strongly challenged by Japan in several key sectors. In steel, Japan now has the biggest producer in the whole world, Nippon Steel, which overtook U.S. Steel about five years before American predictions had envisaged. In cars, Japan now has the number three firm in terms of output, Toyota. Japan leads the world in shipbuilding. However, several important additional considerations must be introduced. First, the extent of U.S. capital control in the key sectors of the Japanese economy – which is still very much greater than vice versa. Second, the much greater power and penetration of U.S. banks (although Japan is now hurriedly trying to right the balance with mergers and the formation of the two giant consortia mentioned earlier).[3] On the other hand, against the strength of the U.S. banks must

1. Arghiri Emmanuel, *Unequal Exchange: A Study of the Imperialism of Trade*, London, 1972, pp. 122, 128.

2. Ernest Mandel, 'Where is America Going?', *NLR*, no. 54, 1969; Martin Nicolaus, 'Who Will Bring the Mother Down?', *Leviathan*, vol. I, no. 5, 1969, reprinted as 'The Universal Contradiction' in *NLR*, no. 59, 1970; Ernest Mandel, 'The Laws of Uneven Development', *NLR*, no. 59.

3. On the importance of banks, see Nicolaus, ibid.; and especially Harry Magdoff, 'The Age of Imperialism', *Monthly Review*, vol. 20, no. 5, October 1968, pp. 23–31 (now available as a book entitled *The Age of Imperialism*, New York, 1969).

be set the much greater centralization of the Japanese banking system, and the whole factor of the greater co-ordination between the state and private capital in Japan which allows much better economic planning and swifter government intervention than in the U.S.A.[1]

The question of technology is equally vexed. As shown above, Japan is still paying out far more on technological imports than it receives. Yet, as the 'borrowed technology' discussion demonstrates, there are definite advantages in purchasing technological know-how from others, provided the terms are strictly controlled. The evidence is that Japan has greatly benefited from its relatively backward situation: the example of the rotary engine, whose basic plan was bought from Wankel for a pittance and then refined by Toyo Kogyo, is only the most striking of many such cases. On the other hand against this, one must set the fact that U.S.A. technological superiority may in some cases have allowed them *de facto* control or veto power in joint ventures where, on paper, the American partner only controlled a small minority of the company.[2] It has to be admitted that the precise situation in

1. The importance of the co-ordination between private capital and the state in Japan cannot be over-emphasized. The decision to concentrate investment in Japan itself, of course, prevented the 'leakage' of capital abroad as happened in Britain, for example. Government intervention can be seen very clearly in the recent textile dispute with America. Although Japan had to concede to the U.S.A., the Sato government immediately provided sizeable sums of money to cushion the effect on the industry: and it is quite probable that more advanced sectors of Japanese capital were not entirely unhappy at seeing this declining sector being given half a *coup de grâce* – since it was scheduled for gradual elimination anyway. In addition, with the vast government subsidy, a big firm like Mitsui has already moved to get round the U.S.A. textile restrictions by setting up joint ventures in the Philippines and Singapore, which were exempt from the agreement (*International Herald Tribune*, 17 March 1972): Mitsui hoped to have the ventures set up by summer 1972. This is a nice case of integrated government 'help' turning an apparent blow into an asset.

2. For example, U.S. General Electric controls 12.6 per cent of the Japanese electrical giant Tokyo Shibaura (Toshiba), and was recently reported to be trying to get a 10 per cent share in another

many cases e.g., in the oil and computer industries, is not visible to the public eye.

It has long been acknowledged that capital investment overseas is not an essential or perhaps even basic feature of contemporary imperialism.[1] Emmanuel argues that it never was.[2] At any rate, it is obvious that the relationship between the U.S.A. and Japan has involved trade as well as investment competitivity – and trade has been, up until the last few years, much more important in Japan's relationship with South-East Asia than has investment. Japan has been running bigger and bigger trade surpluses with its neighbours, especially with South Korea and Taiwan; and this imbalance, which is structurally not eliminable under the present imperialist arrangement, has to be maintained by repeated infusions of Japanese capital in the form of credits, loans (and earlier 'reparations'). The relationship between capital and production is not exclusively one of investment, much less investment abroad.[3]

In the recent economic struggle with Japan, the U.S.A. had fairly clear objectives: first, to protect its own market, which is still much the largest in the world; second, to force Japan to allow more American capital into Japan into the key growth sectors, so that U.S. business could protect its own profit margins (though against the 'national' interest of the U.S.A.); third, to use its power to force Japan into an increased, but continuingly subordinate, relationship with U.S. capital in

---

large firm, Hitachi. As a Soviet economist emphasizes, even a 10–12 per cent share, in the hands of an American mammoth like G.E., can be enough to ensure a high degree of control (Ashik Manukian, 'Situazioni conflittuali nelle relazioni economiche degli Usa', *Critica Marxista*, no. 5–6, 1971, p. 50.

1. On this, see Hamza Alavi, 'Imperialism Old and New', *Socialist Register*, 1964, p. 121; and Rodolfo Banfi, 'A proposito di *Imperialismo* di Lenin', *Rivista Storica del Socialismo*, no. 23, 1964, pp. 424–5.

2. Arghiri Emmanuel, 'White-Settler Colonialism and the Myth of Investment Imperialism', *NLR*, no. 73, 1972, pp. 4–5.

3. On this, see Banfi, op. cit.

South-East Asia – with the captive Japanese market as the objective.

It was correctly pointed out by several writers on imperialism that a successful export drive by a competitor of the U.S.A. would be bound to bring retaliation.[1] But U.S. retaliation can now only take the elementary form of forcing a slowdown in world trade, which has boomeranging effects on the U.S.A. itself. In the race to capture competitors' markets, which is becoming more and more important given the level of unemployment and unused production capacity in all the advanced capitalist countries,[2] Japan is better placed than the U.S.A. to provide government support in planning and credit; combined with the fact that Japan still has a good deal of market 'slack' worldwide,[3] this has enabled Japan to race on again at high speed out of the U.S.-forced recession of 1971: Japanese exports in February 1972 were 25 per cent higher than those for February 1971. It is this capacity continually to increase exports – a capacity which is certain to continue for quite a long time – that has determined the *form* of Japanese imperialism in the recent phase. It simply has not had to form multi-national companies, or let itself be taken over by American capital to survive.[4]

Paradoxically, however, it may well be Japan's own rapid expansion which will weaken its autarchy. The continued growth of Japan's exports demands an ever-wider search for the raw materials to fuel Japanese industry. As we have shown above, in this phase of the process, Japan is still in a position of weakness vis-à-vis the big U.S., Canadian and European

1. See Nicolaus, for example; also Bob Rowthorn, 'Imperialism in the Seventies – Unity or Rivalry?', *NLR*, no. 69, 1971, p. 41.

2. Mandel, *NLR*, no. 59, op. cit., p. 26, discusses the phenomenon of unemployment in inter-imperialist rivalry: will the U.S.A. try to export its unemployment, and why has it got the highest unemployment rate of the major capitalist economies?

3. See p. 214 above for the very low ratio of Japan's exports compared to its GNP.

4. Rowthorn, op. cit., p. 37 raises this question, but does not answer it.

companies. Japanese mining and other interests are being forced into an ever-expanding network of long-term joint ventures and investment deals with more powerful partners: these are overwhelmingly directed at the Japanese market, and this 'external' collaboration must soon wreak its effect internally as well.

In addition, the contradictions between the demands of Japanese capitalism and the interests of the peoples of South-East Asia must become more and more acute. The effects of Japan's trading with South-East Asia in the postwar period are obvious: areas like South Korea and Taiwan have been forced into positions of impossible subordination, and lasting imbalance. It is impossible even to fantasize that the new phase of heavy Japanese investment in the area can be anything but equally deleterious to the masses of the countries concerned. Even under the ferocious dictatorship of General Pak in South Korea the Korean masses rose in protest against the 1965 'normalization' deal with Japan. In Japan, too, this arrangement was seen as a watershed in the re-establishment of a colonial penumbra, along pre-1945 lines, with suitable modification.

This major episode in Japan's postwar expansion in Asia was combated by the masses of both Korea and Japan, fighting together against their common enemy: Japanese imperialism. The Japanese people have continued to fight heroically against the LDP government's alliance with U.S. imperialism. These struggles have centred on the issue of Okinawa, the focal point not just of U.S.–Japanese contradiction, but also of U.S.–Japanese collaboration. Numerous aspects of the Tokyo government's servile relationship with Washington have roused large-scale popular protest: from the manufacture and transport of napalm, to the seizure of farmers' land at Sanrizuka. After the January 1972 meeting at San Clemente Premier Sato was asked if he would invite Nixon back to Japan for a return meeting. 'Out of the question,' Sato replied. And there is no doubt that the active hostility of the Japanese masses to such a visit makes it impossible. The Japanese people have repeatedly demonstrated their desire to oppose all manifestations of imperialism: by opposing the 1965 deal with the Seoul regime, by opposing the Japanese government's collusion with the American wars in Korea and Indochina; and by opposing the underhand arrangement to return Okinawa to Japan as a joint U.S.–Japanese military colony. Despite the enormous economic and military ties between the two countries, popular feeling in Japan has been such as to prevent any American President since the war setting foot in their country. It is this militancy which will surely liberate both the Japanese people themselves and all the peoples of Asia from Japanese imperialism.

APPENDIX I

JAPAN AND THE SOVIET UNION

Since the date of the 1968 lumber agreement Japanese–Soviet collaboration has advanced considerably. By 1971 Japan had overtaken Britain to become the U.S.S.R.'s leading capitalist trading partner.

The Russians have gradually been promoting the idea of a vast joint project covering much of Siberia. This has taken the following form: a plan to construct a large new port, Vrangel, on the Siberian coast near Nakhodka (agreed February 1970); development of the natural gas deposits on the island of Sakhalin, just off the north of Japan, and a bigger scheme for extracting gas from the Yakutsk area, a frozen wasteland in the heart of northern Siberia. The Japanese at first balked at the prospect, but then reconsidered it, as Yakutia also contains large deposits of coking coal and iron ore.[1]

Having enticed Japan into central Siberia, the Russians then began offering the most important commodity of all: oil. The Japanese requested permission to exploit deposits off Sakhalin and the Kamchatka peninsula, both only a fairly short tanker trip from Japan. The Russians countered with an offer to develop the huge field at Tyumen in the middle of Siberia, and extend the trans-Siberian pipeline from its present terminal at Irkutsk through to the Pacific coast, a distance of some 3,000 miles.

As with Japan's relations with the U.S.A., so relations with the U.S.S.R. are tied up with political and territorial questions. The Russians would like to sign a peace treaty with Japan. Japan

1. *Le Monde*, 19 February 1970; *The Times*, 10 February 1970 for the new port; *The Times*, 13 October 1970 for Yakutia.

would like to recover three islands (Shikotan, Kunashiri and Etorofu) and one small archipelago (the Habomais) off the north coast of Hokkaido. The U.S.S.R. has indicated that it might return Shikotan and the Habomais, but will not commit itself without a parallel commitment on a peace treaty. These issues have become entangled in the Siberian scheme, just as Okinawa did in the Tokyo–Washington wrangling over textiles.

The total cost of the Tyumen plan and the pipeline extension is estimated at $4 billion, and the Russians are asking Japan to put up an initial $1 billion to purchase equipment. In return (apart from the huge benefits to Japanese industry), the U.S.S.R. is offering Japan very low-sulphur oil in quantities which could supply about 8–9 per cent of the needs of the Japanese economy for at least twenty years from about 1975. Obviously, this is a grandiose scheme which virtually entails a cast-iron political settlement between the two countries, which in turn would involve Japan breaking or loosening its connections with other suppliers.[1]

Gromyko visited Tokyo in January 1972 to give a powerful push to the Tokyo–Moscow settlement, cashing in on Japanese

1. The best survey of the Tyumen proposals available at the time of writing was the editorial in the *JEJ*, no. 487, 22 February 1972. See also *Newsweek*, 7 February 1972; *The Times*, 22 and 25 February 1972. Published estimates for the cost of the pipeline vary between $2.5 and $4 billion; the planned flow – 50 million tons per year – seems agreed. The pipeline would have enormous military implications for the Soviet Union, and would radically alter supply problems for the Soviet Army on the Chinese frontier and for the Soviet Pacific fleet. It would also help to boost construction of petrochemical plants in eastern Siberia. It should be noted that the U.S.S.R. has already embarked, together with Hungary and Czechoslovakia, on a giant container station at the junction of the three countries to handle the expected Japan–Europe trans-U.S.S.R. container boom. Japan was lured out of a big gas deal in Siberia by the Western cartel in the late sixties, and it may be guessed that considerable pressure will be exerted again now. But the manoeuvring is now multilateral. The West might like Japan to diversify its sources up to a point; the U.S.A. might prefer the U.S.S.R. to develop its resources; and there is the new and major factor of China's oil resources. Recent Japanese missions to China have let it be known, off the record, that China would like technical arrangements to develop its big oil fields, and the U.S.A. and Japan are known to be competing vigorously for an entrée there.

resentment towards the U.S.A. (particularly strong in oil circles) and anti-China feeling. Japan and the U.S.S.R. have arranged for an exchange of visits between 'leaders' and for a general stepping-up of collaboration on all fronts. Japan has recognized both Bangladesh and Mongolia (which was a fairly strong move for Tokyo, involving as it did offending Taiwan).[1] In addition, the Russians have established a level of military collusion with Japan unknown in their relations with other capitalist powers: in 1971 a Japanese military delegation was permitted to tour Soviet military installations in Siberia.[2]

Postscript. Since the above was written a fundamental change has taken place in the nature of the projected Japan–Soviet co-operation in the development of Siberian resources: the two partners have become three, with the inclusion of the United States in virtually all of the projects concerned, following the visit of President Nixon to Moscow in May 1972. Japanese reports indicate that the initiative for drawing American capital into involvement in these projects came from the Japanese side, and for several very plausible reasons.[3] For one thing, Japanese business had been frozen in a stance of hostility and suspicion towards the Soviet Union for a very long time, and also in dependence towards the United States for only slightly less long a

1. *Le Monde*, 24 February 1972: a most useful survey of Tokyo's suddenly stepped-up moves to ameliorate relations with continental Asia. Recognition of Mongolia was officially announced a few days later. For Japan's trade with the Asian Communist countries, 1967–70, see table 30.

2. *Japan Times*, 11 March 1971; *Le Monde*, 17 March 1971. This crucially important new development seems to have been passed over in total silence by the British press. We are most grateful to Alain Bouc of *Le Monde* for providing further information on the trip. It was led by the parliamentary vice-minister for defence, Tsuchiya Yoshihiko, and included 'several' members, both uniformed and civilian personnel. Members of the group said that they 'hoped' to be allowed to visit the naval base at Vladivostok (a closed port), and 'some garrisons along the Sino–Soviet frontier' (*Japan Times*, op. cit.). It would seem that no communiqué was published after the visit, which lasted eleven days from 26 April 1971.

3. Noguchi Yuichiro, 'The Japanese and American Economies in Asia', *Sekai*, September 1972, pp. 112–20.

TABLE THIRTY Japan's Trade with Selected Communist Countries 1967–70 ($mill.)

	1967		1968		1969		1970	
	exp.	imp.	exp.	imp.	exp.	imp.	exp.	imp.
China	288.2	269.4	325.4	224.1	390.8	234.5	568.8	253.8
N. Korea	6.3	29.6	20.7	34.0	24.1	32.1	23.3	34.4
N. Vietnam	1.8	6.6	2.4	6.1	7.2	6.0	5.0	6.3
Mongolia	0.2	0.6	0.3	0.6	0.3	0.3	0.3	0.6
U.S.S.R.	157.6	453.9	179.0	463.5	268.2	461.5	340.9	481.0
Overall	525.2	868.2	581.7	837.3	764.4	847.9	1,045.1	887.4

Source: MITI, *Tsusho Hakusho, Kakuron*, 1970, p. 659; 1971, p. 700.

period; entry upon a long-term relationship of co-operation and dependence with the Russians could be contemplated with more equanimity if the Americans were also drawn into the deal. For another, the Japanese felt that Chinese suspicions and worries about Soviet intentions for the Siberian area would be calmed the more that development projects relating to it were entrusted to multi-national rather than bi-national concerns. Continuing American superiority in most of the technological fields important to the development plans was a further factor, And, finally, American capital seemed to be readily available in much larger amounts than had ever been contemplated by the Japanese. The Tyumen plan, discussed above, was to call for an investment of $1 billion on the Japanese side, and was held up for a long time by reluctance on the part of the Japanese government to back the deal. After a visit to the Soviet Union by a representative Japanese *zaikai*[1] group in late June 1972, Soviet consent to the participation of the American company, Gulf Oil, with the Japanese in the Tyumen project, as also to joint U.S.–Japanese participation in the development of natural gas deposits on Sakhalin, seemed settled.[2] At the same time the Japanese were working to involve the Americans in Yakutsk natural gas and in the long-shelved Udokan copper mine project.[3] But as well as these three-sided co-operative deals, what is even more striking is that there is one bilateral Soviet–American deal under negotiation which dwarfs any of the projects the Japanese have so far been interested in: that is the development of the natural gas fields at Urengoy in western Siberia, plus construction of a 2,500 mile pipeline to Murmansk where the gas is to be liquefied for shipping at the rate of 20 million tons annually to the east coast of the United States – the total cost involved to be a staggering $7·6 billion.[4]

The implications of all this are considerable. Not least is the fact that in one of the few remaining areas in which it might have been possible for Japan to stake out a claim to a source of raw material supply independent of American capital control, the

1. *Zaikai:* Japanese term for 'big business/financial circles'.

2. ibid.: also 'Last Resort Diplomacy of the *Zaikai*' (editorial), *Sekai*, July 1972, pp. 154–7.

3. Noguchi, op. cit.

4. 'America Cutting in on Siberian Development' (editorial), *Asahi Journal*, 9 June 1972, pp. 103–4.

Japanese in the end either chose, or were forced (by American pressure), to co-operate with the Americans. Siberia thus provides only the most recent example of the structural co-ordination of U.S. and Japanese business interests that frequently underlies the surface of contradiction and hostility. As in the case of Indonesian resources, American capital has shown itself to be, once again, vastly more powerful than the Japanese and, despite all the shocks and disputes in U.S.–Japanese relations in 1971–2, Japanese business has remained subordinate in the partnership with the Americans. However, even though this partnership in Siberian development may be a mutually satisfactory one for the time being, since Siberian reserves are vast in quantity, it should be remembered that the U.S.A. is expected to become a net importer of raw materials some time in the late 1970s, and by 1985 will have to import some 54 per cent, or 720 million kilolitres, of its annual oil consumption.[1] In a situation of increasing scarcity there may no longer be any room for co-operation.

3 October 1972

1. ibid.

APPENDIX II

JAPAN AND AUSTRALASIA

The most striking change in Pacific trading relations has been that between Japan and Australia. Only a few years ago Australia was pursuing an almost racist anti-Japanese policy. Yet, by 1969, it was the first 'Western' nation to take part in joint naval manoeuvres with Japan (and Malaysia). In April 1971 it was host to the single most important business mission which had to date left Japan.

Since 1966–7 Japan has been Australia's leading export market, and in 1970 Australia exported goods worth $1,507.7 mill. to Japan (second only to the U.S.A. as a source of imports for the latter). By that year exports to Japan were double those to Britain (25 and 12.6 per cent, respectively). The basis of this expansion has been Australian mining, in which Japan has invested heavily, often in joint companies, as Australia has promoted a protective investment policy not unlike Japan's. Already by late 1969 Japan was taking 85 per cent of Australia's exports of iron ore, 98 per cent of its coal exports, and 60 per cent of all minerals.[1]

This has made Australian mining heavily dependent on the state of the Japanese economy, and the slowdowns in Japan in key sectors such as steel, shipbuilding and automobiles had serious effects during 1971 on the Australian economy. By early

1. For a useful survey up to 1969 see Peter Drysdale, 'Minerals and Metals in Japanese–Australian Trade', *Developing Economies*, vol. 8, no. 2, June 1970. See also the *Economist*, 15 November 1969 (a survey of Australian mineral resources to date), *The Times*, 27 October 1970 and 5 April 1971; the *Observer*, 14 March and 18 April 1971; *Time*, 5 April 1971.

1972 it was being estimated that Japanese crude steel production in the year ending 31 March 1972 would have been cut back to about 88 million tons from the 1971 level of 92 million tons: the exact effect of this on the Australian economy was not clear at the time of writing, but most of the Japanese–Australian contracts (written in U.S. dollars) allow for a 15 per cent oscillation either side of the agreed figure – which could mean a 30 per cent drop in estimated sales. The two sectors worst affected are iron ore and copper. Of Japan's annual imports of 40mill. tons of iron ore from Australia, two mines, Hamersley and Mount Newman, each supplied more than 15mill. tons. Japan is also reported trying to cut back its copper imports from the island of Bougainville (an Australian colony, with a powerful working-class political opposition) by up to 20 per cent.[1]

In spite of the current recession, however, the future looks good for mining interests: by 1975 it is estimated that Japan's crude steel output could reach 145 million tons, which would result in an iron ore deficit of 30 million tons a year. In 1971–2 Australia was already providing Japan with 42 per cent of its iron ore imports, and by 1975 this percentage will rise to 60 per cent on present contractual commitments, and 71 per cent if the present additional sales offers were to be accepted. It is unlikely that Japan will want this degree of dependence on one supplier. Yet a heavy degree of dependence is inevitable.[2]

Japan has recently been pouring gigantic sums of capital into investment in gas and oil in Australia. In January 1971 three Japanese companies announced a plan to invest some £476mill. (over one billion U.S. dollars) in a project to extract natural gas in northern Australia for export to Japan. The three Japanese firms, Marubeni Corporation, Okura Shoji and Nippon Kokan Kaisha (Japan Steel Tube Corporation) are in partnership with one Australian company: Magellan Petroleum. Almost simultaneously, the Mitsubishi group announced that it was forming an oil-development group to invest U.S. $119mill. in a major petroleum exploration project in Australia. Mitsui is involved in the huge Robe River iron ore project in western

1. For the cutbacks, see the Business Section of *The Times*: particularly 7, 8 and 31 January and 2, 5 and 8 February 1972; cf. *FEER*, no. 52, 1971, p. 34.

2. *The Times*, 10 January 1972.

Australia, along with two U.S. firms and an Australian company. Four Japanese companies (Sumitomo Chemical, Showa Denko, Marubeni Corporation and Sumitomo Shoji Kaisha) announced a deal in February 1972 with two U.S. firms (America Metal Climax and Holland Aluminum) to build an alumina plant in Australia with an initial output, in 1975, of one million tons a year. The initial Japanese stake will be ¥35,200mill. (about £44.5mill.), ultimately rising to ¥132,000-mill.[1]

Japan is also an excellent market for Australia's forest and agricultural exports. Early in 1971 two Japanese companies (Mitsubishi Trading and Sumitomo Trading) signed a $321.5 mill. deal to import 10 million tons of eucalyptus wood chips from Australia – reportedly the largest single wood-chip contract on record, and enough to supply Japan's paper industry with pulp material for ten years.[2]

By early 1971, too, Australia was supplying 71 per cent of Japan's beef imports, 35 per cent of its diary products, and 25 per cent of its sugar. A 1970 Japanese forecast predicted that foodstuff imports from Australia would rise from their then current level of $A161mill. (£75mill.) a year to $A572mill. by 1980. This increase, which is likely, would about equal the total loss Australia expects from Britain joining the EEC . . .

1. Respectively, *The Times*, 21 January 1972 (natural gas project); *Newsweek*, 24 January 1972 (Mitsubishi oil project); *The Times*, 18 February 1972 (Mitsui and Robe River); *The Times*, 21 February 1972 (alumina plant).

2. *Newsweek*, 7 February 1972.

APPENDIX III

THE 1969 SATO-NIXON COMMUNIQUÉ

1. President Nixon and Prime Minister Sato met in Washington on Nov. 19, 20, and 21 to exchange views on the present international situation and on other matters of mutual interest to the United States and Japan.

2. The President and the Prime Minister recognized that both the United States and Japan have greatly benefited from their close association in a variety of fields, and they declared that, guided by their common principles of democracy and liberty, the two countries would maintain and strengthen their fruitful co-operation in the continuing search for world peace and prosperity and in particular for the relaxation of international tensions. The President expressed his and his Government's deep interest in Asia, and stated his belief that the United States and Japan should co-operate in contributing to the peace and prosperity of the region. The Prime Minister stated that Japan would make further active contributions to the peace and prosperity of Asia.

3. The President and the Prime Minister exchanged frank views on the current international situation, with particular attention to developments in the Far East. The President, while emphasizing that the countries in the area were expected to make their own efforts for the stability of the area, gave assurance that the United States would continue to contribute to the maintenance of international peace and security in the Far East by honouring its defence treaty obligations in the area. The Prime Minister, appreciating the determination of the United States, stressed that it was important for the peace and security of the Far East that the United States should be in a position to carry

out fully its obligations referred to by the President. He further expressed his recognition that, in the light of the present situation, the presence of U.S. forces in the Far East constituted a mainstay for the stability of the area.

4. The President and the Prime Minister specifically noted the continuing tension over the Korean peninsula. The Prime Minister deeply appreciated the peace-keeping efforts of the United Nations in the area and stated that the security of the Republic of Korea was essential to Japan's own security. The President and the Prime Minister shared the hope that Communist China would adopt a more co-operative and constructive attitude in its external relations. The President referred to the treaty obligations of his country to the Republic of China, which the United States would uphold. The Prime Minister said that the maintenance of peace and security in the Taiwan area was also a most important factor for the security of Japan. The President described the earnest efforts made by the United States for a peaceful and just settlement of the Vietnam problem. The President and the Prime Minister expressed the strong hope that the war in Vietnam would be concluded before return of the administration rights over Okinawa to Japan. In this connexion they agreed that, should peace in Vietnam not have been realized by the time reversion of Okinawa is scheduled to take place, the two Governments would fully consult with each other in the light of the situation at that time so that reversion would be accomplished without affecting the United States' efforts to assure the South Vietnamese people the opportunity to determine their own political future without outside interference. The Prime Minister stated that Japan was exploring what role she could play in bringing about stability in the Indo-China area.

5. In light of the current situation and the prospects in the Far East, the President and the Prime Minister agreed that they highly valued the role played by the [U.S.–Japanese] Treaty of Mutual Co-operation and Security in maintaining the peace and security of the Far East including Japan, and they affirmed the intention of the two Governments firmly to maintain the treaty on the basis of mutual trust and common evaluation of the international situation. They further agreed that the two Governments should maintain close contact with each other on matters affecting the peace and security of the Far East including Japan,

and on the implementation of the Treaty of Mutual Co-operation and Security.

6. The Prime Minister emphasized his view that the time had come to respond to the strong desire of the people of Japan, of both the mainland and Okinawa, to have the administrative rights over Okinawa returned to Japan on the basis of the friendly relations between the United States and Japan, and thereby to restore Okinawa to its normal status. The President expressed appreciation of the Prime Minister's view. The President and the Prime Minister also recognized the vital role played by U.S. forces in Okinawa in the present situation in the Far East. As a result of their discussion it was agreed that the mutual security interests of the United States and Japan could be accommodated within arrangements for the return of the administrative rights over Okinawa to Japan. They therefore agreed that the two Governments would immediately enter into consultations regarding specific arrangements for accomplishing the early reversion of Okinawa without detriment to the security of the Far East including Japan. They further agreed to expedite the consultations with a view to accomplishing the reversion, hopefully during 1972, subject to the conclusion of these specific arrangements with the necessary legislative support. In this connexion, the Prime Minister made clear the intention of his Government, following reversion, to assume gradually the responsibility for the immediate defence of Okinawa as part of Japan's defence efforts for her own territories. The President and the Prime Minister agreed also that the United States would retain under the terms of the Treaty of Mutual Co-operation and Security such military facilities and areas in Okinawa as required in the mutual security of both countries.

7. The President and the Prime Minister agreed that, upon return of the administrative rights, the Treaty of Mutual Co-operation and Security and its related arrangements would apply to Okinawa without modification thereof. In this connexion, the Prime Minister affirmed the recognition of his Government that the security of Japan could not be adequately maintained without international peace and security in the Far East, and therefore the security of countries in the Far East was a matter of serious concern for Japan. The Prime Minister was of the view that, in the light of such recognition on the part of the Japanese Government, the return of the administrative rights over Okin-

awa in the manner agreed above should not hinder the effective discharge of the international obligations assumed by the United States for the defence of countries in the Far East including Japan. The President replied that he shared the Prime Minister's view.

8. The Prime Minister described in detail the particular sentiment of the Japanese people against nuclear weapons and the policy of the Japanese Government reflecting such sentiment. The President expressed his deep understanding and assured the Prime Minister that, without prejudice to the position of the U.S. Government with respect to the prior consultation system under the Treaty of Mutual Co-operation and Security, the reversion of Okinawa would be carried out in a manner consistent with the policy of the Japanese Government as described by the Prime Minister.

13. The President and the Prime Minister agreed that attention to the economic needs of the developing countries was essential to the development of international peace and stability. The Prime Minister stated the intention of the Japanese Government to expand and improve its aid programmes in Asia commensurate with the economic growth of Japan. The President welcomed this statement and confirmed that the United States would continue to contribute to the economic development of Asia. The President and Prime Minister recognized that there would be major requirements for the post-war rehabilitation of Vietnam and elsewhere in South-East Asia. The Prime Minister stated the intention of the Japanese Government to make a substantial contribution to this end.

Source: *Keesing's*, 1969, p. 23699 (clauses 9, 10, 11, 12, 14 and 15 have been omitted).

POSTSCRIPT

Important developments have occurred since this book was originally completed in March 1972.

Although Japan was pulling out of its recession at the time of writing, the Japanese economy is still beset by the same structural problems as before. Excess production capacity continues to fuel demands for both an increased military budget and larger and larger markets overseas. The demand for raw materials continues to foster aggressiveness towards the South-East Asian countries and compromises with Japan's capitalist rivals. American and European pressure continues to elbow open chinks in Japan's protective investment barriers.

First, the military budget. Behind a smokescreen of whirlwind diplomatic activity, the thoroughly reactionary Tanaka government managed to keep news of its domestic activities fairly well concealed. Little attention was given to the draft budget for 1973 presented by the Defence Agency at the end of August 1972, calling for ¥978,200mill. (£1,223mill.) – an increase of 22 per cent over 1972 (the highest percentage increase ever made from one year to the next). The budget requests included sixty tanks, three destroyers and thirty F-4EJ Phantom jets.[1]

As the former Minister of International Trade and Industry in Sato's last cabinet, it was not to be expected that Tanaka as Premier would ease up on Japan's export drive. And indeed, in tandem with his equally aggressive partner, Nakasone Yasuhiro

1. The *Financial Times*, 30 August 1972. The cuts in the defence budget reported by the *Sunday Times* among others (see ch. 3) certainly did not seem to be materializing, cf. Bix, 'Report on Japan 1972', for more details on the mystifications of the defence budget.

(head of MITI in the new Tanaka cabinet), he has not. The September 1972 agreement with South Korea (see below) is crystal clear confirmation that the Tanaka government is continuing the policies of its predecessors.

As well as larger markets, Japan also desperately needs new sources of raw materials. Tanaka has moved to streamline government backing for overseas investment by Japanese firms (thus, of course, helping to ease foreign pressure on Japan by reducing the external reserves and ultimately promoting 'Japanese' exports which cannot be attributed to Japan itself). At the end of August 1972 the Finance Ministry announced a new system of lending dollars from external reserves to Japanese companies. This can be done through a number of organizations, including the Export-Import Bank, the Petroleum Resources Development Corporation, the Metallic Minerals Exploration Corporation and the Overseas Economic Co-operation Fund (OECF).[1] The OECF subsequently announced, at the end of September, that the government would cover fully any future losses private investors might incur through a further yen revaluation if they availed themselves of the OECF lending scheme. And the next day commercial banks were authorized for the first time to extend foreign currency loans to domestic corporations to finance direct investment overseas.[2] In effect this removes the last barrier on Japanese investment abroad (domestic lending rates higher than those applicable to foreign currency), and a further upsurge in Japanese investment abroad, particularly in the hunt for raw materials, is to be expected.

At the same time, Japan is gradually yielding to foreign (particularly American) pressure to ease restrictions on investment in Japan itself. In September 1972 the Foreign Investment Council, with the backing of the Finance Ministry (but against MITI opposition), called on the government to liberalize all industries for 100 per cent foreign investment in Japan.[3] The

1. *The Times*, 21 August 1972; the Finance Ministry estimated that this move would reduce Japan's reserves by $1,500mill. by March 1973.

2. *The Times*, 21 and 22 September 1972.

3. *The Times*, 12 September 1972; cf. the *Financial Times*, 30 August 1972 and *FEER*, 16 September 1972, p. 32 for further details.

government was also expected to raise the ceiling on the percentage of shares of Japanese corporations which can be bought by foreign interests. However, this is bound to be a gradual process, with Japan continuing to protect vital, vulnerable sectors, such as computers. The U.S.A. is making a major drive to penetrate Japan's retailing sector and a number of big American stores have recently muscled their way into Japan: given the structure of Japanese retailing (a multiplicity of very small shops, and general absence of chain stores), this process will bear watching, since American control of outlets within Japan can be expected to lead to a big increase in sales of American products there. This is particularly true of agricultural products and foodstuffs, which Washington is urging on Japan.

One of the main items of the Hawaii meeting between Nixon and Tanaka (31 August–1 September 1972) was the trade imbalance between Japan and the U.S.A., which may come to $4 billion in 1972.[1] A great fanfare was made over Japan's agreement to an 'emergency' package of imports from the U.S.A.: agricultural, forestry and fishery products ($440mill. 'extra' – i.e., in the year to 31 March 1973, than in the previous year); helicopters and jets ($320mill. up to 31 March 1974); uranium enrichment services ($320mill.). In fact, as *The Times* put it, 'the $1,100mill. figure is overwhelmingly attributable to orders that would have occurred in the natural course of trade'.[2] Although this is perfectly true, it should not be allowed to obscure the fact that Japan, under intense pressure from its capitalist rivals, is definitely moving towards freeing restrictions on imports (into Japan). In September 1972 the government nullified the nine-year old 'Buy Japan' decree – except for the computer industry and peripheral equipment – and took a number of steps to promote imports.[3] However, it should not be assumed, even with the problem of Japan's huge reserves, that this process can go too far, since domestic Japanese producers will not allow

1. $4 billion is the estimate in *FEER*, 9 September 1972, p. 12 (a good survey of the Hawaii talks). *Pacific Imperialism Notebook*, vol. 3, no. 4 (April 1972), p. 143 clarifies the different methods of calculating the trade balance (on a 'payments basis' and on a 'customs clearance basis') and the discrepancies which result therefrom.

2. *The Times*, 2 September 1972.

3. *The Times*, 12 September 1972. cf. *The Times* 22 September 1972.

their market to be eroded beyond a certain limited point. Furthermore, as of September 1972, the average Japanese tariffs on finished consumer goods were still 12 per cent – well above the average of 7.7 per cent maintained by most other industrialized nations.[1]

Perhaps the most important item to emerge from the Hawaii meeting was the agreement to study the feasibility of a joint venture for a $1,000mill. 'gaseous diffusion enrichment facility for peaceful uses'.[2] If realized, this would be the first such joint venture of its kind ever undertaken, and would, of course, effectively sidetrack Japan from its tentatively projected plans for nuclear collaboration schemes with other countries, such as France and Australia.

This deal, although so far only on paper, is a reminder of the very close relationship between the U.S.A. and Japan, a relationship with a unique combination of co-operation and contradiction. In particular, the Hawaii agreements point up the continuing phenomenon that no matter how acute purely economic contradictions may be between Japan and the U.S.A., their military relationship remains extremely close, with Japan's military growth inextricably entwined with the American military machine.

The Hawaii meeting between Nixon and Tanaka was, of course, also arranged to review Japanese–American relations prior to Tanaka's visit to China. The Nixon–Tanaka communiqué reaffirmed the maintenance of the 1960 Treaty, under which the U.S.A. is authorized to use Japanese bases to protect Taiwan, to which the U.S.A. is still bound by treaty. Tanaka's success in not having Taiwan specifically mentioned in the Hawaii communiqué has to be measured against this reaffirmation of the aggressive anti-communist Security Treaty. At his press conference after the communiqué was issued Tanaka stated that he might press for the relocation of some of the American bases in Japan, since his party, the LDP, had been losing too many elections in constituencies near the bases.[3] So far Tanaka's position, based on the bland claim that the Security

1. *Time*, 11 September 1972.

2. *The Times*, 2 September 1972.

3. *FEER*, 9 September 1972, p. 12; cf. *The Times*, 2 September 1972, and *PR* 36, 8 September 1972, p. 20 for China's cautious reaction to the Hawaii meeting.

Treaty does not matter since there is no likelihood of armed action in the Taiwan–China Sea area (in which case, of course, the Treaty is redundant), seems to have carried him along successfully. But it must be emphasized that, in spite of China's willingness to 'normalize' relations with Tokyo, the Japanese regime remains tightly knitted into America's reactionary network in East Asia – a situation which is not satisfactorily changed by Tanaka's statement on his return from China that the Security Treaty would 'not be reactivated'.[1] America's drive in the autumn of 1972 to get Japan a seat on the UN Security Council was a payoff to an ally, not a sop to a foe.

Moreover, it must be repeated that, with the single possible exception of China, in every area where Japan may go to seek raw materials it will be obliged to continue to enter into an essentially subordinate relationship with U.S. capital. This is as true of Siberia as it is of South-East Asia.

This provides part of the context for the 1972 rapprochement between Japan and China. But it is also important to stress that the Tokyo–Peking rapprochement is the result of a change in policy by Japan and is, in effect, the successful outcome of the diplomatic offensive launched by Chou En-lai early in 1970 aimed at prising loose Japan's grip on the areas politically and strategically of importance to Peking: Taiwan and the southern part of Korea. Japanese media misinformation and LDP-fabricated euphoria cannot disguise the fact that it was Japan which had to recognize China, Japan which had to alter its policies.

With hindsight, it is possible to better appreciate the impact of China's revolutionary diplomacy: to see how China used the Nixon visit to stimulate unease in Tokyo, so that China was able, so to speak, to double up the impact of its diplomatic initiatives by hitting Japan with the boomerang 'Nixon shocks' rather than 'Chou shocks' or 'Mao shocks'. The double punches, from Chou En-lai and Richard Nixon, left the Japanese ruling class reeling and meant that the policies described above associated with the period of Sato's premiership (particularly those in chapter 5) were no longer viable. Tactically, too, it must be remembered that the LDP was desperately in need of new policies by the end of Sato's rule and a change in China policy

1. The *Sunday Telegraph*, 1 October 1972.

was a sure winner, given the overwhelming majority of public opinion in favour of 'normalization' of relations.

This crisis coincided with a period of economic recession and of growing resistance to Japan's export drive in many parts of the world (especially from Japan's main capitalist rivals), and with increasing unease about securing supplies of raw materials needed for further economic expansion. Thus, while China's initiatives led to the frustration of established Japanese policies on the one hand, on the other they held out the prospect of a solution to some of Japanese business's structural problems – if the China market and China's raw material sources could be opened up to Japan. The moves preceding Japanese recognition of China show that big business was the main agent of the change in government policy. Tanaka and much of his cabinet belong to the far right of the LDP[1] and would not have undertaken such a switch without the backing and pressure of big business, which still controls the LDP purse-strings.

Doubtless there is a good deal of wishful thinking, mystification and self-deceit involved in Japanese big business's China drive, particularly as regards the possibility of Japan's exports to China: the People's Republic will not tolerate either the kind of imbalance which Japan consistently runs with areas like South Korea or excessive (more than about 20 per cent) dependence on any one supplier. However, as far as Japan being able to buy vital raw materials from China is concerned, there are definitely real prospects for a big increase in trade. At the present stage of development of Japanese capitalism, access to raw materials, particularly oil, is no less important than access to export markets. The relatively small barter agreement between Toyota and China in early 1972 whereby China paid for Toyota trucks by the shipment of oil was a pointer to the future. Oil was discussed during the Tanaka visit to China, but no details were forthcoming as of the time of writing.

Another central issue in Japan–China relations which was not clarified at the time of the Tanaka visit was the ownership of the Tiaoyu Islands. From the end of Sato's premiership in mid-

1. For a fuller description of the Tanaka cabinet and evidence of its reactionary nature, see Muto Ichiyo, 'Nothing to Offer – Tanaka Kakuei Steps into Power', *Ampo* no. 13–14, May–July 1972, pp. 3–6. cf. p. 255-6.

summer, China eased up its attacks on the Japanese ruling class, concentrating on the one issue of detaching the new government from its liaison with Taipei. Unofficial reports prior to the Tanaka visit alleged that Chou En-lai had let it be known that the Tiaoyu issue could be shelved for the time being in the interests of achieving agreement on fundamental questions with Japan. Tanaka's version, after his visit to China, was that Chou refused to discuss the Tiaoyu Islands with him at all. The non-settlement – indeed, the non-appearance of the issue in any official statement – is surprising, since Japan's seizure of the islands played such a central part in Chinese attacks on the Japanese regime up to the middle of 1972, and also because the islands lie in the middle of the China Sea oil field and some solution to the question has to be found if co-operation in oil exploration is to go ahead.

Japan's relationship to Taiwan, the key thorny issue, was settled with only a minimum of diplomatic *legerdemain.* Having got Taiwan left out of the Hawaii communiqué entirely, Tanaka was able to get Chinese agreement to a curious split-level arrangement whereby Japan disowned the Kuomintang regime in Taipei: while the official communiqué states that 'Japan fully understands and respects this stand of the government of China [that Taiwan is an inalienable part of the territory of the People's Republic of China]' it did not embody Japan's abrogation of the 1952 peace treaty with Taiwan. This was announced, in an apparently pre-agreed move, by Foreign Minister Ohira, at a separate press conference on the same day. The Taiwan government immediately severed diplomatic relations 'in view of the perfidious action of the Japanese Government in total disregard of treaty obligations'.[1]

At the time of writing it was still too early to see the exact new shape of Japan–Taiwan relations. Before Tanaka reached China the Taiwan regime initiated economic moves to reduce its trade ties to Japan: it allocated $100mill. to local companies wishing to purchase raw materials from countries other than Japan, and it refused to authorize purchases of goods worth more than $20,000 from Japan.[2] It seems not unlikely that Japan will continue trading with Taiwan on something like the same basis

1. *The Times*, 30 September 1972.
2. *The Times*, 26 September 1972.

as it traded with China prior to the establishment of diplomatic relations – through 'friendly firms' and something like the 'Memorandum Trade' arrangement.

It is as well to repeat here that the convergence of interest between Japan and China outlined above need not necessarily mean much more than that. Recognition and 'normalization' were in the interests of both the Soviet Union and Japan in 1925, but certainly did not imply any agreement on fundamental political issues – and indeed signalled the beginning of a massive assault on communists and radicals in Japan. The cabinet which recognized China in 1972 represented the unreformed reactionary mainstream of the LDP. Tanaka's reference to the 'troubles' Japan caused China earlier hardly qualifies as a thorough reconsideration of the long record of Japanese aggression against, and exploitation of, China for which the predecessors of this present leadership (or, indeed, in some cases the very same individuals) were responsible.[1]

Although Tanaka's rapprochement with China must affect Tokyo–Taipei links, it is important to note that the new Japanese government has, if anything, intensified links with the Seoul regime. Foreign Minister Ohira attended the sixth session of the Japan–R.O.K. ministerial talks in Seoul on 5 and 6 September 1972. In return for $170mill. in Japanese government loans to Seoul, with a further $135mill. to be considered favourably, the Pak regime signed an 'agreement on ownership of industry' under which Japanese interests can further consolidate their grip on the South Korean economy. North Korea roundly denounced the September 1972 deal which, it said,

> indicate[s] that the present rulers of Japan have not detached themselves from the aggressive line which the ex-Prime Minister Sato and other Japanese militarists followed in a desperate effort to subjugate South Korea and realise their militarist ambition for overseas expansion at the instigation of the U.S. imperialists.[2]

1. The communiqué stated that: 'The Japanese side is keenly aware of Japan's responsibility for causing enormous damages in the past to the Chinese people through war, and deeply reproaches itself.' Tanaka only said that he was engaging in 'profound self-examination' over the 'troubles'.

2. *Pyongyang Times*, 16 September 1972, p. 6. For further details of the talks, see *FEER*, 23 September 1972, pp. 13–14. For information on the background to the talks, including Japanese determination

It is reasonable to suppose that the weakening of ties with Taiwan may lead to a reinforcement of those with South Korea.

In the new and fluid situation in the Far East, this will not prevent the Japanese government from expanding its relations with the D.P.R.K., even though Seoul is hostile to this. Both MITI head, Nakasone, and the Keidanren are vigorously backing expanded trade with Pyongyang; and Japan's trade with North Korea in the six months January to June 1972 was up 75.3 per cent over the corresponding period in 1971.[1]

Japan's relationship with Korea is likely to continue to provide the clearest concentrated evidence of its relationship to Asia in general. Japan will be trying to expand its trade with both North and South Korea, steering between Seoul's feeble attempts to restrict Tokyo's trade with the North and the D.P.R.K.'s deeply-felt political protests about the increasing Japanese grip on the South's economy. Interestingly, the application of Chou En-lai's Principles to South Korea would seem to be in abeyance. At any rate, China ceased voicing the Principles when Tanaka succeeded Sato as premier. Clearly, it makes little sense to discriminate against individual Japanese companies and 'accept' the Japanese government which is simultaneously the key agent in propping up the Pak dictatorship.

Throughout the rest of South-East Asia, too, there is no reason to think that Japanese policy, based on pure capitalist considerations, will undergo any substantial changes. In the Philippines Japanese business interests are deeply involved in the Marcos

---

to tighten control over use of loans to the R.O.K., see Nakagawa Nobuo, 'The End of the ASPAC Period', *Sekai*, August 1972, pp. 127–34. ASPAC is the Asian and Pacific Council, founded in Seoul, largely on South Korean initiative, as a diehard anti-communist East and South-East Asian group.

1. *FEER*, 12 August 1972, p. 28. The January–June trade was heavily unbalanced in Japan's favour, although up to now Tokyo–Pyongyang trade has been in balance. The increase in early 1972 followed on the signing in January of a private trade pact calling for an increase in two-way trade up to $500mill. by the end of 1976 (see *Pacific Imperialism Notebook*, vol. 3, no. 4 April 1972, pp. 124–5). Japan has been involved behind the scenes in manipulating the North-South talks: on the talks, see Nakagawa Nobuo, 'The End of the ASPAC Period'; and Saito Takashi, 'New Developments in the Korean Unification Problem', *Sekai*, September 1972, pp. 88–98.

dictatorship. The same goes for Indonesia: just before Sato left the premiership Suharto paid an unannounced one-week visit to Tokyo in May 1972 to consolidate the ties between the Japanese oil industry and the Djakarta junta. Sato gave Suharto a loan of $300mill. At the same time Sato's Minister of International Trade and Industry, Tanaka, tried to railroad a special bill through the Diet allotting the Petroleum Development Public Corporation an extra $1·5 billion. On 23 May 1972 Tanaka addressed the General Assembly of Keidanren and grovelled before the business leaders: 'Please use the money royally and freely,'[1] he proclaimed. Although Tanaka has agreed to modify policy on the China question, it would be quite wrong to think that this will in any way mitigate the role of Japanese imperialism in South-East Asia as a whole. Changes in the forms of imperialism will, of course, take place. As the resistance to the flood of Japanese consumer goods in South-East Asian markets grows, the Japanese government is switching to a policy of promoting long-term development projects in the area, but for this sort of commitment, it should be noted, Japanese government and business will have to be assured of the security of the area, and renewed calls for military guarantees of the South-East Asian status quo can be expected.[2]

Such considerations naturally do not apply to Japan's relations with the Soviet Union. The main economic developments in relations between the two countries are dealt with in Appendix I. The Siberian settlement will, of course, have its political as well as its economic side. The Soviet Union currently has fifty divisions on the Chinese frontier (one third its entire army) and very much wants the Tyumen-Pacific pipeline, which would greatly facilitate oil supplies to its vast armed forces in Siberia. China, naturally, can hardly be expected to welcome a Japanese commitment to the pipeline. Decisions on these issues are expected some time in the winter of 1972–3, since Tokyo and Moscow have announced their intention of signing a peace treaty at that time.

1. Murata Goro, 'Japanese Imperialism and Oil in Asia', (Economic Analysis 3), *Ampo* no. 13–14, May–July 1972, p. 58. This three-part study by Murata is an invaluable source on Japanese imperialism.

2. Noguchi Yuichiro, 'The Japanese and American Economies in Asia', *Sekai*, September 1972, pp. 112–20.

The other main issue in a Soviet-Japanese peace treaty will be the four islands, Kunashiri, Etorofu, Shikotan and Habomai. The Japanese are pressing for the return of these islands as part of the Siberian package deal. Shortly after taking office as premier, Tanaka asked the Finance Ministry to more than double the funds for the campaign to secure the return of what the Japanese refer to as 'the Northern islands'.[1] With the so-called 'reversion' of Okinawa accomplished, and a formal settlement achieved with China, the Tanaka government was quick to foster the concentration of Japanese nationalism and channel it into a well-financed anti-Russian campaign, whose funds could be turned on and off at the whim of the Prime Minister's office.

The exploitation of this territorial issue to promote chauvinism is a good example of the intimate relationship between foreign and domestic policies. Likewise, one must recognize that big business and the LDP forced a change both of premier and of China policy because they saw this as a quick way to shore up their rapidly eroding electoral position inside Japan. By the end of Sato's term of office, his support (applying both to him personally and to the policies of his cabinet) was a mere 12 per cent. With less than half the popular vote and the support of less than one third the electorate at the last general election in 1969, the LDP was in danger of seeing its major losses at the local level (of some importance in Japan) extended to the national level. The 'cost' of normalized relations with China is the demobilization of some of the mass popular hostility to LDP rule: the capitulation of the entire national press and all the main opposition parties, including JSP and JCP, to the LDP position on Tiaoyu is extremely ominous in this respect [2]

Nor should the slick coverage given to Tanaka's China visit by the international media be allowed to hide the fact that his first cabinet belongs to the far right, particularly as regards the key domestic posts. Apart from the presence of Tanaka himelf and Nakasone, whose views have been outlined above, at MITI two very important rightists hold key posts in the government: Kimura Takeo as Chairman of the National Security Agency,

1. The *Financial Times*, 30 August 1972. *Peking Review* reported appreciatively on a fairly small demonstration in Hokkaido over the islands.

2. Nomura Koichi, 'The Ideological Composition of Sino-Japanese Relations', *Sekai*, August 1972, p. 18.

and Inaba Osamu as Education Minister. Inaba, a notorious right-winger, can be expected to continue the out-and-out reactionary education policies of the Sato government.[1] The element of continuity between Sato and Tanaka is very strong. Tanaka, it must be remembered, not only served as head of MITI, but earlier as Secretary General of the LDP under Sato. In this position he was the key person behind the main reactionary achievements of the Sato regime. At his first press conference after becoming president of the LDP Tanaka went out of his way to pay homage to Sato's 'three great deeds' – the conclusion of the Japan–South Korea Treaty, the railroading through the Diet of the special anti-student law, and the Okinawa 'reversion' treaty[2] Tanaka, of course, was Sato's partner and aide in all these events.

Immediately after his nomination, Tanaka spoke to a joint breakfast meeting of Keidanren and Keizai Doyukai leaders, on 13 July 1972. In case they needed any reassuring about his willingness to collaborate with them, he told his audience that he would step up government assistance to business. 'To teach civil servants the spirit of business in future [men from] each government department will be sent to study in business,' he told his listeners. And the government would make even more strenuous efforts to promote expansion overseas: 'Till now overseas government offices have been cold towards enterprises expanding overseas; in future they will give positive aid.'[3] *Zaikai* leaders in turn expressed their hopes that Tanaka's domestic popularity would blunt the edge of the mass reform movements on pollution and suchlike issues.

It is still too soon to see how successful the LDP's strategy will be. Certainly Tanaka's record popularity cannot hurt the LDP in the general election. But the Tokyo government's record on the really basic domestic issues which affect the lives of the Japanese people is an atrocious one. The re-occupation of Okinawa after 'reversion' in May 1972 was a searing experience.

1. Muto, *Ampo* no. 13–14, op. cit.; *FEER*, 15 July 1972, p. 11 ('Inaba is a known hawk . . . He favours curtailment of some civil liberties and advocates military rearmament . . . Evidently there is a rightist slant in the more important Cabinet posts.').

2. Muto, *Ampo* no. 13–14, op. cit., p. 6.

3. 'The Tanaka Administration and its Honeymoon with the *Zaikai*', *Sekai* (editorial), September 1972, p. 158.

The tragedy and cruelty of this deception has made a deep mark among the Japanese masses. Moreover, Tanaka is a willing liege of business. His plans for coping with Japan's awful environmental problems mainly consist of spreading pollution more widely over the rest of the country (called 'decentralization'). He has neither the inclination nor the ability to reverse big business's entrenched policies, which are directly inimical to the interests of the masses. With a man like Inaba in charge of education, repression against the students and increasingly reactionary policies throughout the whole educational field can be expected, with chauvinism and militarism being more and more stressed. The chauvinism can be supported by the dire new Immigration Bill on the cards. The projected new arms budget is up 22 per cent. Imperialism is still rampant.

3 October 1972

Maps

EAST AND SOUTH-EAST ASIA

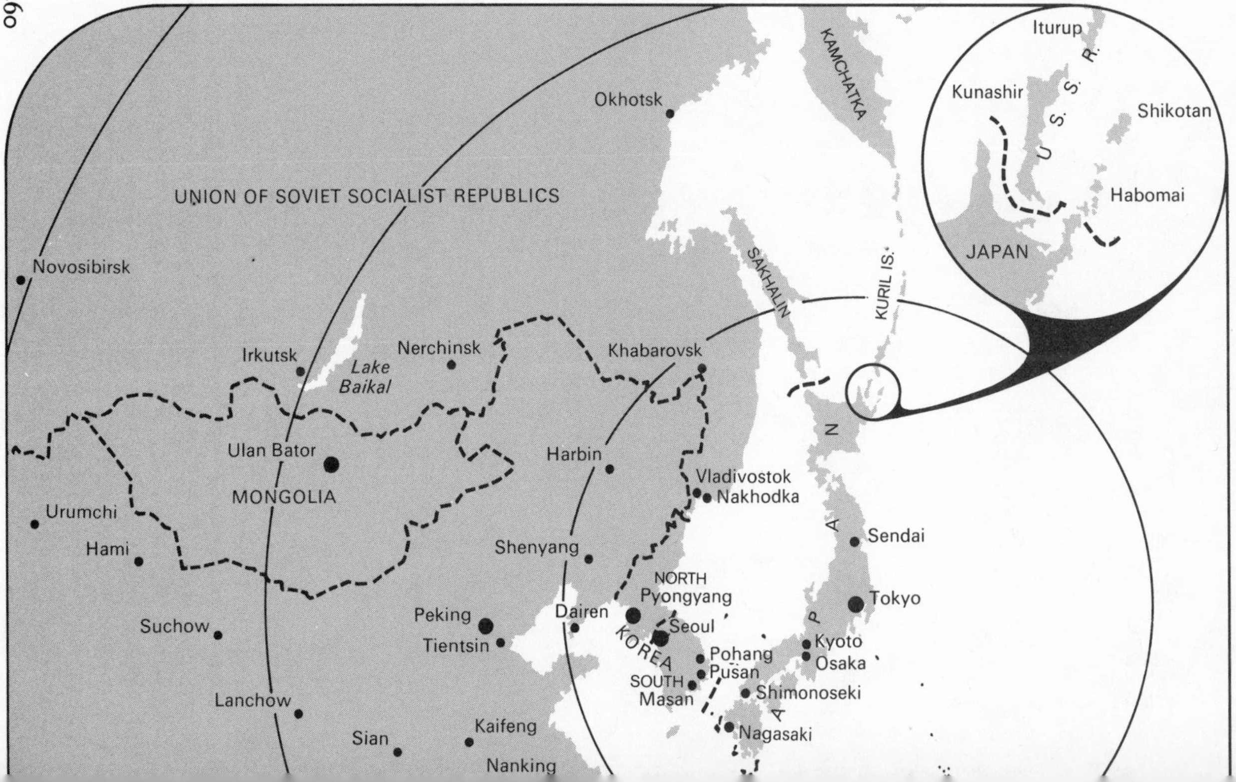

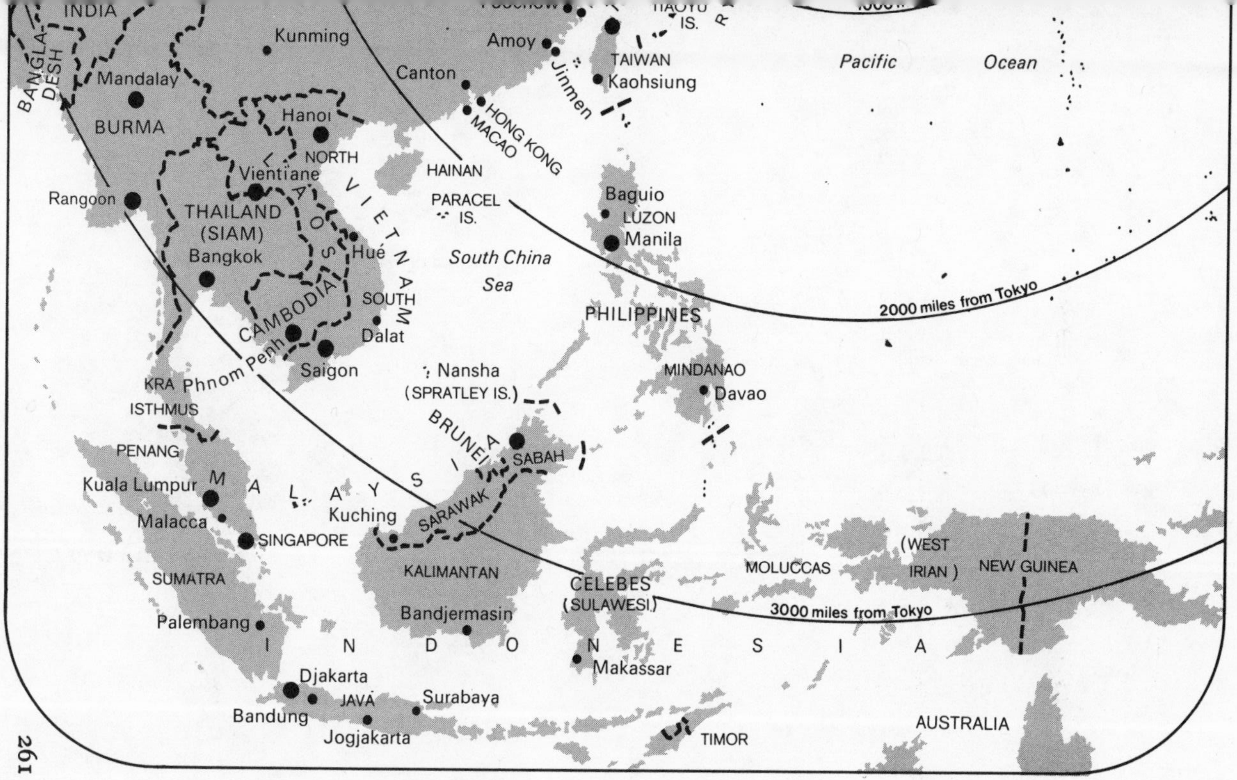
INDIA
BANGLA-DESH
Mandalay
BURMA
Rangoon
Kunming
Hanoi
NORTH
Vientiane
LAOS
VIETNAM
THAILAND (SIAM)
Bangkok
Hué
SOUTH
CAMBODIA
Phnom Penh
Dalat
Saigon
KRA ISTHMUS
PENANG
Kuala Lumpur
Malacca
SINGAPORE
MALAYSIA
Kuching
SARAWAK
BRUNEI
SABAH
SUMATRA
Palembang
KALIMANTAN
Bandjermasin
Djakarta
Bandung
JAVA
Jogjakarta
Surabaya
INDONESIA
CELEBES (SULAWESI)
Makassar
TIMOR
MOLUCCAS
(WEST IRIAN)
NEW GUINEA
AUSTRALIA
Canton
HONG KONG
MACAO
HAINAN
PARACEL IS.
South China Sea
Nansha (SPRATLEY IS.)
Amoy
Jinmen
TAIWAN
Kaohsiung
IS.
Baguio
LUZON
Manila
PHILIPPINES
MINDANAO
Davao
Pacific Ocean
2000 miles from Tokyo
3000 miles from Tokyo

TIAOYU ISLANDS

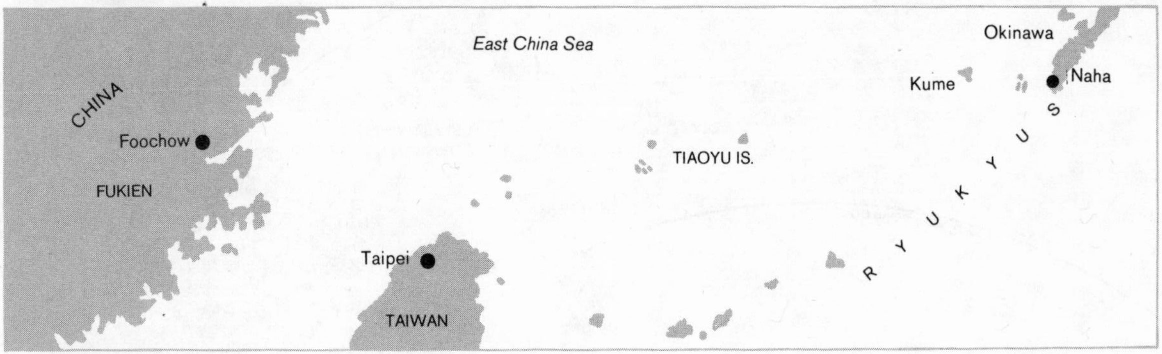

INDEX

All Chinese, Japanese, Korean and Vietnamese names (except Nguyen Van Thieu) are given with surname first and no comma after the surname. Important events which have no recognized 'name' – such as the 1969 meeting between Nixon and Sato – are entered under the name of the Japanese participant (Sato, Tanaka). Other meetings, treaties and so on, between Japan and, say, South Korea, are entered with the name of Japan first. In cases where a meeting is better known by another name (e.g., the April 1970 meeting between Chou En-lai and Kim Il Sung) we have entered it under that name – viz., Pyongyang. Where treaties have an established, fixed name – e.g., the U.S.–Japan Security Treaty – they are entered under their official title.

There are no entries for China, Japan, Taiwan, South Korea and the U.S.A.